# DOCTOR 13

## ARCHITECTURE

## & MORTALITY

BRIAN
AZZARELLO

CLIFF
CHIANG

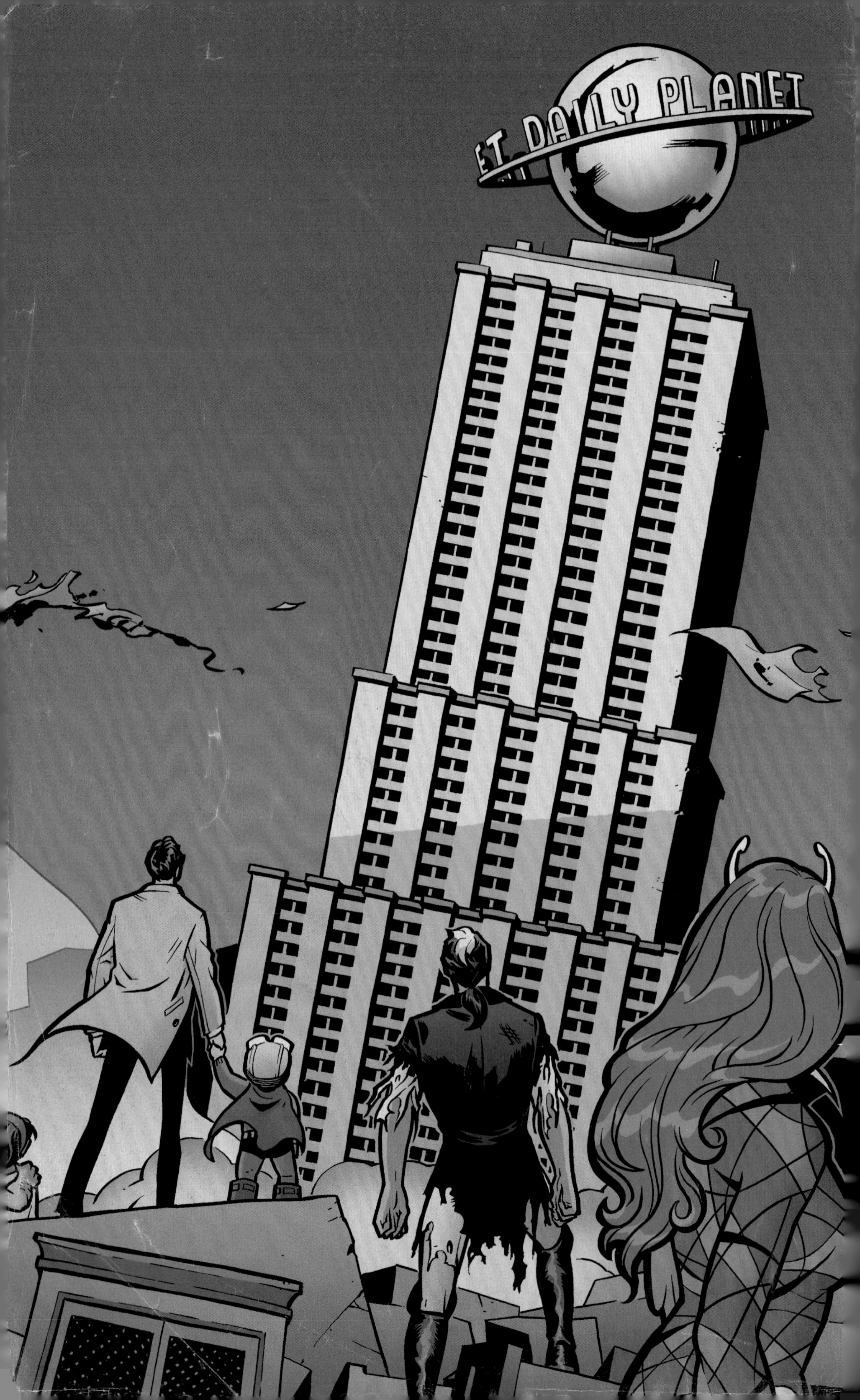
ET DAILY PLANET

# DOCTOR 13

## ARCHITECTURE & MORTALITY

**BRIAN AZZARELLO**
WRITER

**CLIFF CHIANG**
ARTIST

**PATRICIA MULVIHILL**
COLORIST

**JARED K. FLETCHER**
LETTERER

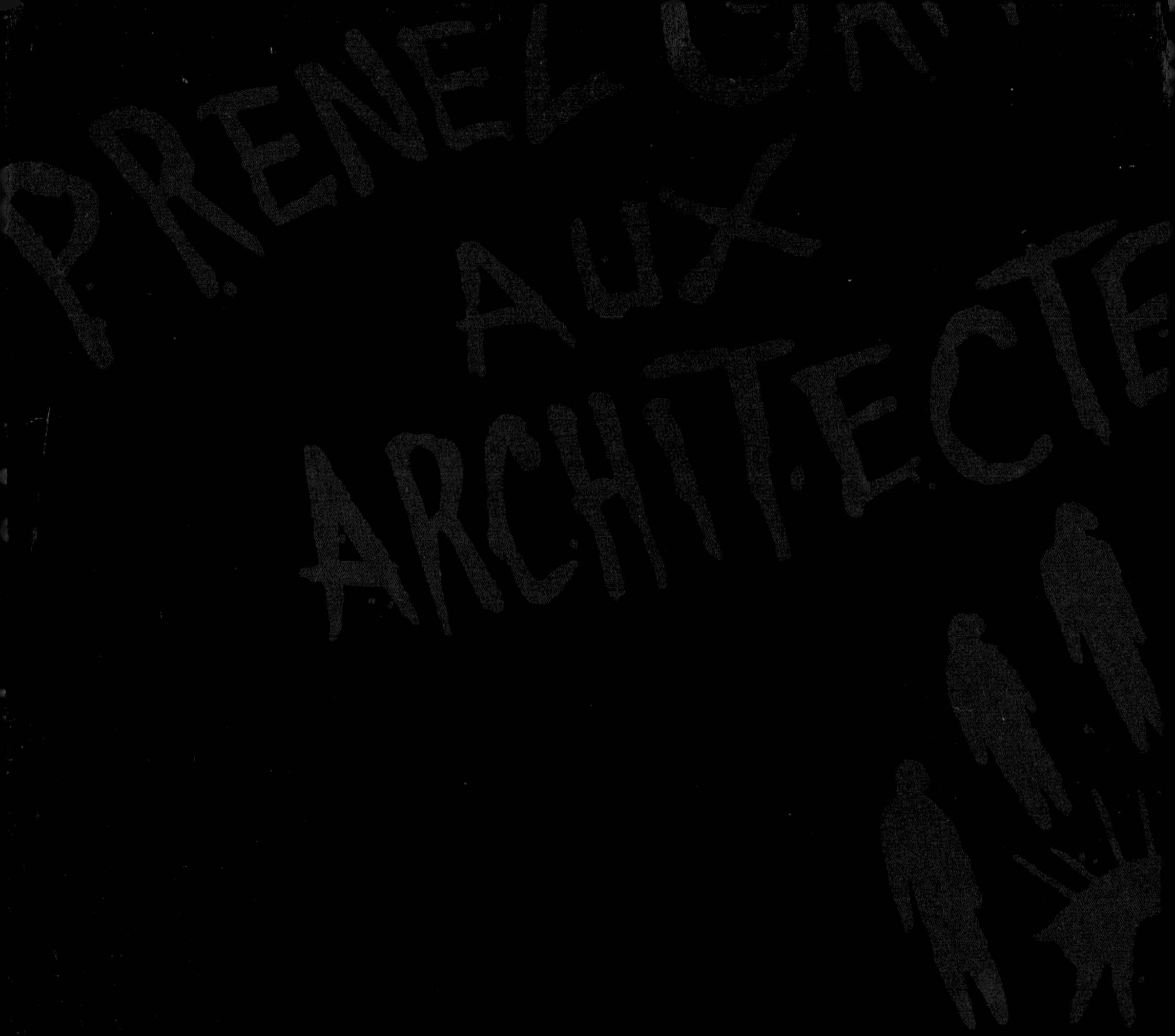
AUX

DAN DIDIO *Senior VP-Executive Editor*
BOB SCHRECK *Editor-original series*
BRANDON MONTCLARE *Assistant Editor-original series*
SCOTT NYBAKKEN *Editor-collected edition*
ROBBIN BROSTERMAN *Senior Art Director*
PAUL LEVITZ *President & Publisher*
GEORG BREWER *VP-Design & DC Direct Creative*
RICHARD BRUNING *Senior VP-Creative Director*
PATRICK CALDON *Executive VP-Finance & Operations*
CHRIS CARAMALIS *VP-Finance*
JOHN CUNNINGHAM *VP-Marketing*
TERRI CUNNINGHAM *VP-Managing Editor*
ALISON GILL *VP-Manufacturing*
HANK KANALZ *VP-General Manager, WildStorm*
JIM LEE *Editorial Director-WildStorm*
PAULA LOWITT *Senior VP-Business & Legal Affairs*
MARYELLEN MCLAUGHLIN *VP-Advertising & Custom Publishing*
JOHN NEE *VP-Business Development*
GREGORY NOVECK *Senior VP-Creative Affairs*
SUE POHJA *VP-Book Trade Sales*
CHERYL RUBIN *Senior VP-Brand Management*
JEFF TROJAN *VP-Business Development, DC Direct*
BOB WAYNE *VP-Sales*

Cover illustration by Cliff Chiang.
Publication design by Brainchild Studios/NYC.

DOCTOR 13: ARCHITECTURE & MORTALITY
Published by DC Comics. 

DC Comics
1700 Broadway
New York, NY 10019
A Warner Bros. Entertainment Company.
Printed in Canada. Second printing.
ISBN: 978-1-4012-1552-1

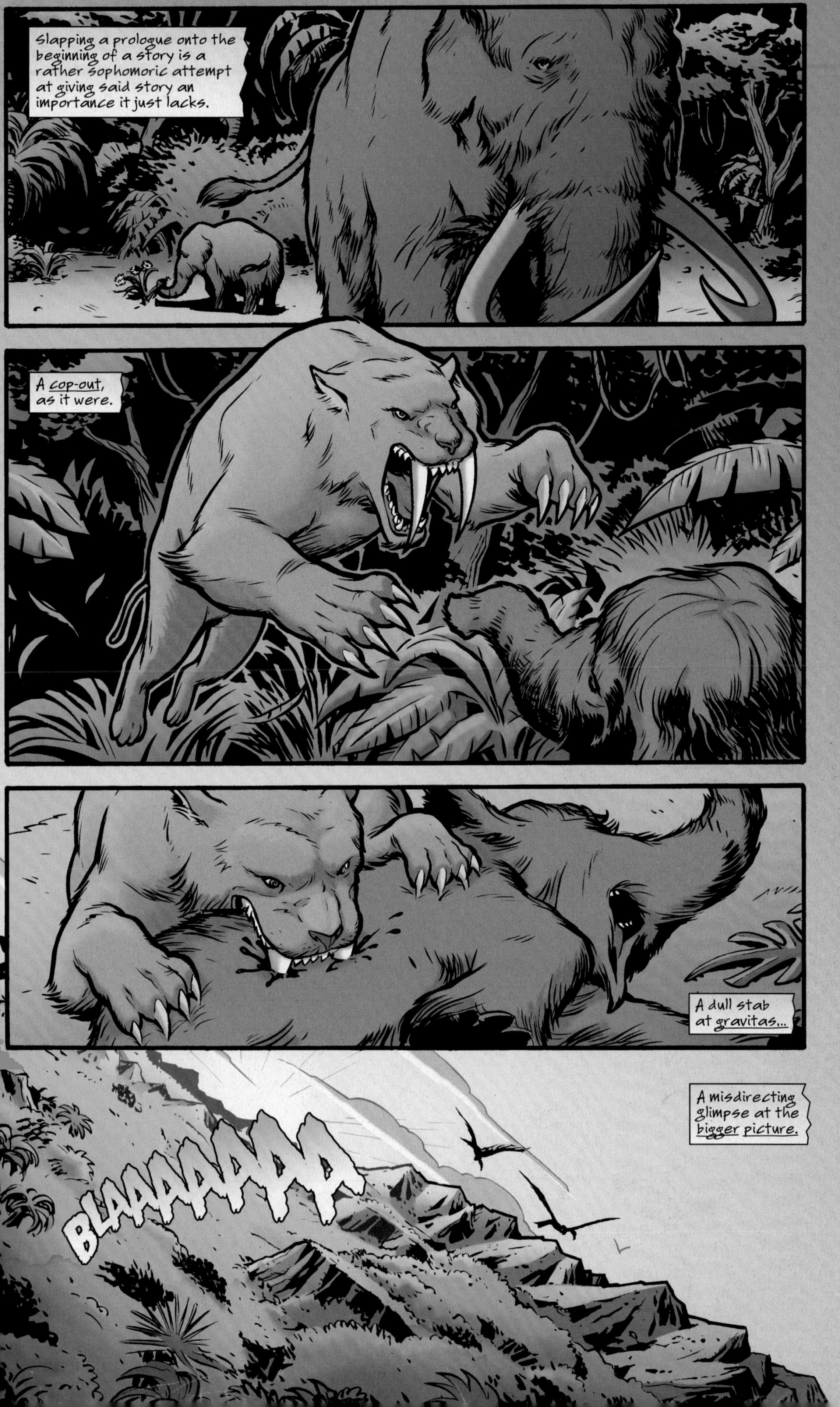
Slapping a prologue onto the beginning of a story is a rather sophomoric attempt at giving said story an importance it just lacks.
A cop-out, as it were.
A dull stab at gravitas...
A misdirecting glimpse at the bigger picture.
BLAAAAAAA

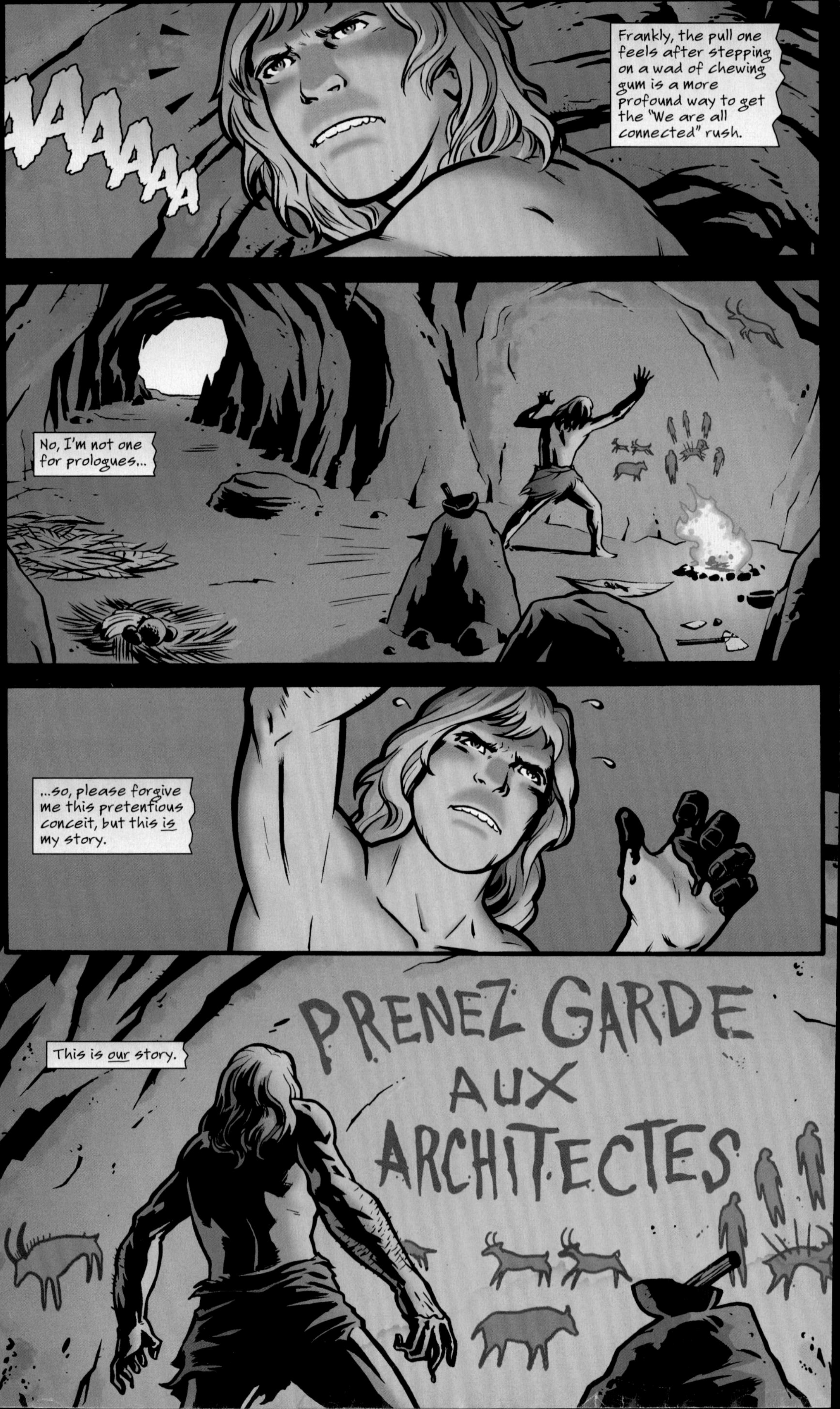
AAAAAAAA
Frankly, the pull one feels after stepping on a wad of chewing gum is a more profound way to get the "We are all connected" rush.
No, I'm not one for prologues...
...so, please forgive me this pretentious conceit, but this is my story.
This is our story.
PRENEZ GARDE AUX ARCHITECTES

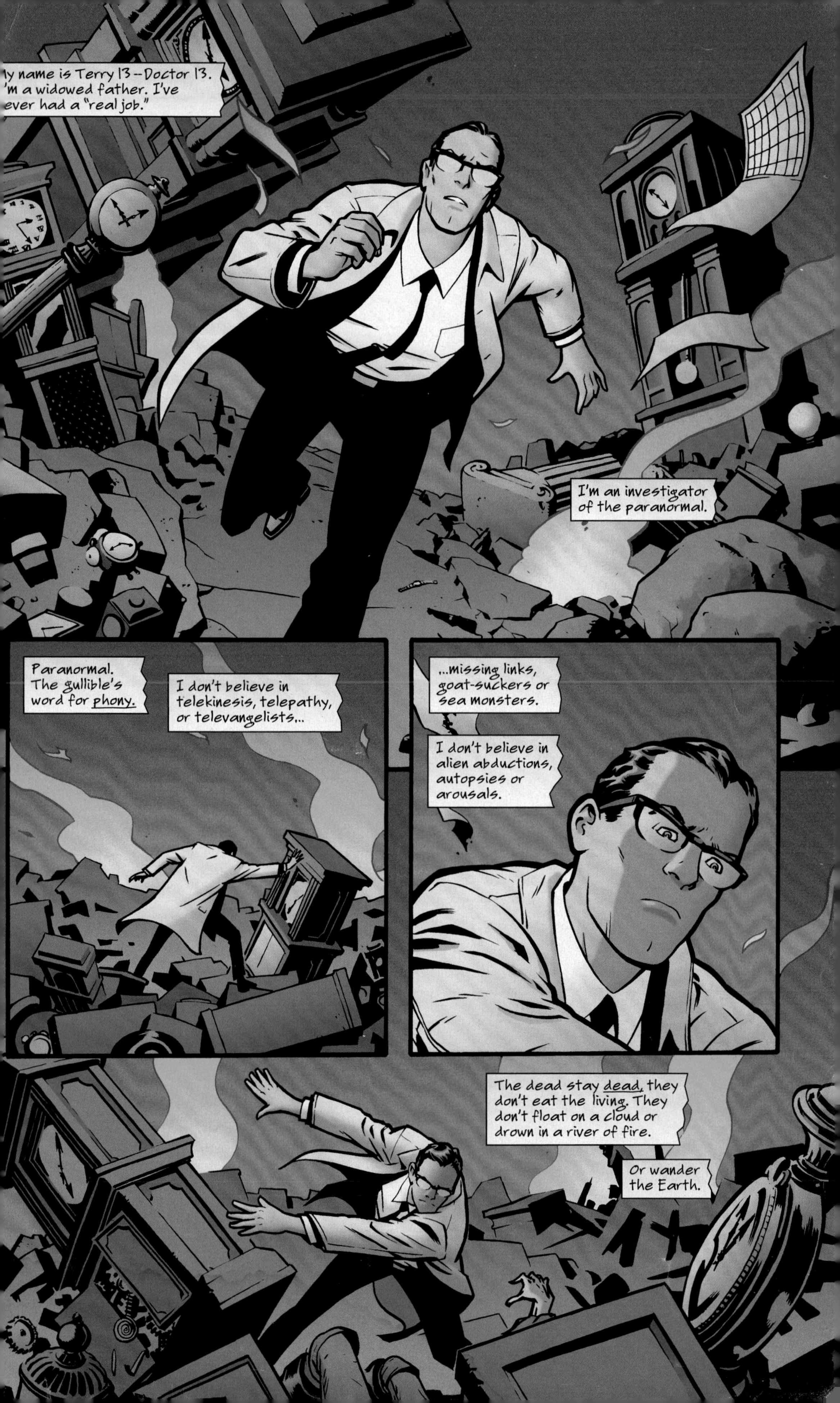
ly name is Terry 13 --Doctor 13. 'm a widowed father. I've ever had a "real job."
I'm an investigator of the paranormal.
Paranormal. The gullible's word for phony.
I don't believe in telekinesis, telepathy, or televangelists...
...missing links, goat-suckers or sea monsters.
I don't believe in alien abductions, autopsies or arousals.
The dead stay dead, they don't eat the living. They don't float on a cloud or drown in a river of fire.
Or wander the Earth.

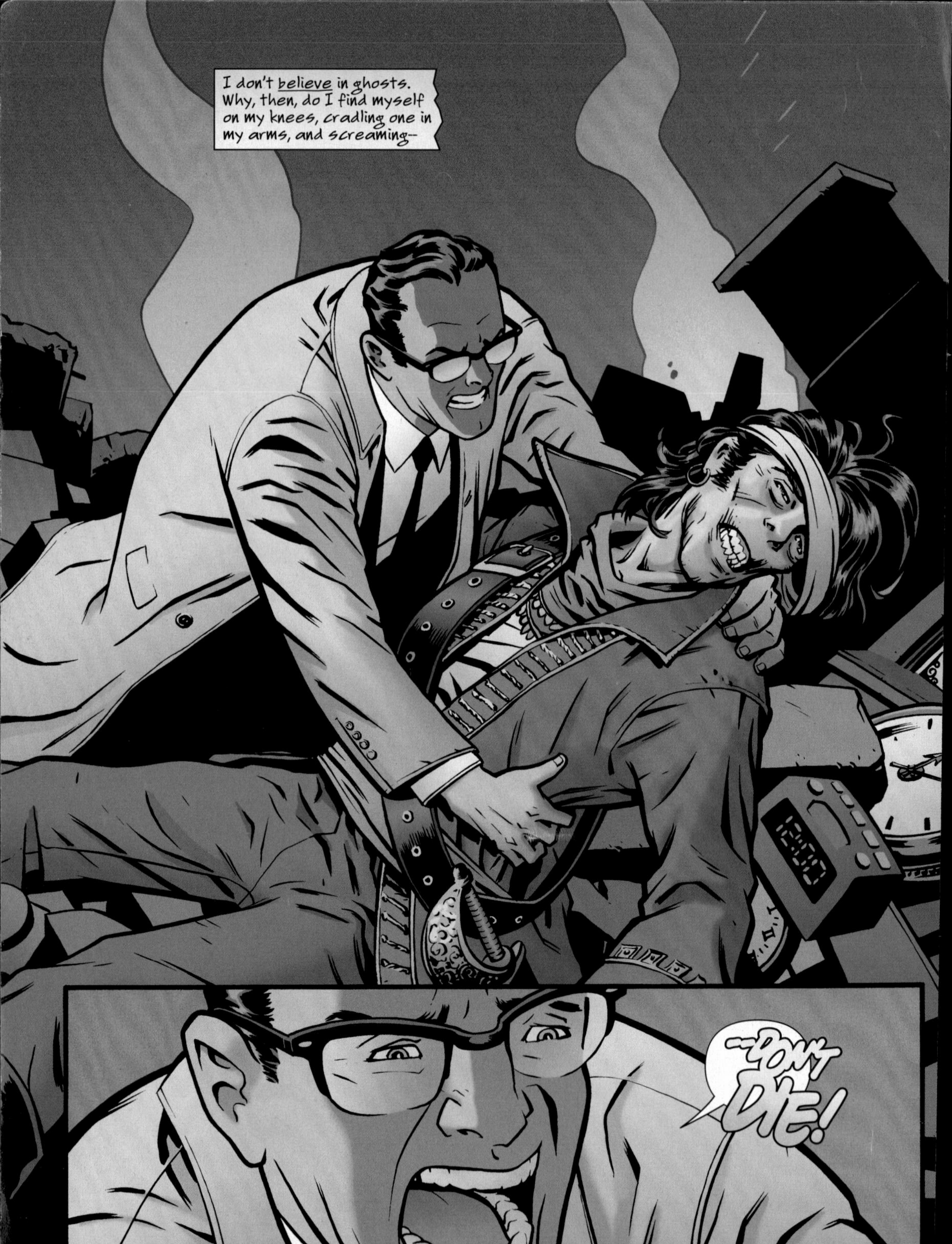
I don't believe in ghosts. Why, then, do I find myself on my knees, cradling one in my arms, and screaming--
--DON'T DIE!

CHAPTER 1

# THE NEW STONE AGE

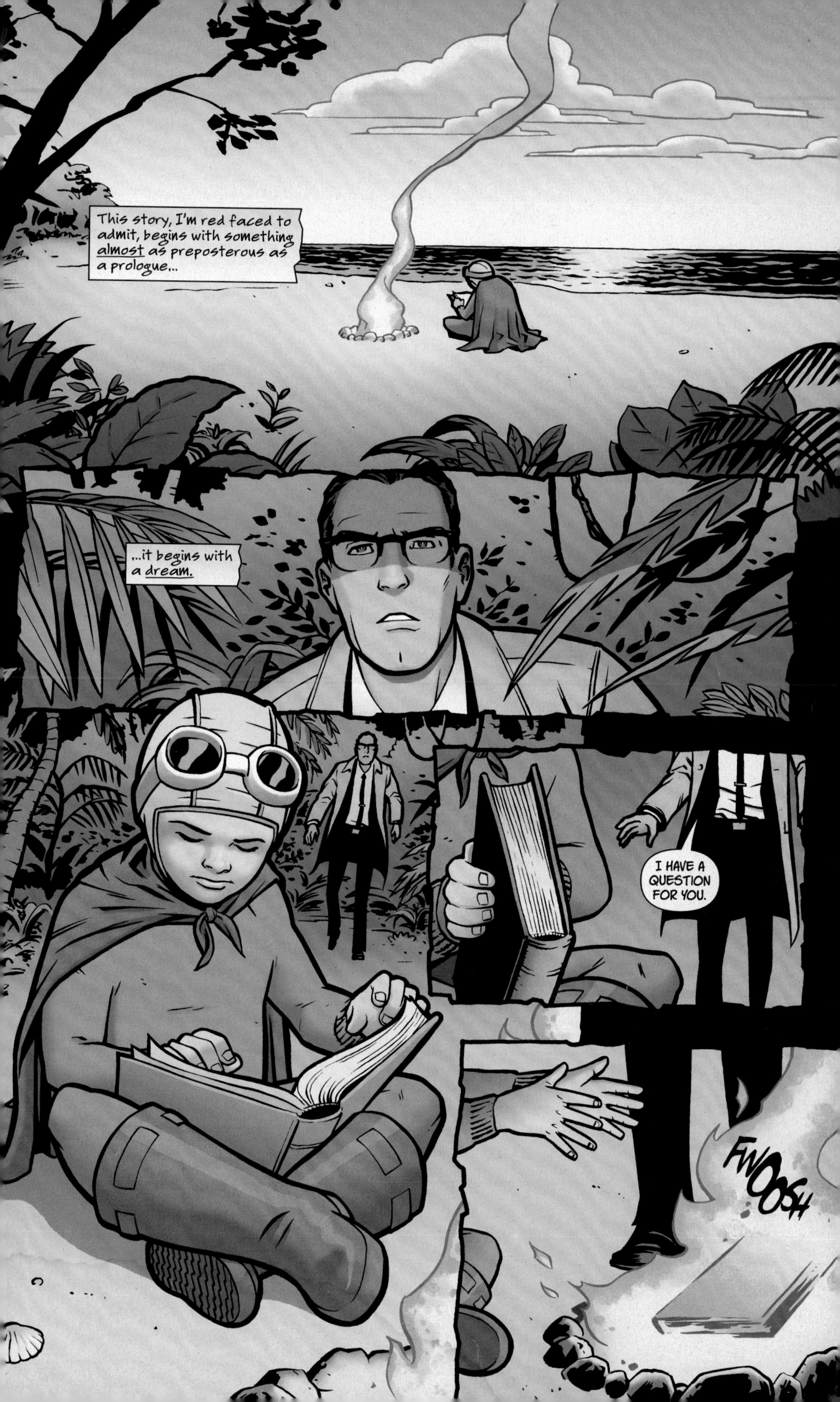
This story, I'm red faced to admit, begins with something almost as preposterous as a prologue...
...it begins with a dream.
I HAVE A QUESTION FOR YOU.
FWOOSH

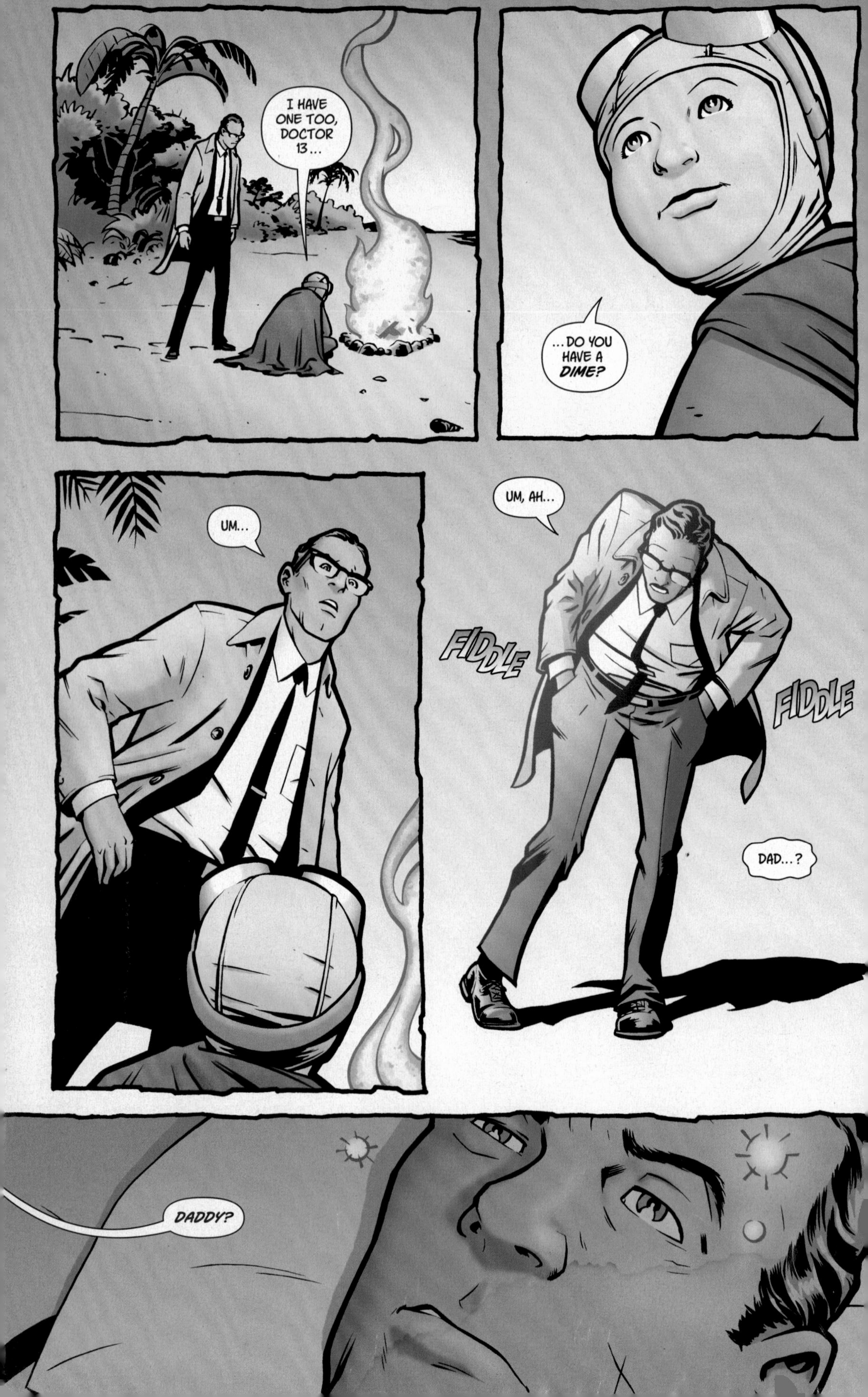
I HAVE ONE TOO, DOCTOR 13...
...DO YOU HAVE A *DIME?*
UM...
UM, AH...
FIDDLE
FIDDLE
DAD...?
*DADDY?*

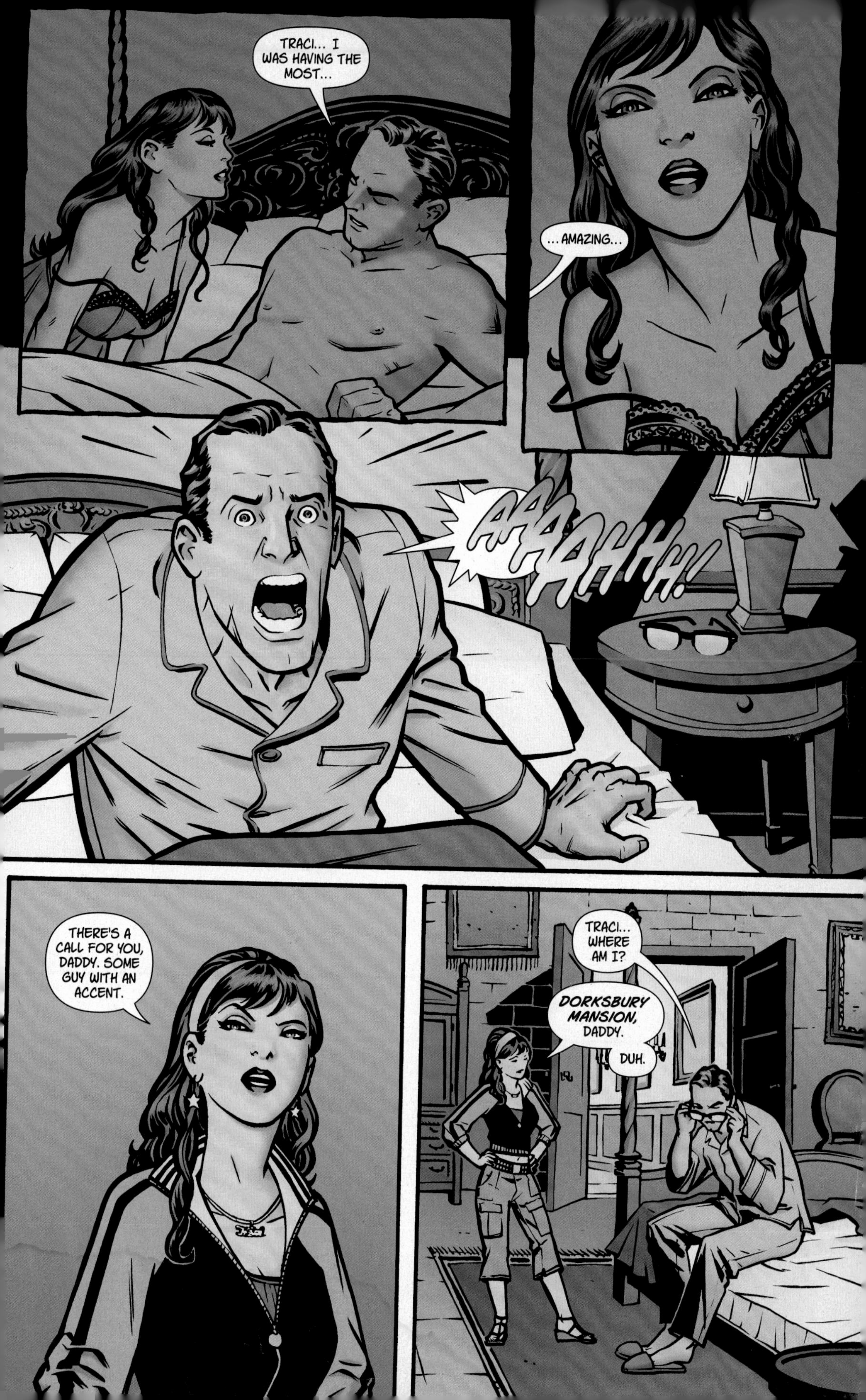
TRACI... I WAS HAVING THE MOST...
...AMAZING...
AAAAHHHH!
THERE'S A CALL FOR YOU, DADDY. SOME GUY WITH AN ACCENT.
TRACI... WHERE AM I?
DORKSBURY MANSION, DADDY.
DUH.

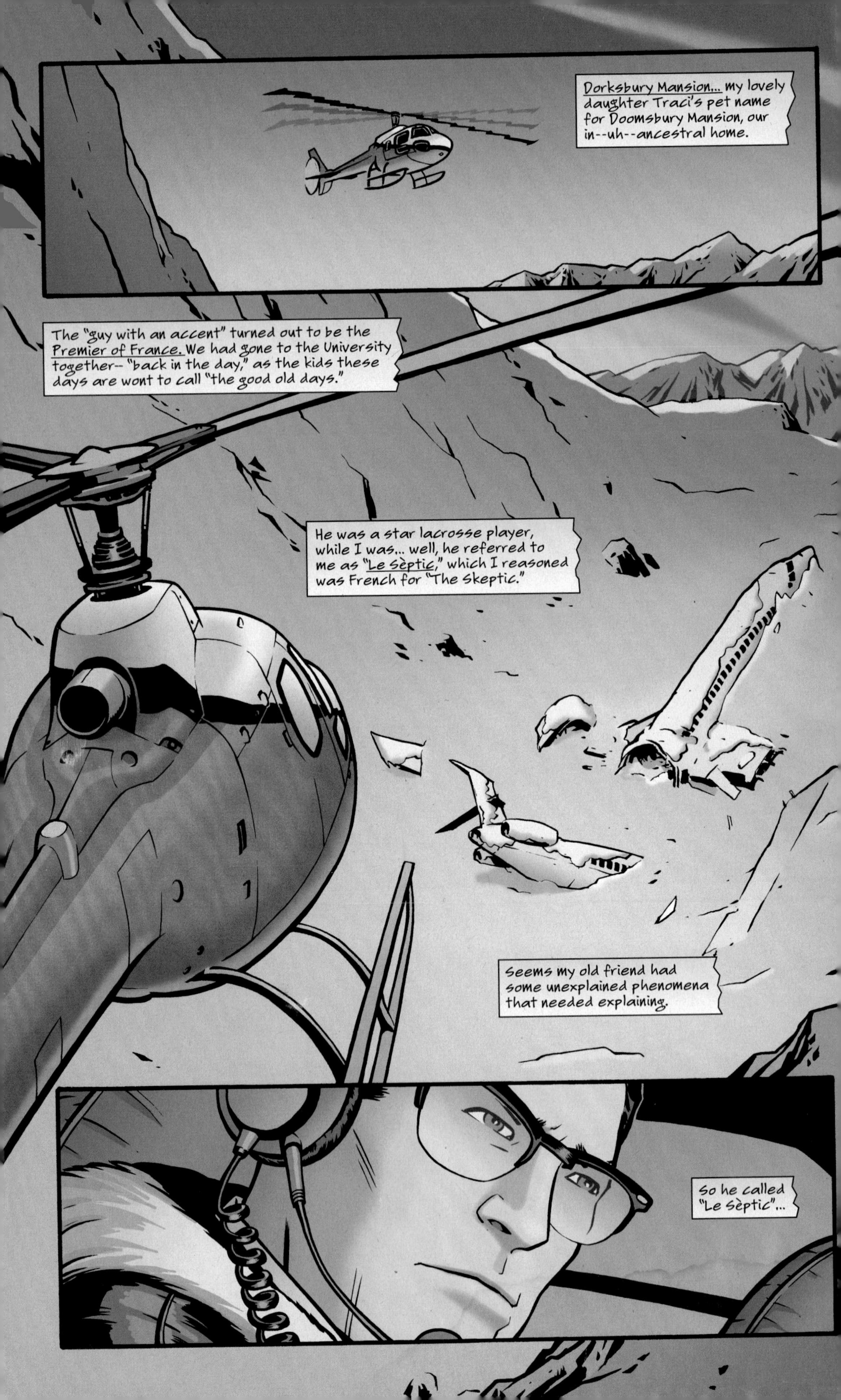

Dorksbury Mansion... my lovely daughter Traci's pet name for Doomsbury Mansion, our in--uh--ancestral home.
The "guy with an accent" turned out to be the Premier of France. We had gone to the University together-- "back in the day," as the kids these days are wont to call "the good old days."
He was a star lacrosse player, while I was... well, he referred to me as "Le Sèptic," which I reasoned was French for "The Skeptic."
Seems my old friend had some unexplained phenomena that needed explaining.
So he called "Le Sèptic"...

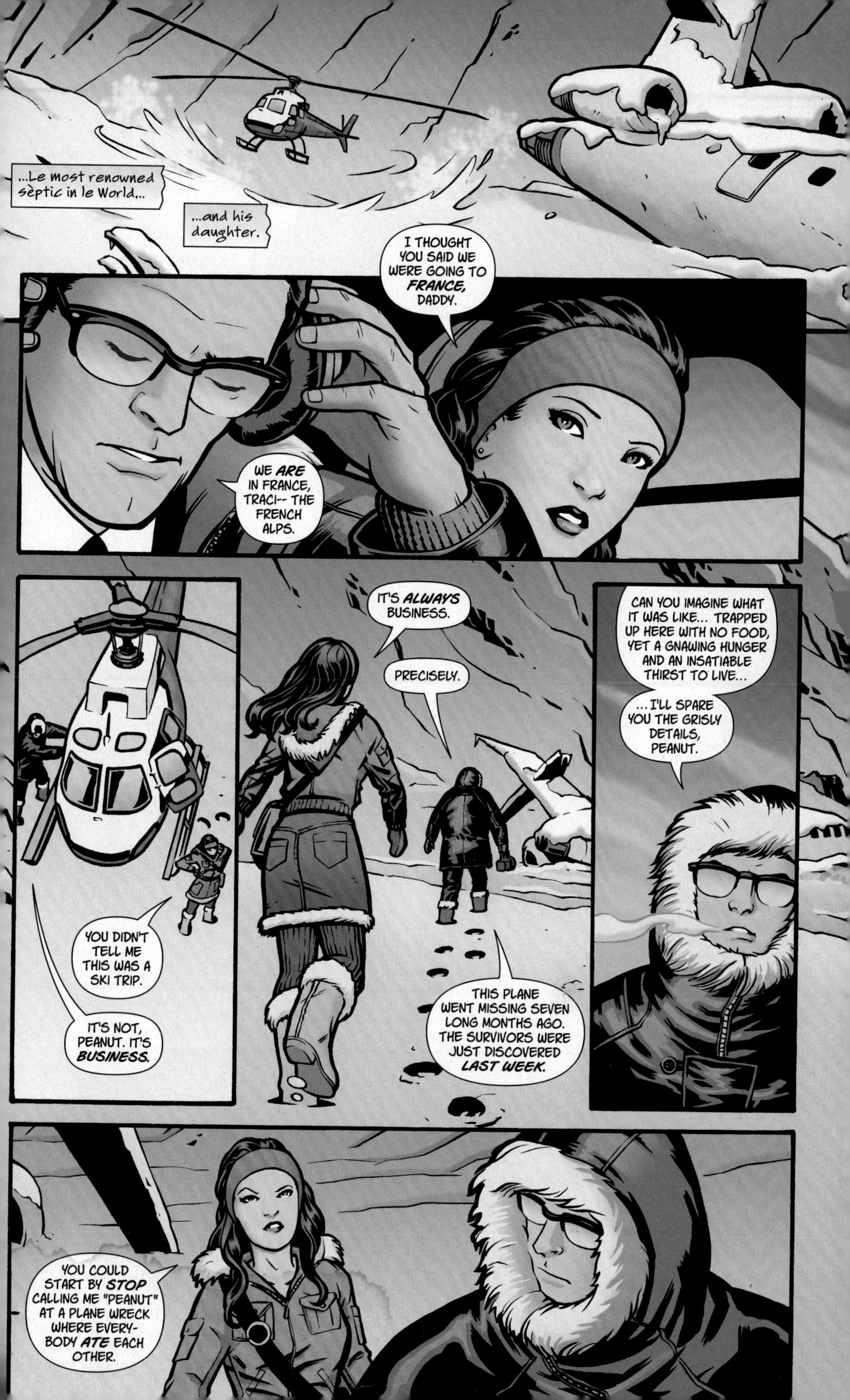
...Le most renowned sèptic in le World,..
...and his daughter.
I THOUGHT YOU SAID WE WERE GOING TO *FRANCE,* DADDY.
WE *ARE* IN FRANCE, TRACI-- THE FRENCH ALPS.
YOU DIDN'T TELL ME THIS WAS A SKI TRIP.
IT'S NOT, PEANUT. IT'S *BUSINESS.*
IT'S *ALWAYS* BUSINESS.
PRECISELY.
THIS PLANE WENT MISSING SEVEN LONG MONTHS AGO. THE SURVIVORS WERE JUST DISCOVERED *LAST WEEK.*
CAN YOU IMAGINE WHAT IT WAS LIKE... TRAPPED UP HERE WITH NO FOOD, YET A GNAWING HUNGER AND AN INSATIABLE THIRST TO LIVE...
...I'LL SPARE YOU THE GRISLY DETAILS, PEANUT.
YOU COULD START BY *STOP* CALLING ME "PEANUT" AT A PLANE WRECK WHERE EVERY-BODY *ATE* EACH OTHER.

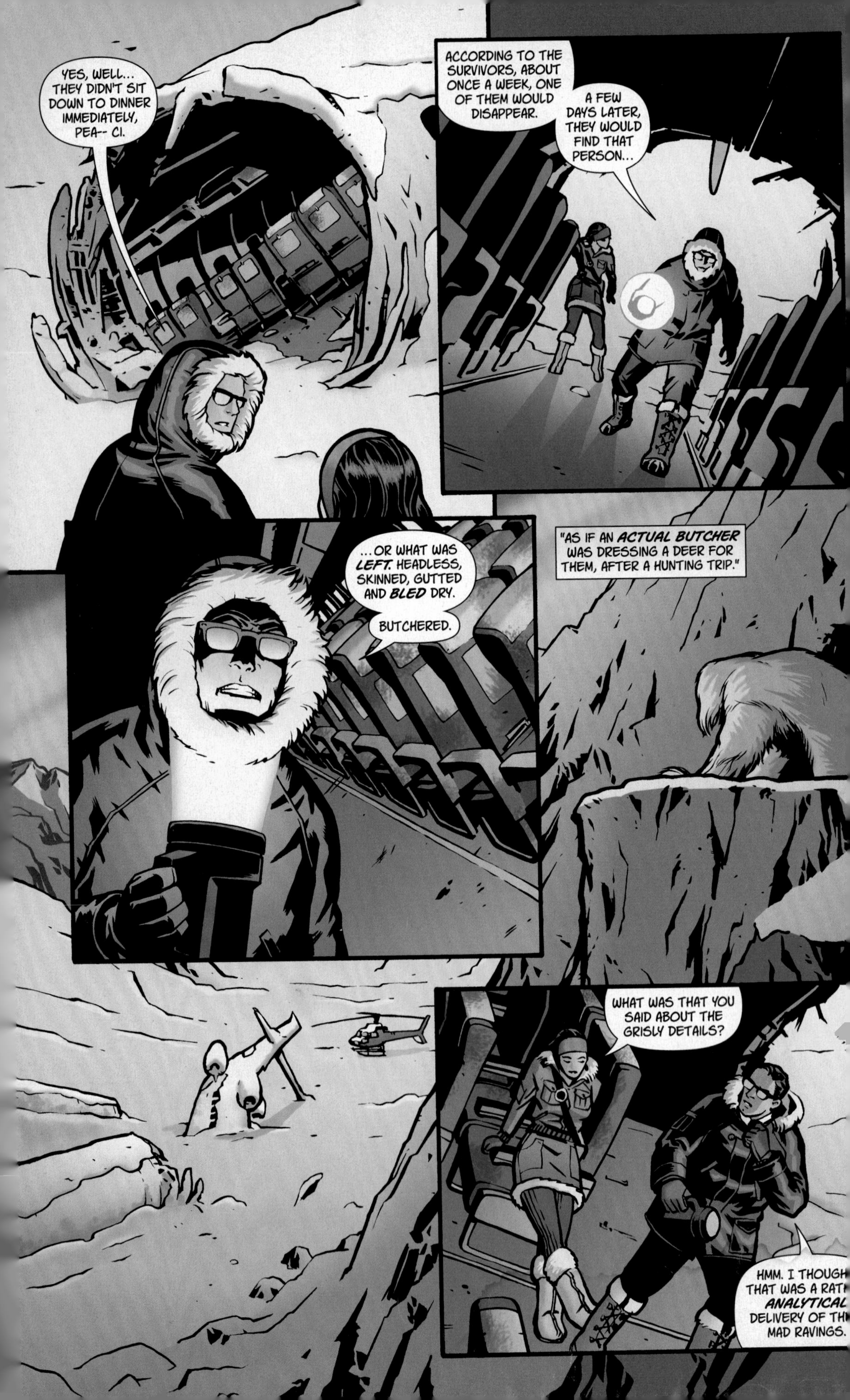
YES, WELL... THEY DIDN'T SIT DOWN TO DINNER IMMEDIATELY, PEA-- CI.
ACCORDING TO THE SURVIVORS, ABOUT ONCE A WEEK, ONE OF THEM WOULD DISAPPEAR.
A FEW DAYS LATER, THEY WOULD FIND THAT PERSON...
...OR WHAT WAS LEFT. HEADLESS, SKINNED, GUTTED AND BLED DRY.
BUTCHERED.
"AS IF AN ACTUAL BUTCHER WAS DRESSING A DEER FOR THEM, AFTER A HUNTING TRIP."
WHAT WAS THAT YOU SAID ABOUT THE GRISLY DETAILS?
HMM. I THOUGH THAT WAS A RAT ANALYTICAL DELIVERY OF TH MAD RAVINGS.

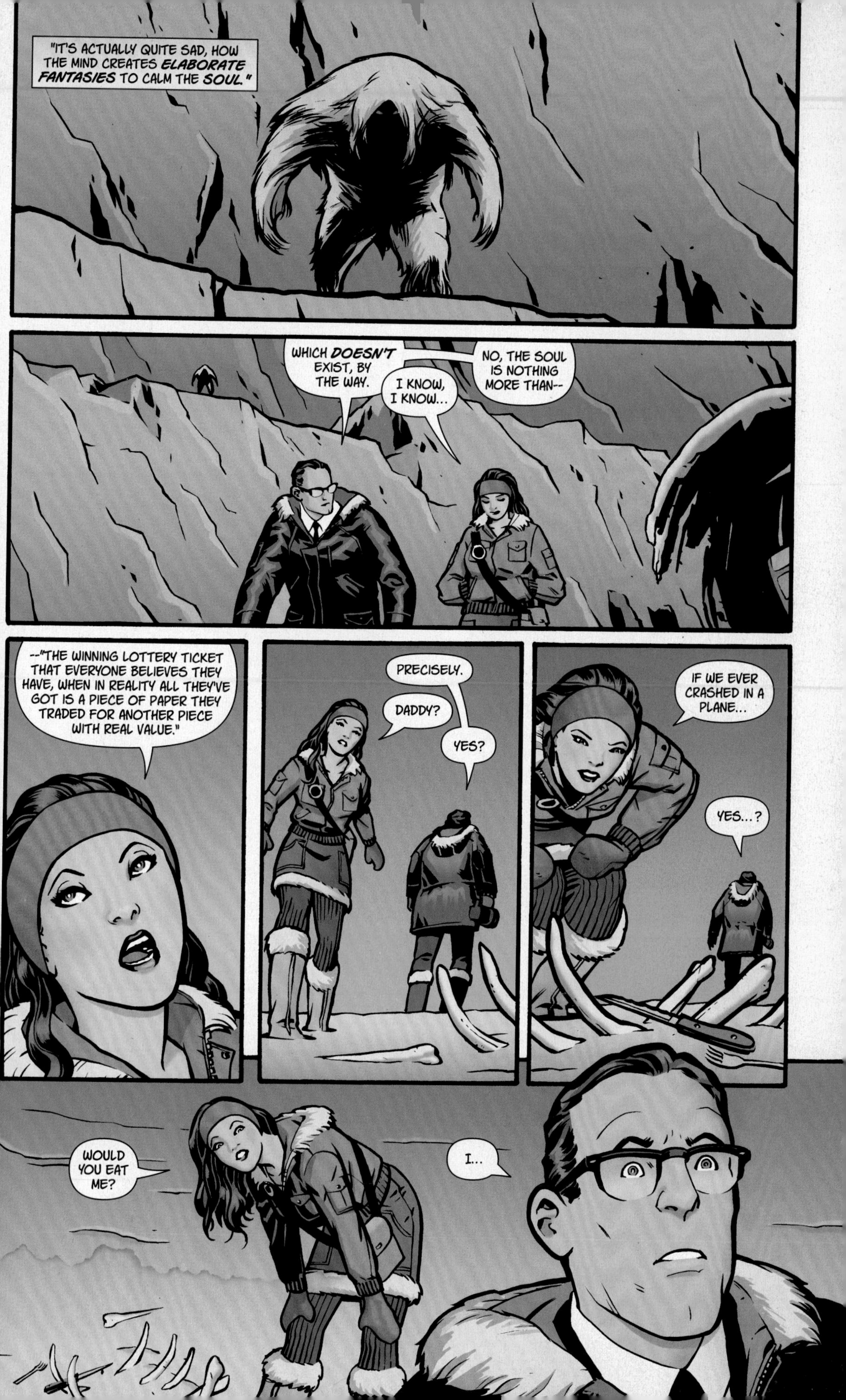
"IT'S ACTUALLY QUITE SAD, HOW THE MIND CREATES ELABORATE FANTASIES TO CALM THE SOUL."
WHICH DOESN'T EXIST, BY THE WAY.
I KNOW, I KNOW...
NO, THE SOUL IS NOTHING MORE THAN--
--"THE WINNING LOTTERY TICKET THAT EVERYONE BELIEVES THEY HAVE, WHEN IN REALITY ALL THEY'VE GOT IS A PIECE OF PAPER THEY TRADED FOR ANOTHER PIECE WITH REAL VALUE."
PRECISELY.
DADDY?
YES?
IF WE EVER CRASHED IN A PLANE...
YES...?
WOULD YOU EAT ME?
I...

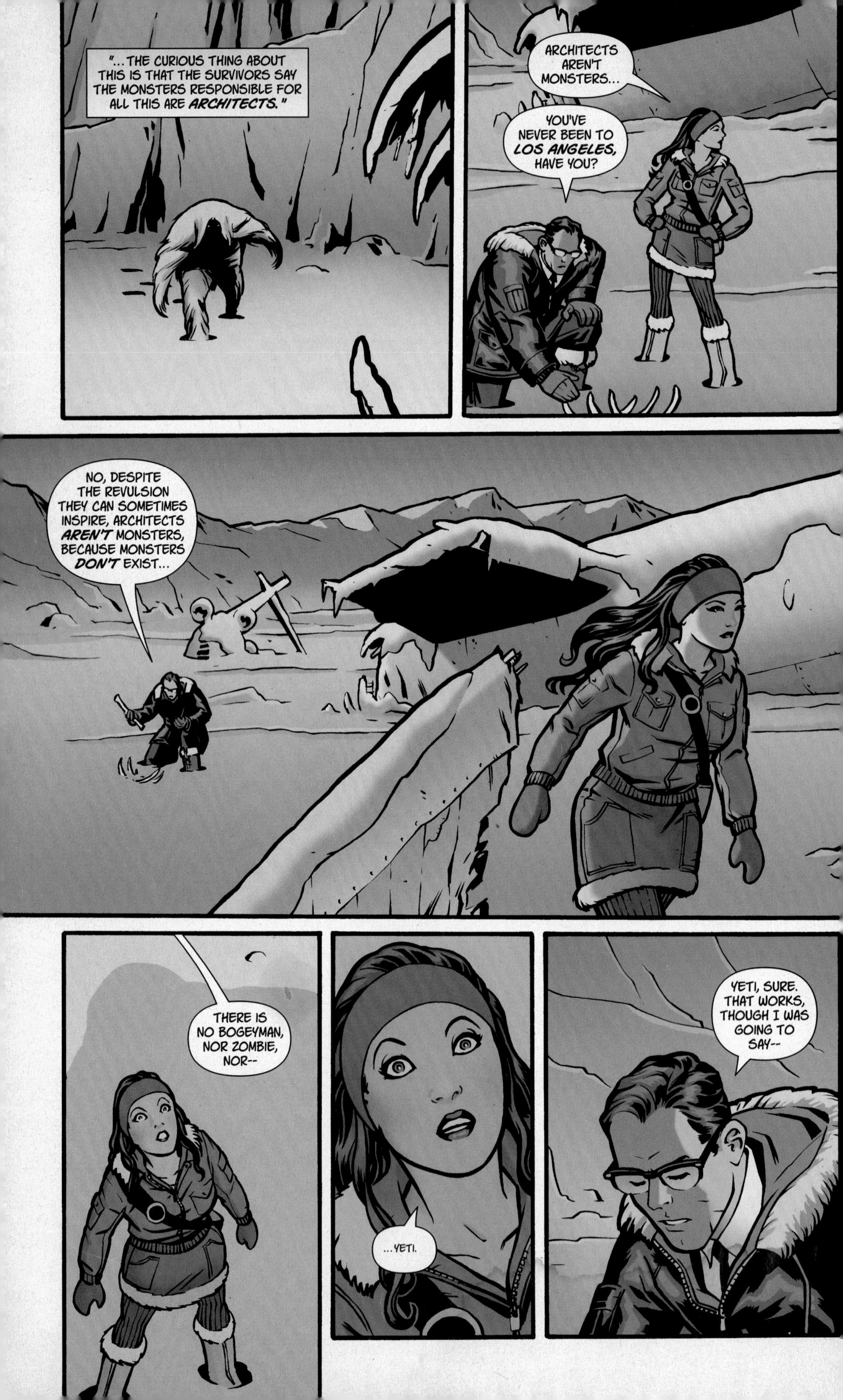
"...THE CURIOUS THING ABOUT THIS IS THAT THE SURVIVORS SAY THE MONSTERS RESPONSIBLE FOR ALL THIS ARE ARCHITECTS."
ARCHITECTS AREN'T MONSTERS...
YOU'VE NEVER BEEN TO LOS ANGELES, HAVE YOU?
NO, DESPITE THE REVULSION THEY CAN SOMETIMES INSPIRE, ARCHITECTS AREN'T MONSTERS, BECAUSE MONSTERS DON'T EXIST...
THERE IS NO BOGEYMAN, NOR ZOMBIE, NOR--
...YETI.
YETI, SURE. THAT WORKS, THOUGH I WAS GOING TO SAY--

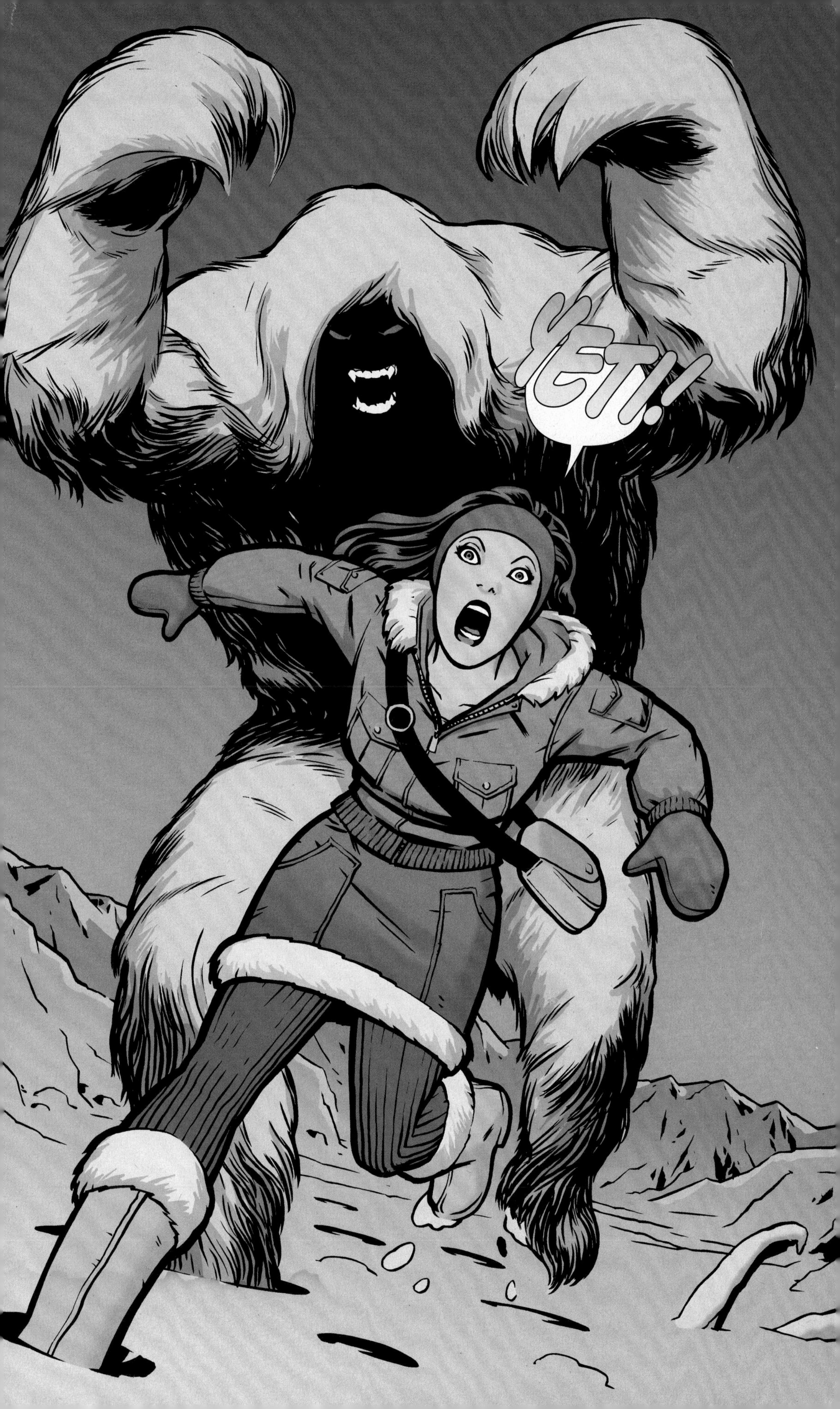
YETI!!

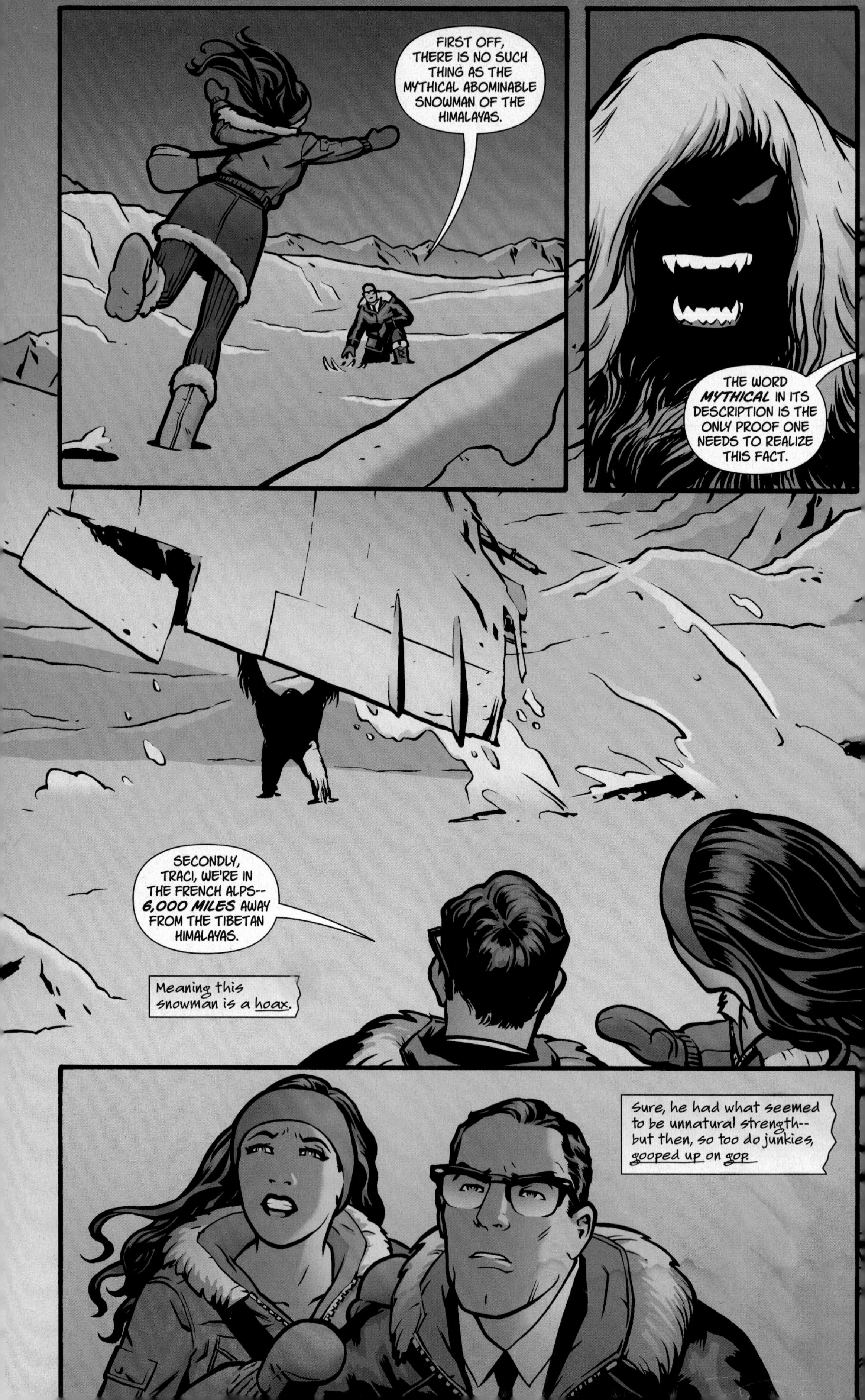
FIRST OFF, THERE IS NO SUCH THING AS THE MYTHICAL ABOMINABLE SNOWMAN OF THE HIMALAYAS.
THE WORD MYTHICAL IN ITS DESCRIPTION IS THE ONLY PROOF ONE NEEDS TO REALIZE THIS FACT.
SECONDLY, TRACI, WE'RE IN THE FRENCH ALPS-- 6,000 MILES AWAY FROM THE TIBETAN HIMALAYAS.
Meaning this snowman is a hoax.
Sure, he had what seemed to be unnatural strength-- but then, so too do junkies, gooped up on gop.

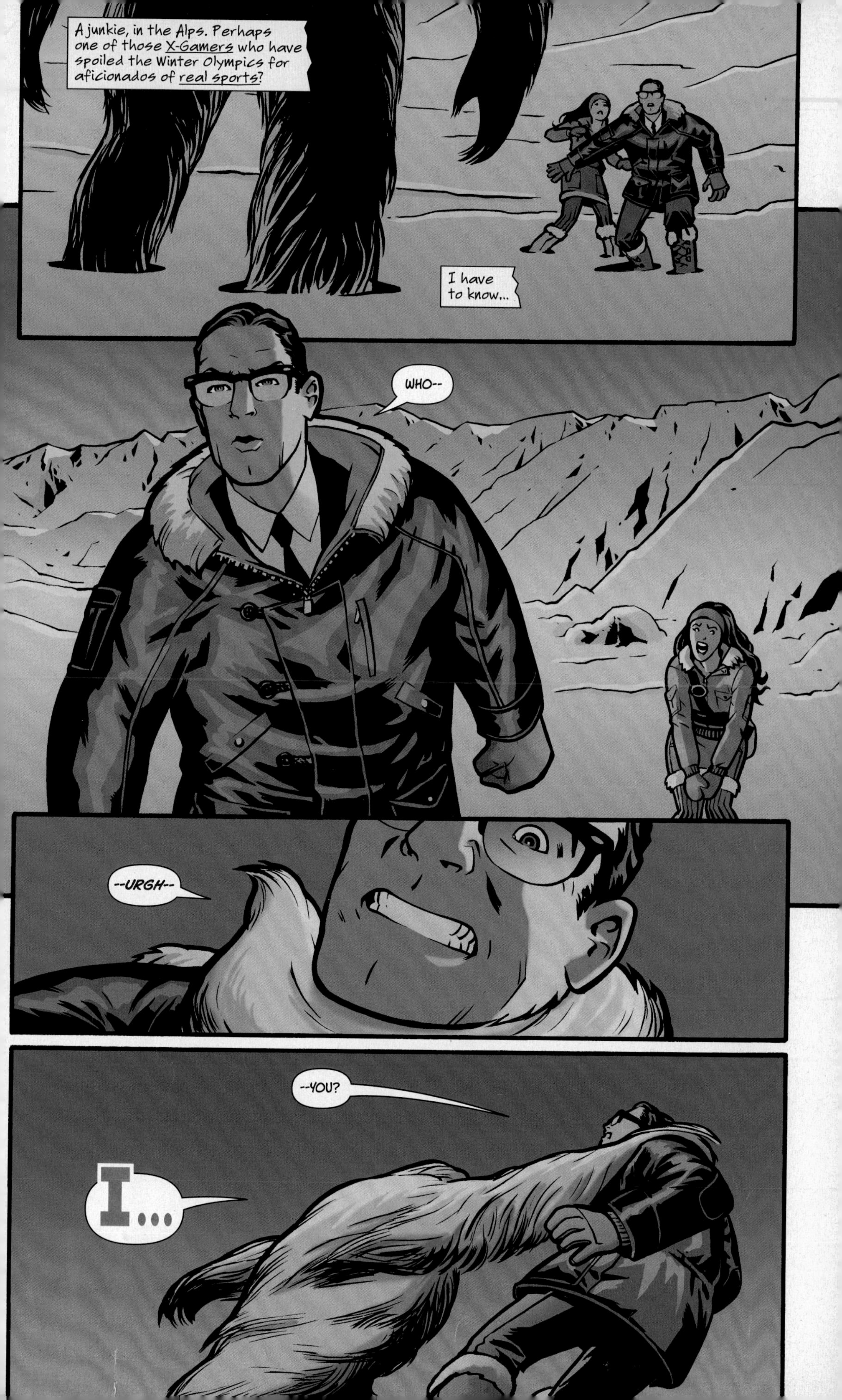
A junkie, in the Alps. Perhaps one of those X-Gamers who have spoiled the Winter Olympics for aficionados of real sports?
I have to know...
WHO--
--URGH--
--YOU?
I...

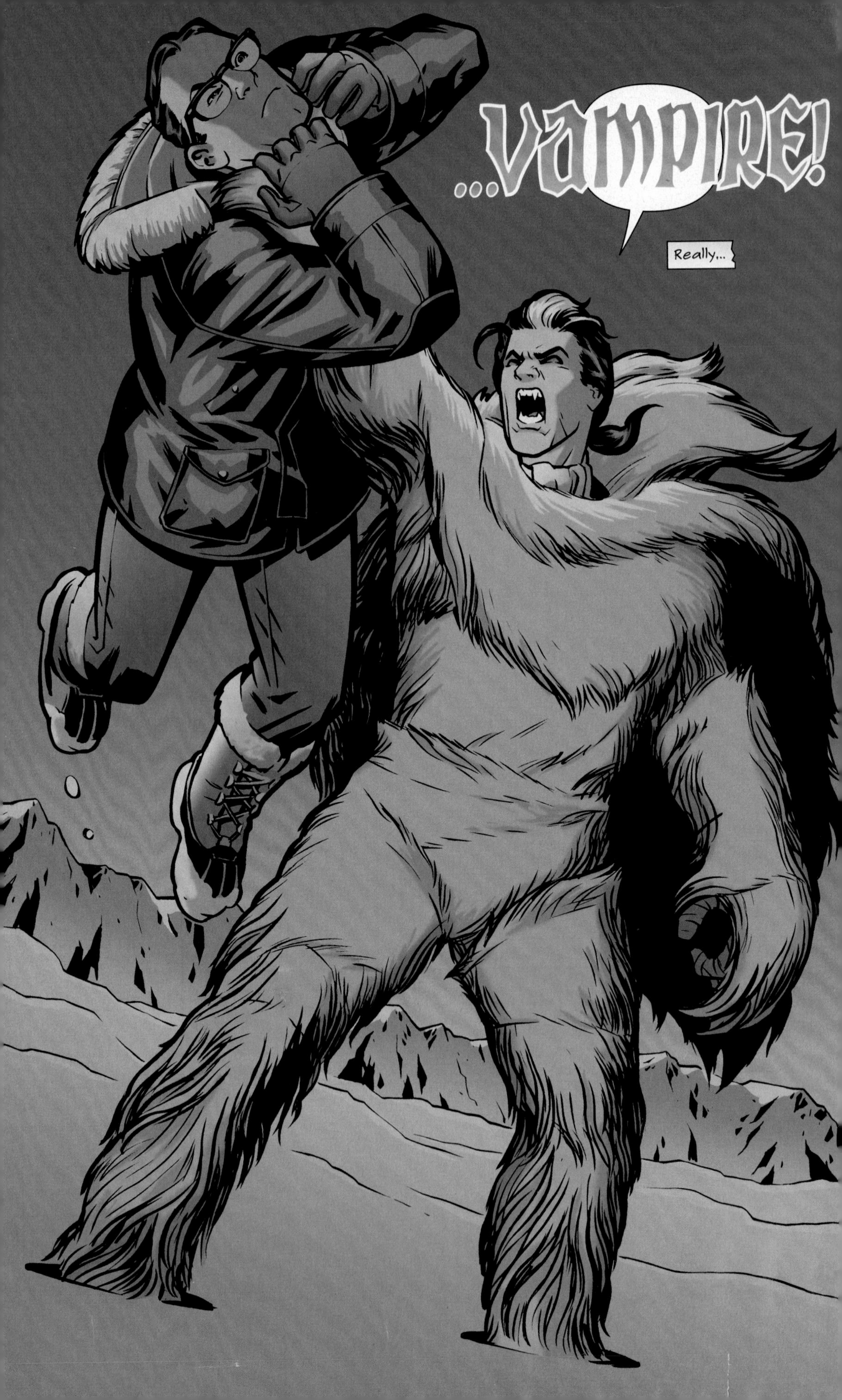

...VAMPIRE!
Really...

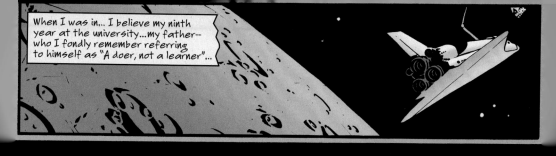

When I was in... I believe my ninth year at the university...my father-- who I fondly remember referring to himself as "A doer, not a learner"...

...muttered either under his breath or over the ice in his ninth _bourbon_ as he wrote my tuition check, that if I stayed in school long enough they'd have to make me a _doctor._

And like so many other fathers, dismissed by their offspring as "know-nothings" or "not the boss of me's"...

...he proved to be _right._ And so I dedicated my degree-- and the fortune he _doerdly_ amassed, to disproving one inescapable truth...

...one man's _fiction_ is another _fact_ for the masses.

My name is Terry 13

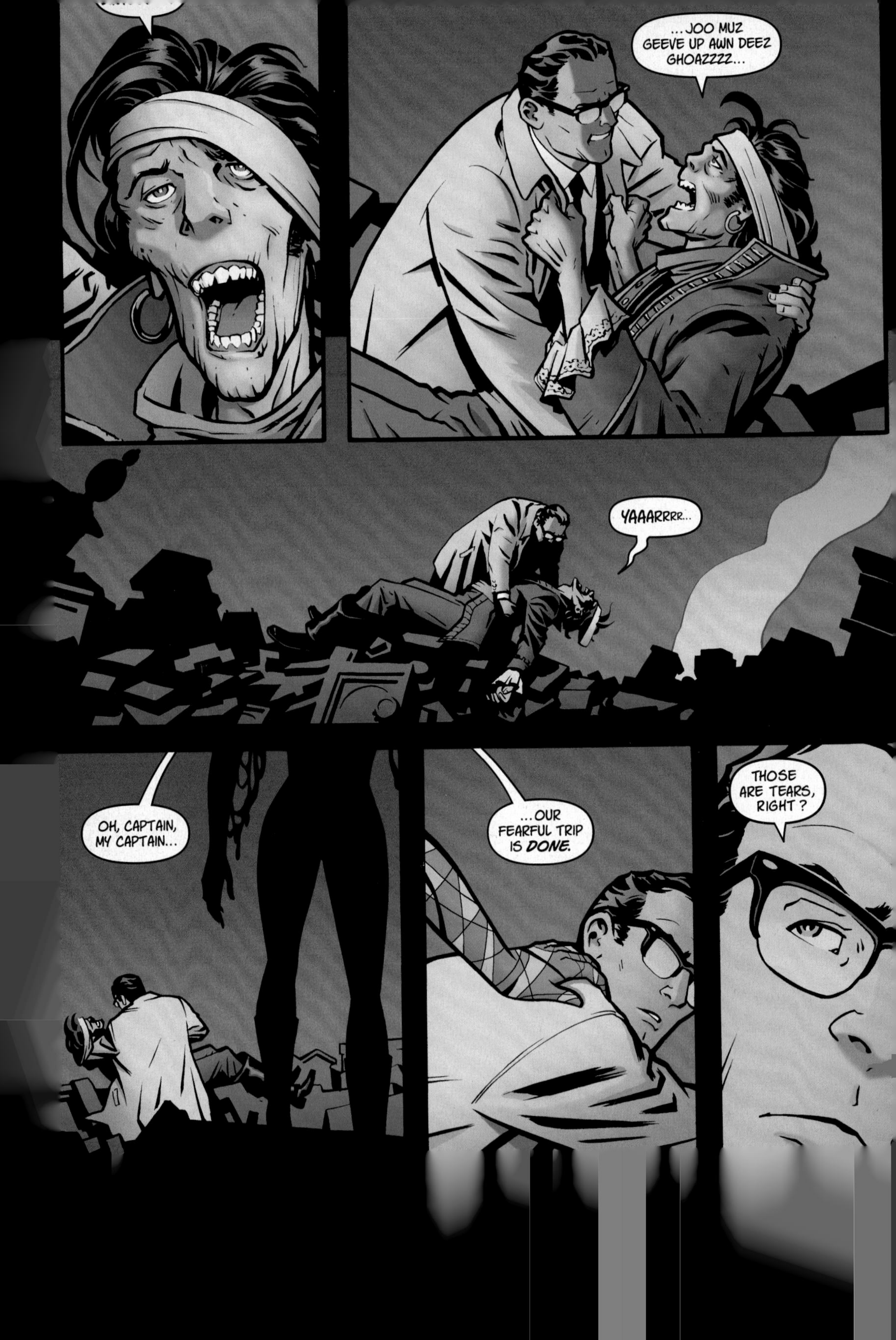
...JOO MUZ GEEVE UP AWN DEEZ GHOAZZZZ...
YAAARRRR...
OH, CAPTAIN, MY CAPTAIN...
...OUR FEARFUL TRIP IS DONE.
THOSE ARE TEARS, RIGHT?

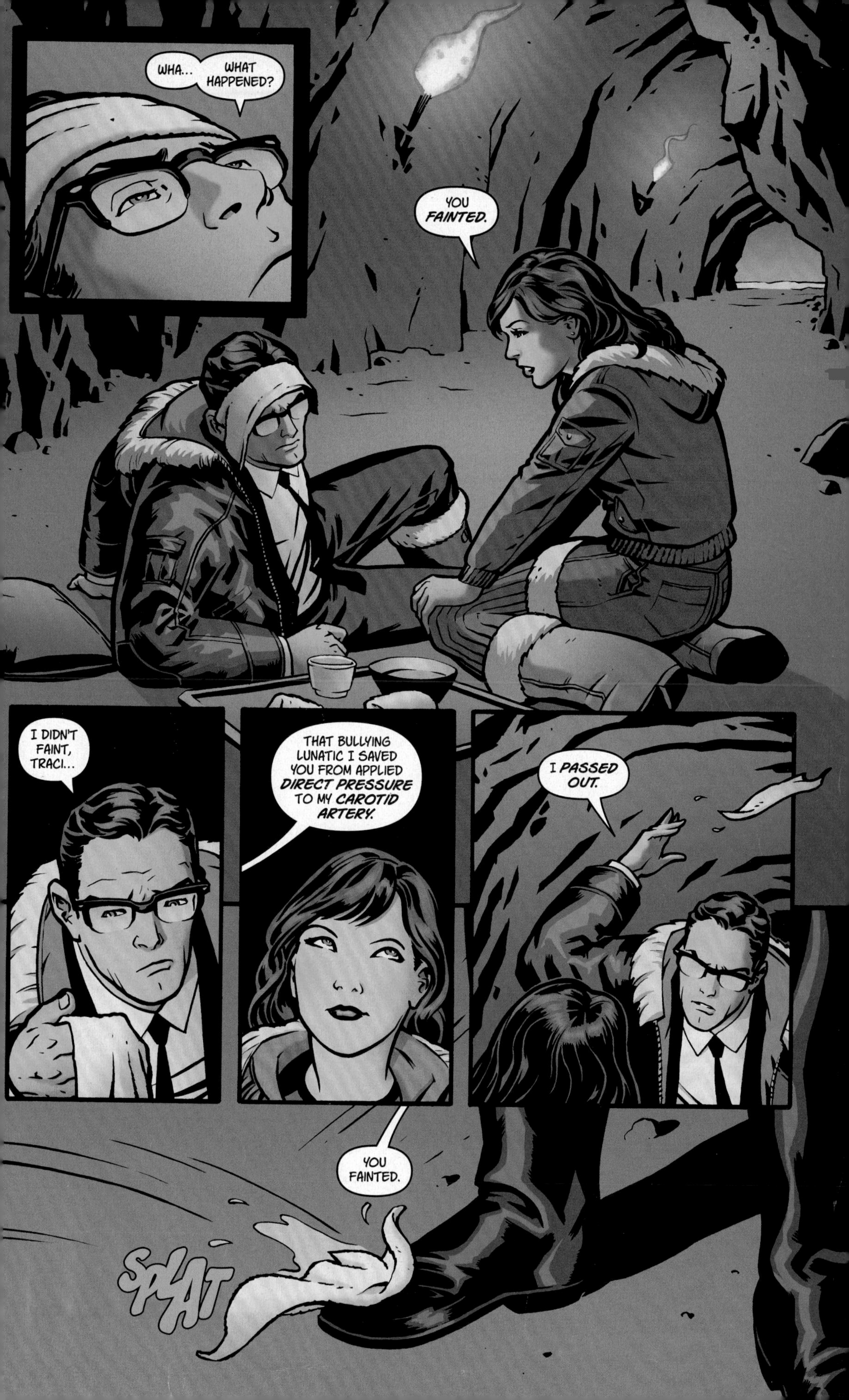
WHA...
WHAT HAPPENED?
YOU FAINTED.
I DIDN'T FAINT, TRACI...
THAT BULLYING LUNATIC I SAVED YOU FROM APPLIED DIRECT PRESSURE TO MY CAROTID ARTERY.
I PASSED OUT.
YOU FAINTED.
SPLAT

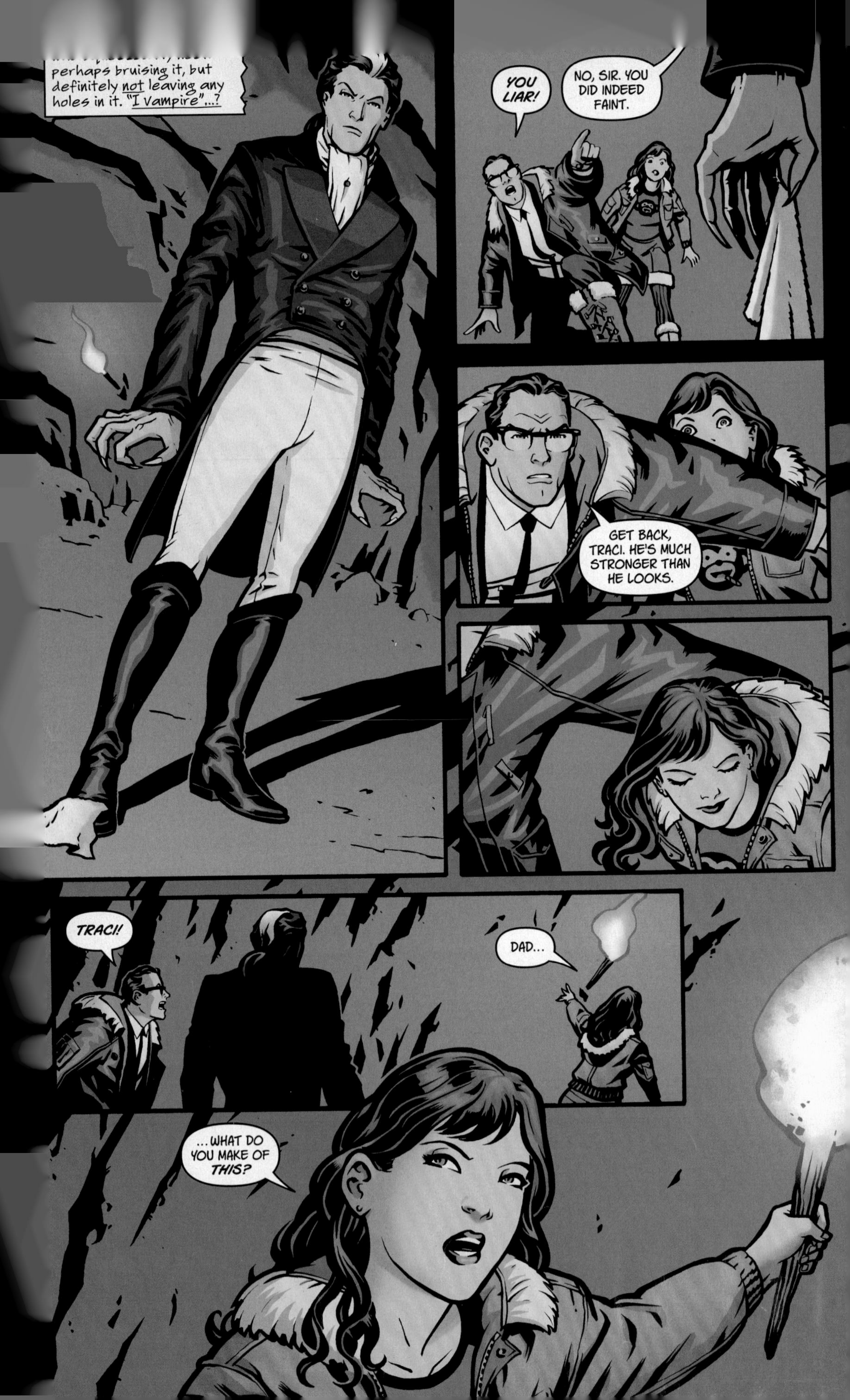
perhaps bruising it, but definitely not leaving any holes in it. "I Vampire"...?
YOU LIAR!
NO, SIR. YOU DID INDEED FAINT.
GET BACK, TRACI. HE'S MUCH STRONGER THAN HE LOOKS.
TRACI!
DAD...
...WHAT DO YOU MAKE OF THIS?

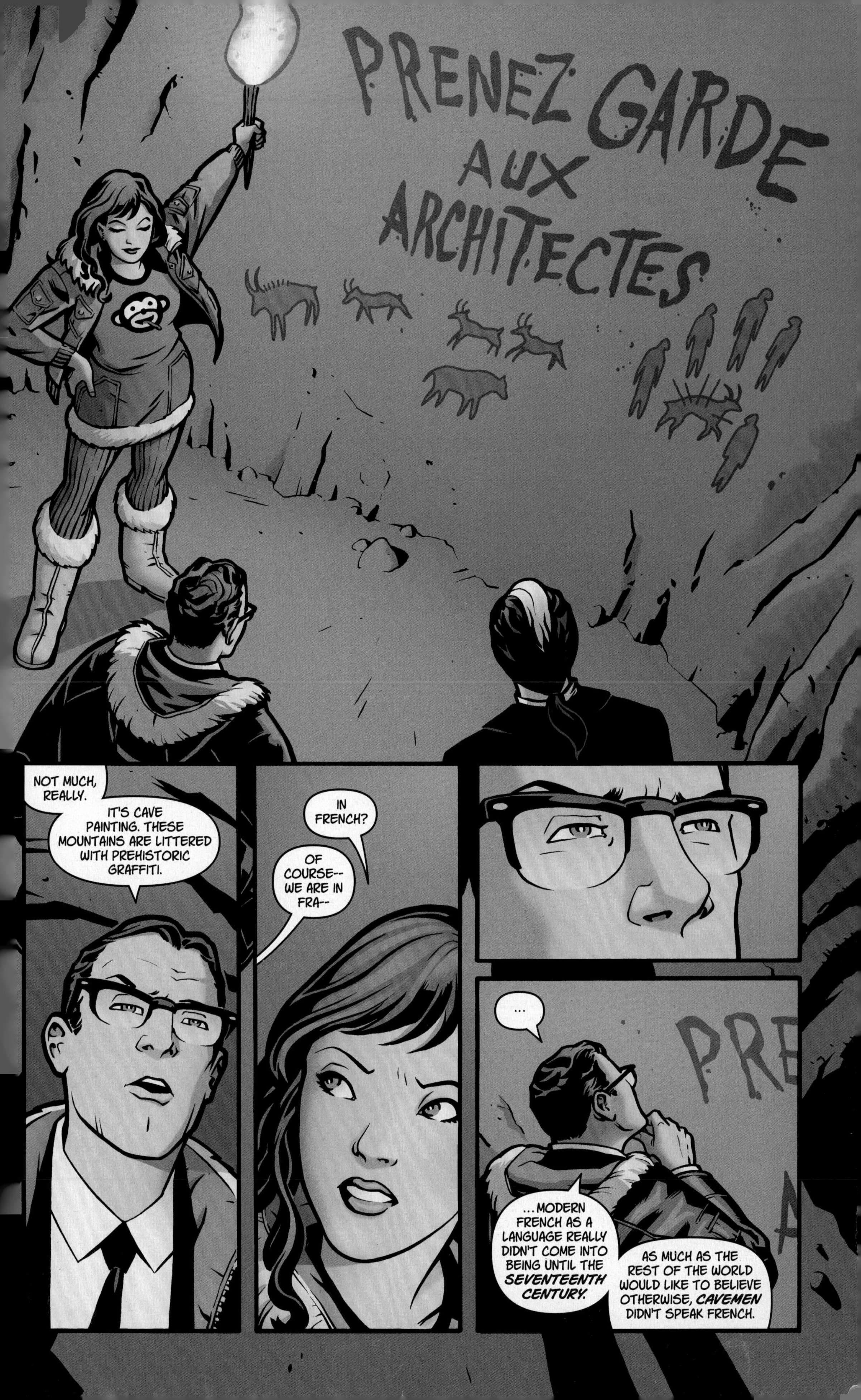
PRENEZ GARDE AUX ARCHITECTES
NOT MUCH, REALLY.
IT'S CAVE PAINTING. THESE MOUNTAINS ARE LITTERED WITH PREHISTORIC GRAFFITI.
IN FRENCH?
OF COURSE-- WE ARE IN FRA--
...
PRE
...MODERN FRENCH AS A LANGUAGE REALLY DIDN'T COME INTO BEING UNTIL THE ***SEVENTEENTH CENTURY.***
AS MUCH AS THE REST OF THE WORLD WOULD LIKE TO BELIEVE OTHERWISE, ***CAVEMEN*** DIDN'T SPEAK FRENCH.

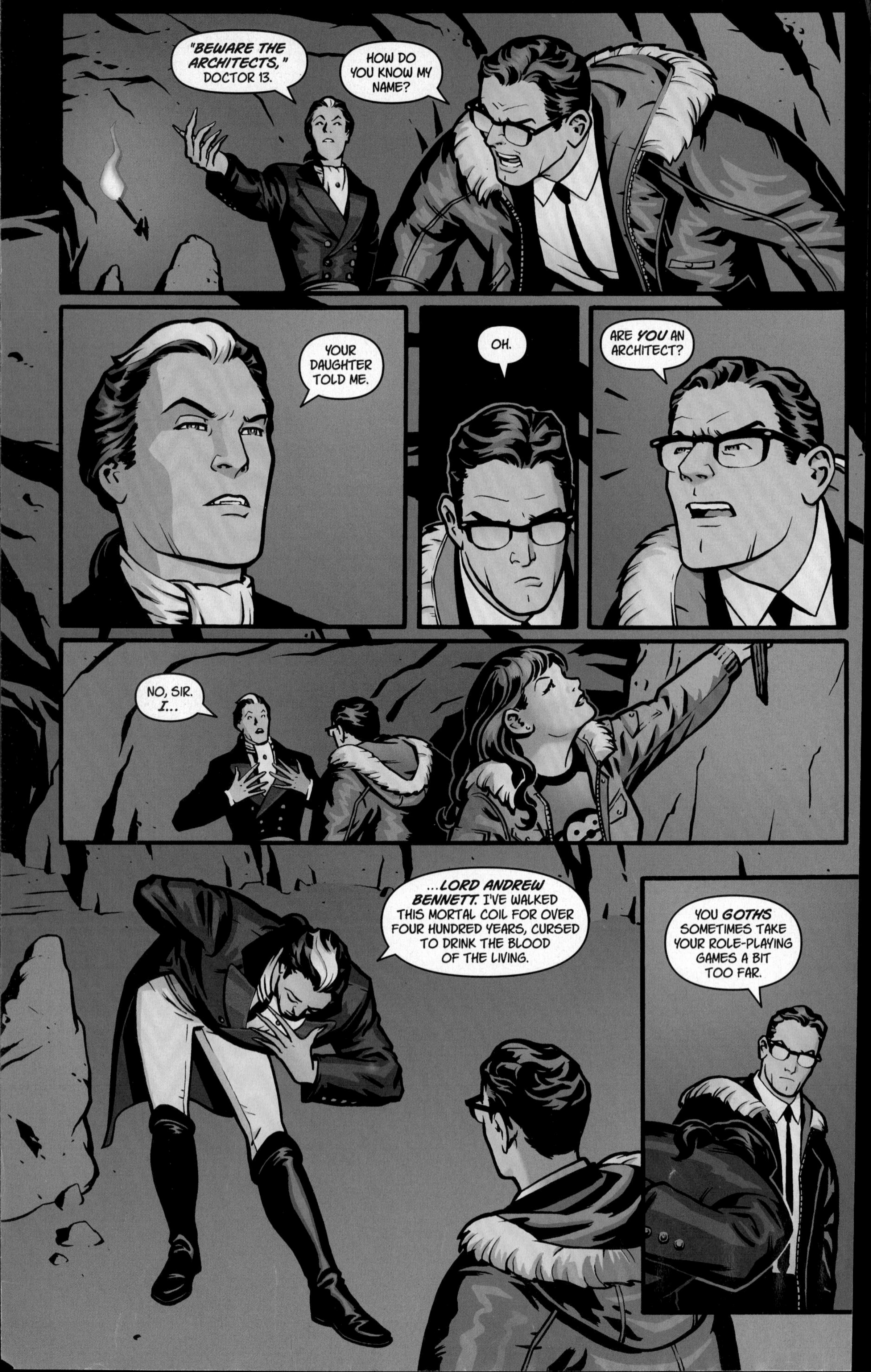
"BEWARE THE ARCHITECTS," DOCTOR 13.
HOW DO YOU KNOW MY NAME?
YOUR DAUGHTER TOLD ME.
OH.
ARE YOU AN ARCHITECT?
NO, SIR. I...
...LORD ANDREW BENNETT. I'VE WALKED THIS MORTAL COIL FOR OVER FOUR HUNDRED YEARS, CURSED TO DRINK THE BLOOD OF THE LIVING.
YOU GOTHS SOMETIMES TAKE YOUR ROLE-PLAYING GAMES A BIT TOO FAR.

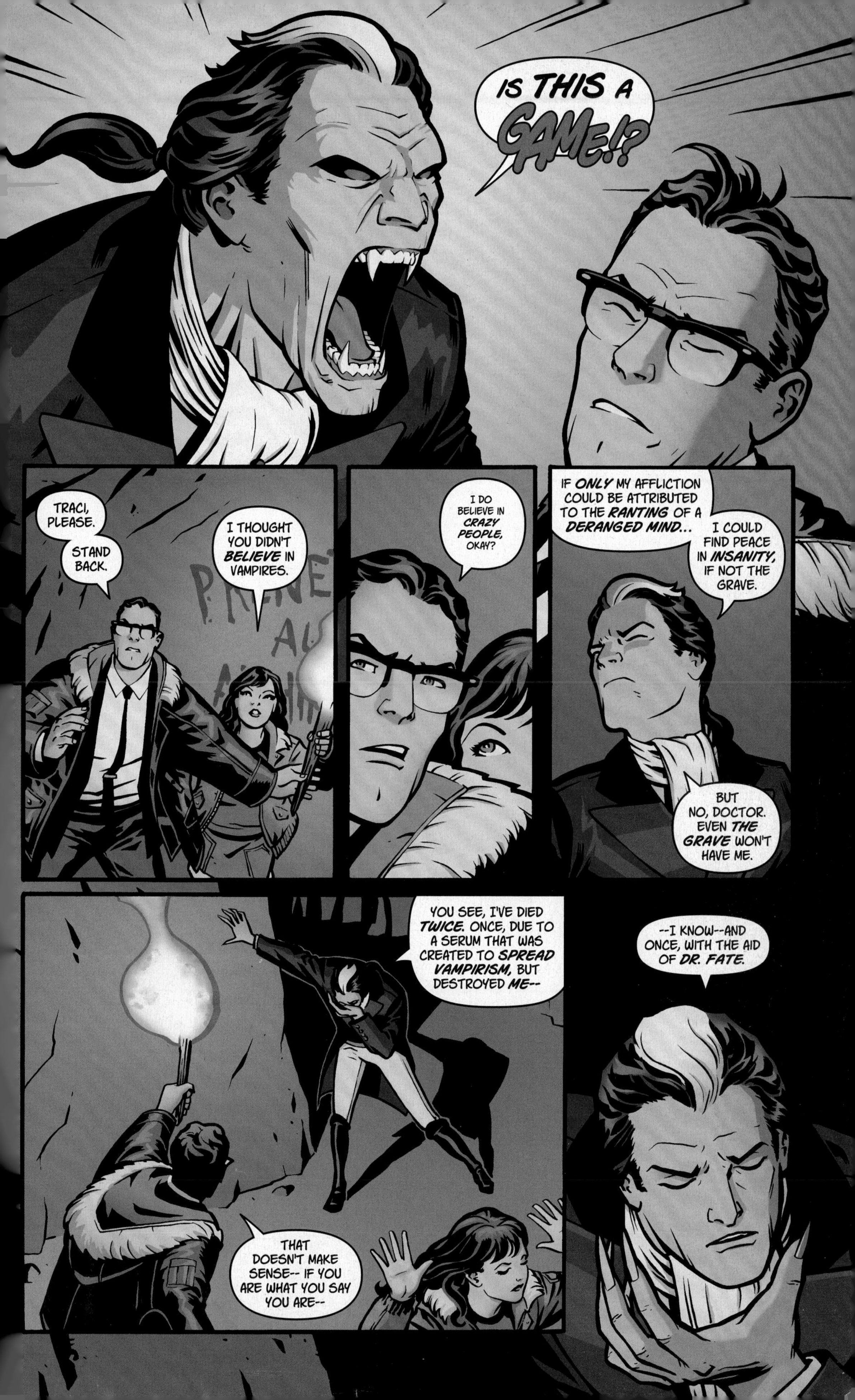

IS THIS A GAME!?
TRACI, PLEASE.
STAND BACK.
I THOUGHT YOU DIDN'T BELIEVE IN VAMPIRES.
I DO BELIEVE IN CRAZY PEOPLE, OKAY?
IF ONLY MY AFFLICTION COULD BE ATTRIBUTED TO THE RANTING OF A DERANGED MIND...
I COULD FIND PEACE IN INSANITY, IF NOT THE GRAVE.
BUT NO, DOCTOR. EVEN THE GRAVE WON'T HAVE ME.
YOU SEE, I'VE DIED TWICE. ONCE, DUE TO A SERUM THAT WAS CREATED TO SPREAD VAMPIRISM, BUT DESTROYED ME--
THAT DOESN'T MAKE SENSE-- IF YOU ARE WHAT YOU SAY YOU ARE--
--I KNOW--AND ONCE, WITH THE AID OF DR. FATE.

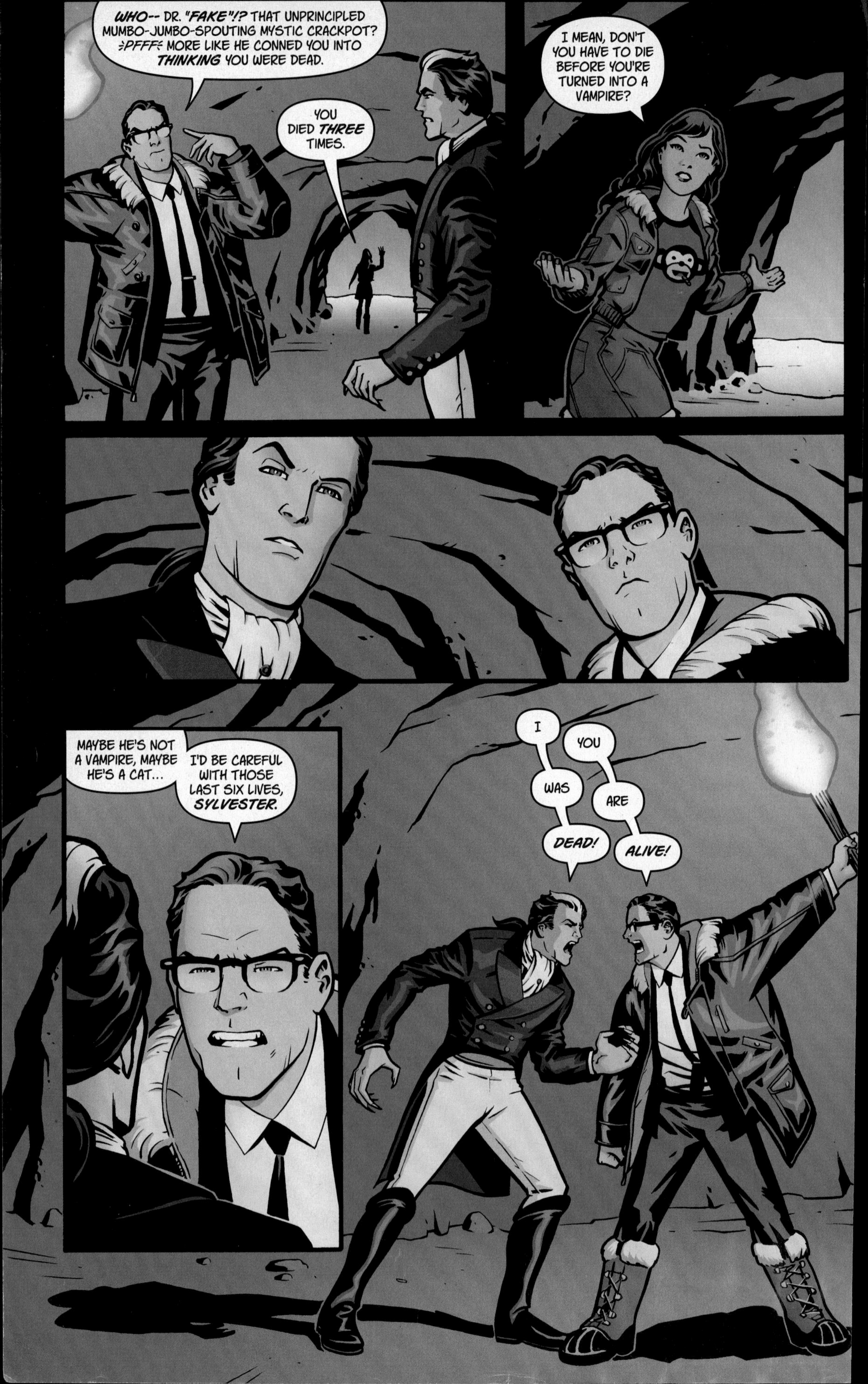
WHO-- DR. "FAKE"!? THAT UNPRINCIPLED MUMBO-JUMBO-SPOUTING MYSTIC CRACKPOT? ≠PFFF≠ MORE LIKE HE CONNED YOU INTO THINKING YOU WERE DEAD.
YOU DIED THREE TIMES.
I MEAN, DON'T YOU HAVE TO DIE BEFORE YOU'RE TURNED INTO A VAMPIRE?
MAYBE HE'S NOT A VAMPIRE, MAYBE HE'S A CAT...
I'D BE CAREFUL WITH THOSE LAST SIX LIVES, SYLVESTER.
I WAS DEAD!
YOU ARE ALIVE!

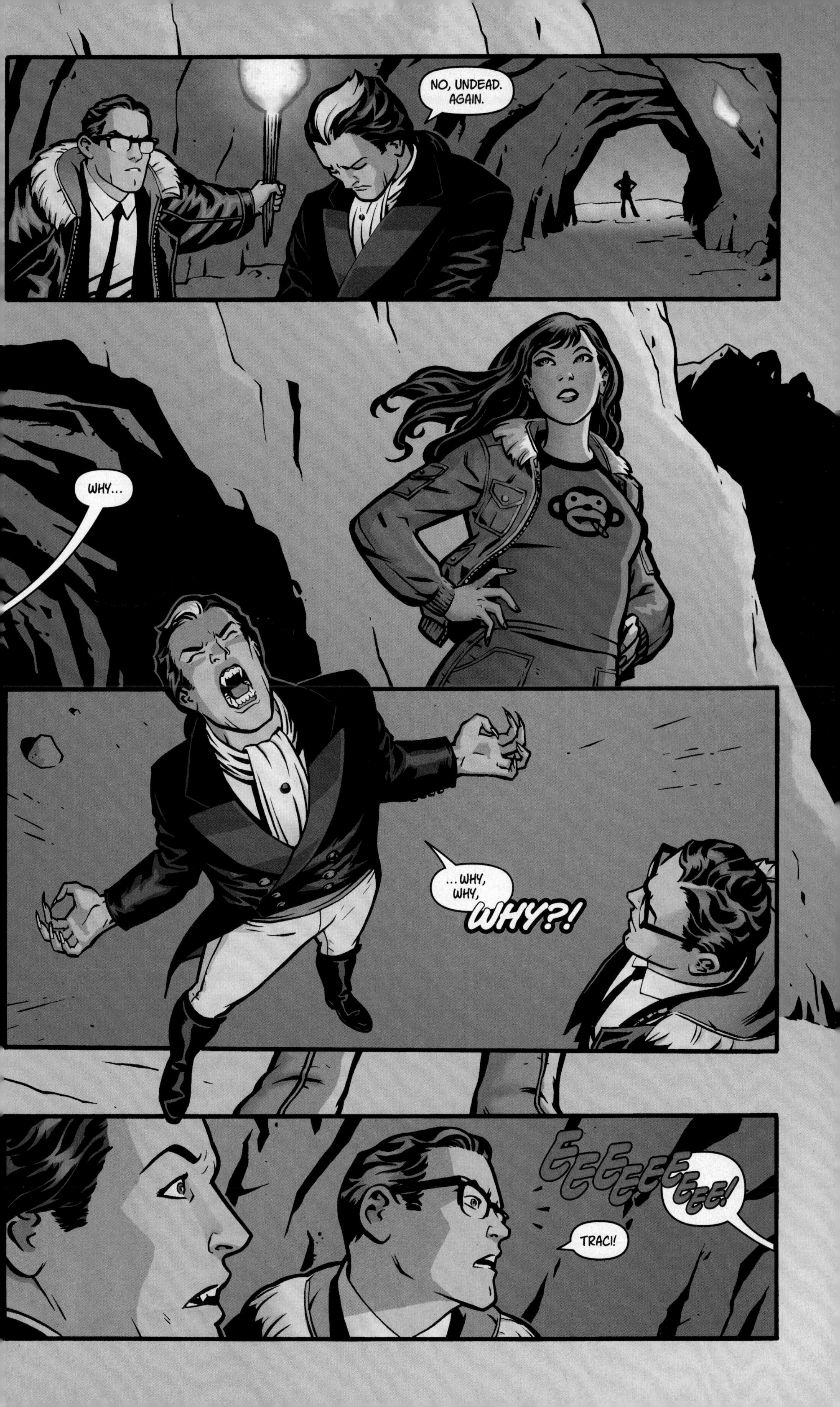
NO, UNDEAD. AGAIN.
WHY...
...WHY, WHY, WHY?!
EEEEEEEEEEEE!
TRACI!

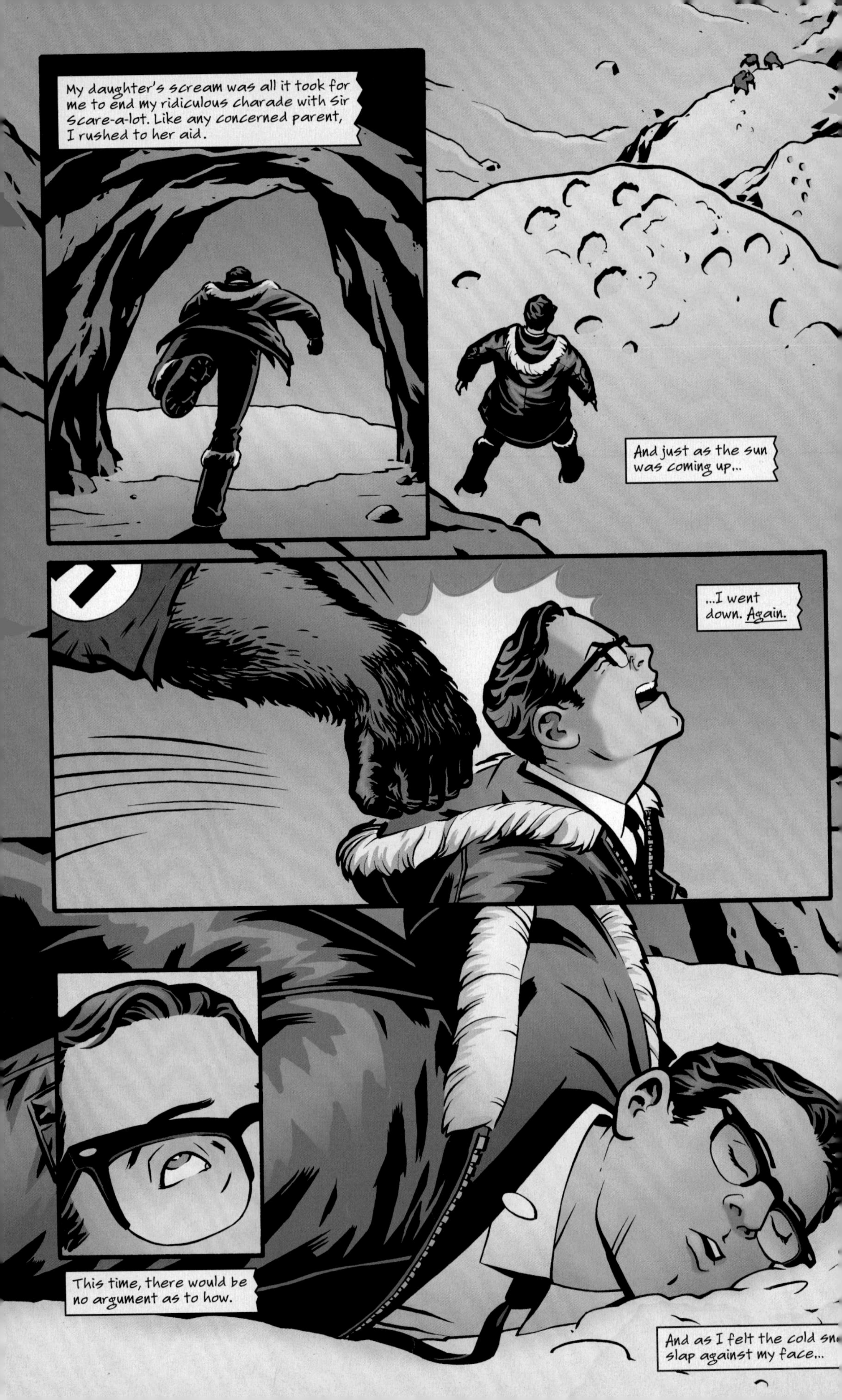
My daughter's scream was all it took for me to end my ridiculous charade with Sir Scare-a-lot. Like any concerned parent, I rushed to her aid.
And just as the sun was coming up...
...I went down. Again.
This time, there would be no argument as to how.
And as I felt the cold sn
slap against my face...

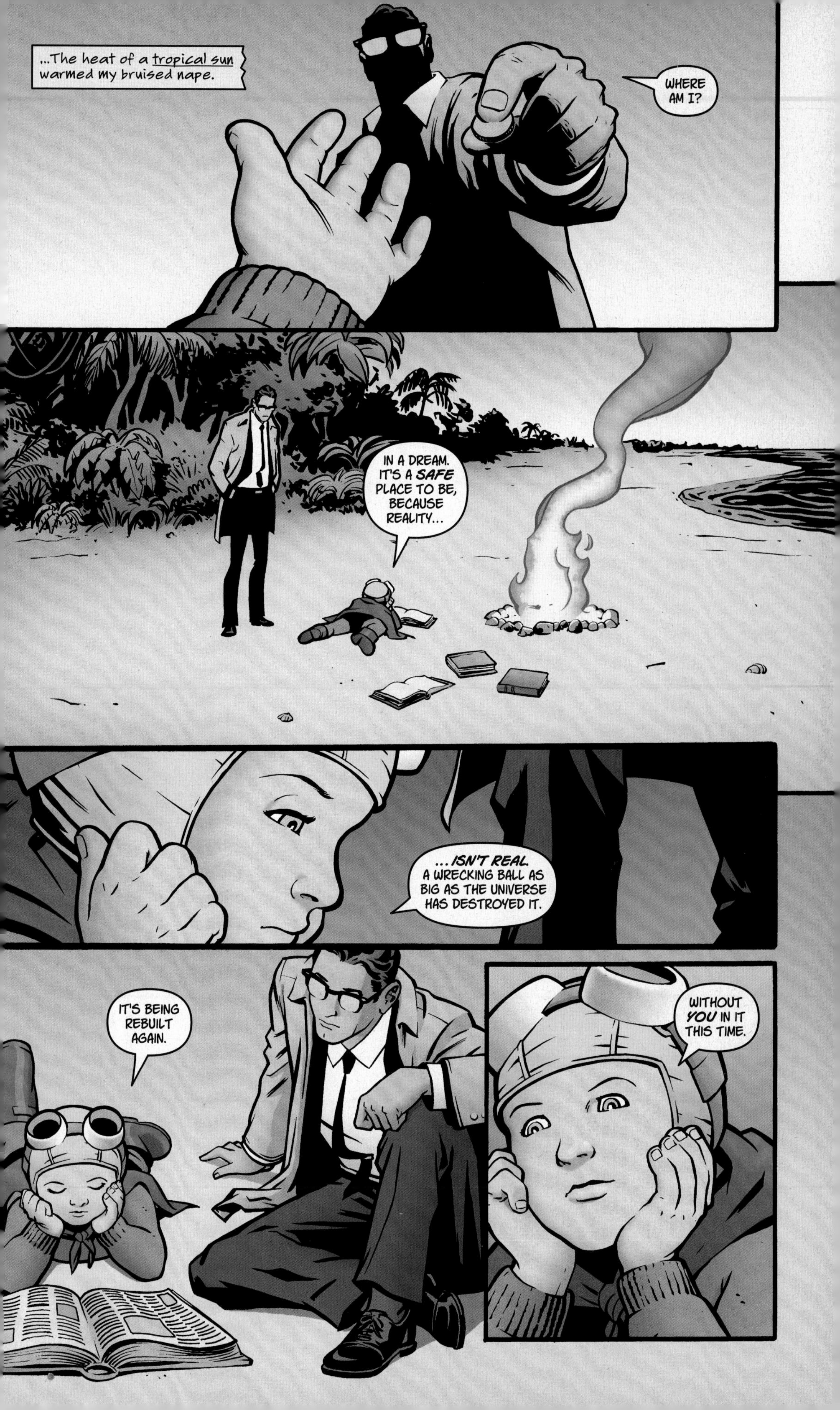

...The heat of a tropical sun warmed my bruised nape.
WHERE AM I?
IN A DREAM. IT'S A SAFE PLACE TO BE, BECAUSE REALITY...
...ISN'T REAL. A WRECKING BALL AS BIG AS THE UNIVERSE HAS DESTROYED IT.
IT'S BEING REBUILT AGAIN.
WITHOUT YOU IN IT THIS TIME.

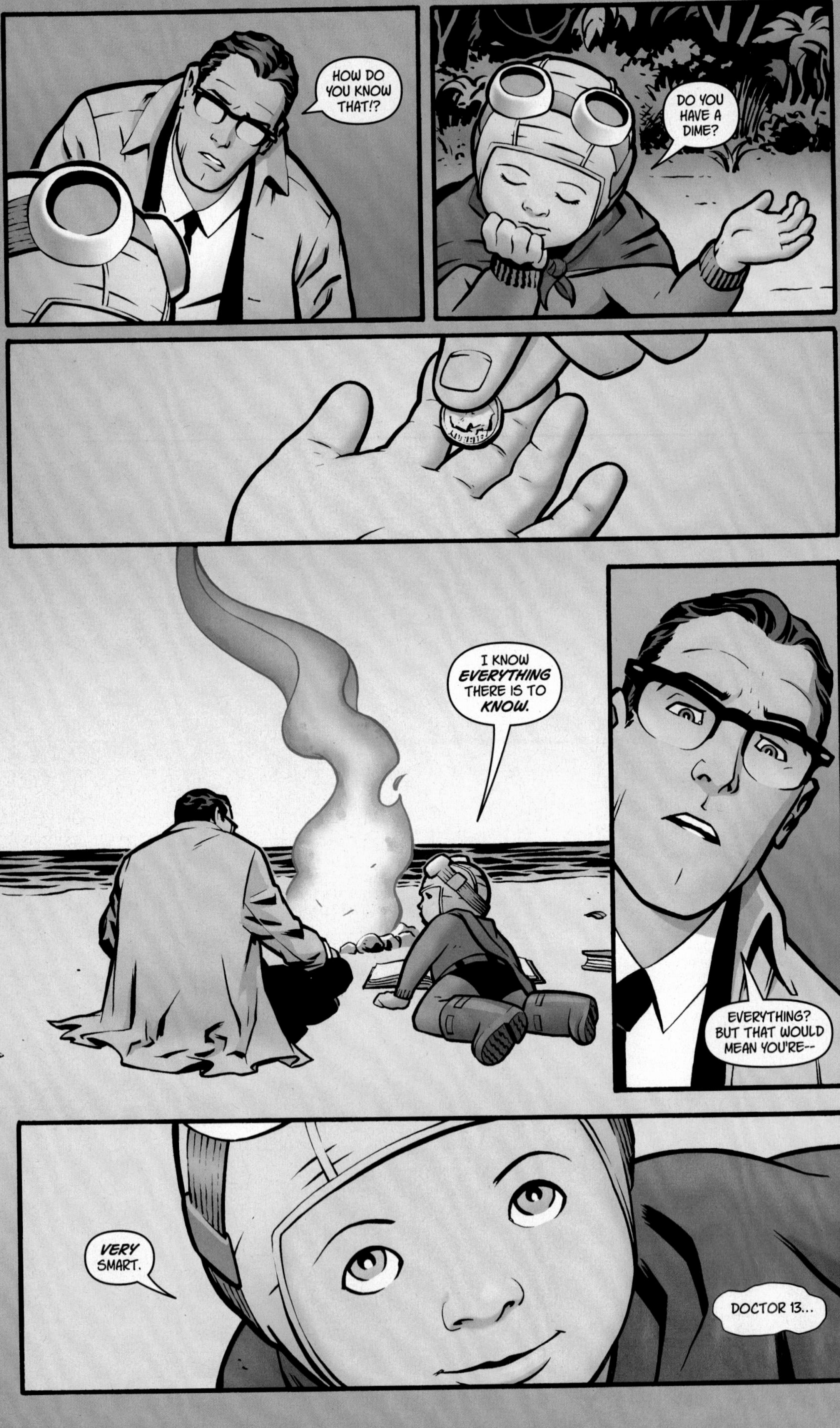

HOW DO YOU KNOW THAT!?
DO YOU HAVE A DIME?
I KNOW *EVERYTHING* THERE IS TO *KNOW*.
EVERYTHING? BUT THAT WOULD MEAN YOU'RE--
*VERY* SMART.
DOCTOR 13...

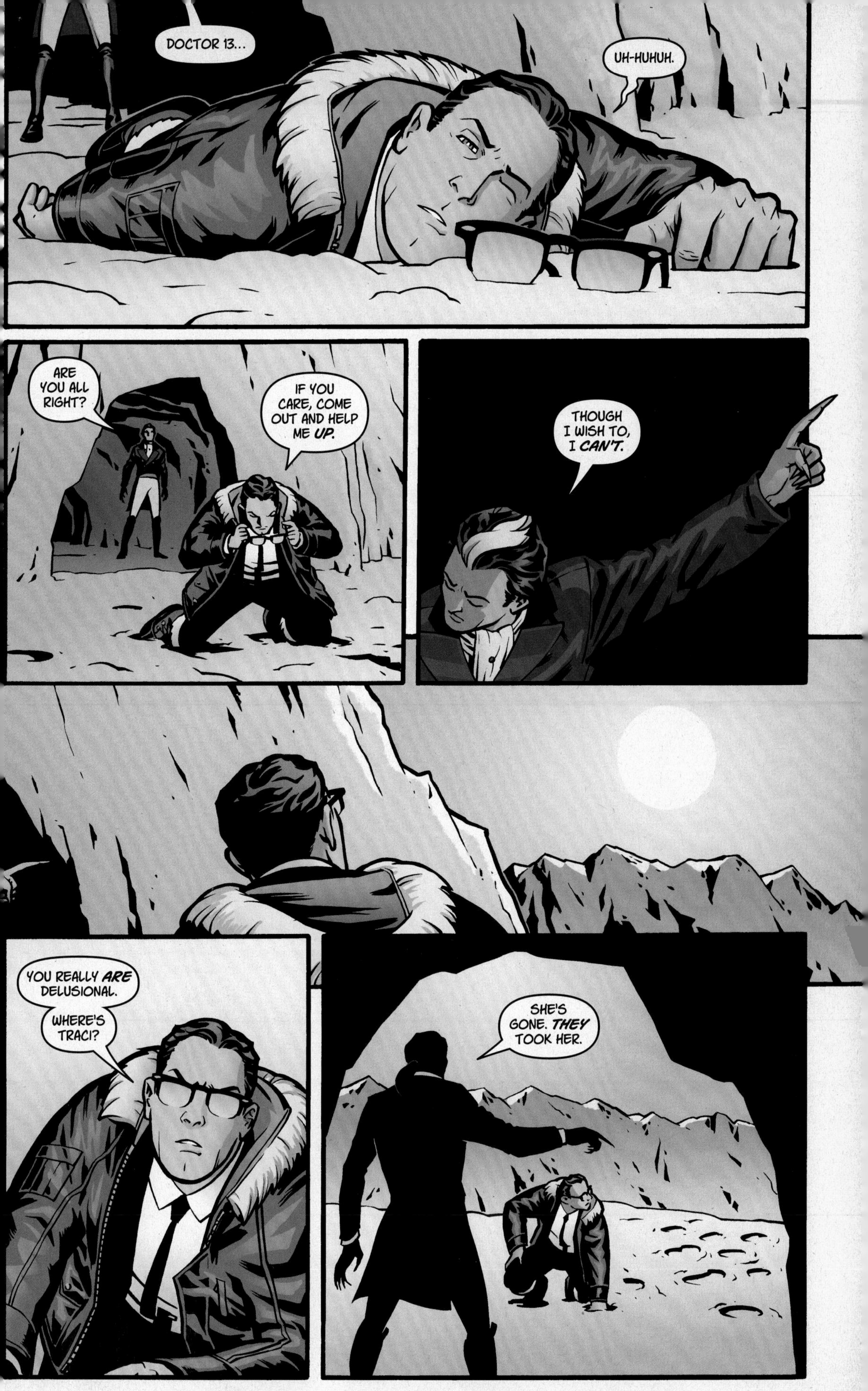

DOCTOR 13...
UH-HUHUH.
ARE YOU ALL RIGHT?
IF YOU CARE, COME OUT AND HELP ME UP.
THOUGH I WISH TO, I CAN'T.
YOU REALLY ARE DELUSIONAL.
WHERE'S TRACI?
SHE'S GONE. THEY TOOK HER.

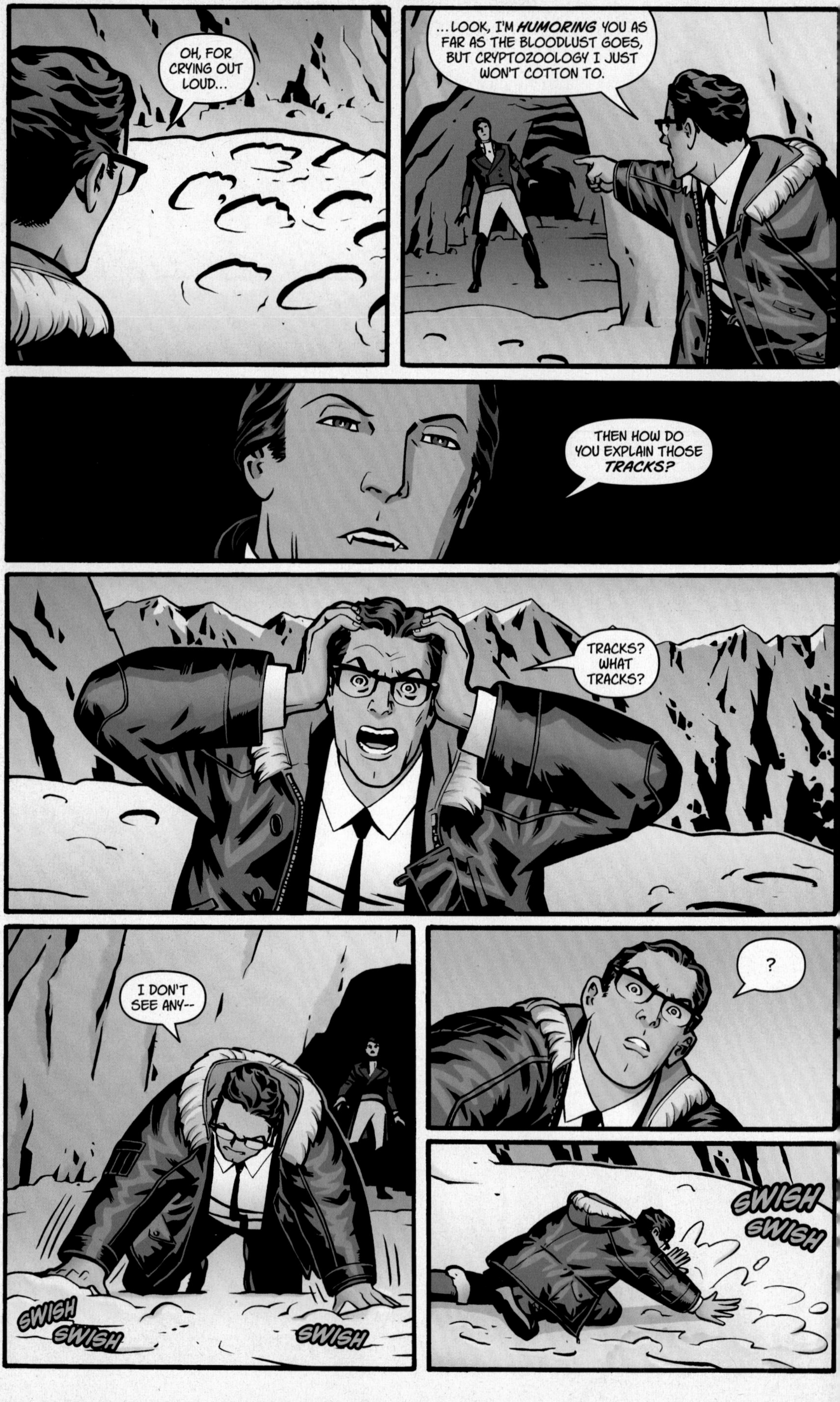
OH, FOR CRYING OUT LOUD...
...LOOK, I'M HUMORING YOU AS FAR AS THE BLOODLUST GOES, BUT CRYPTOZOOLOGY I JUST WON'T COTTON TO.
THEN HOW DO YOU EXPLAIN THOSE TRACKS?
TRACKS? WHAT TRACKS?
I DON'T SEE ANY--
SWISH SWISH
SWISH
?
SWISH SWISH

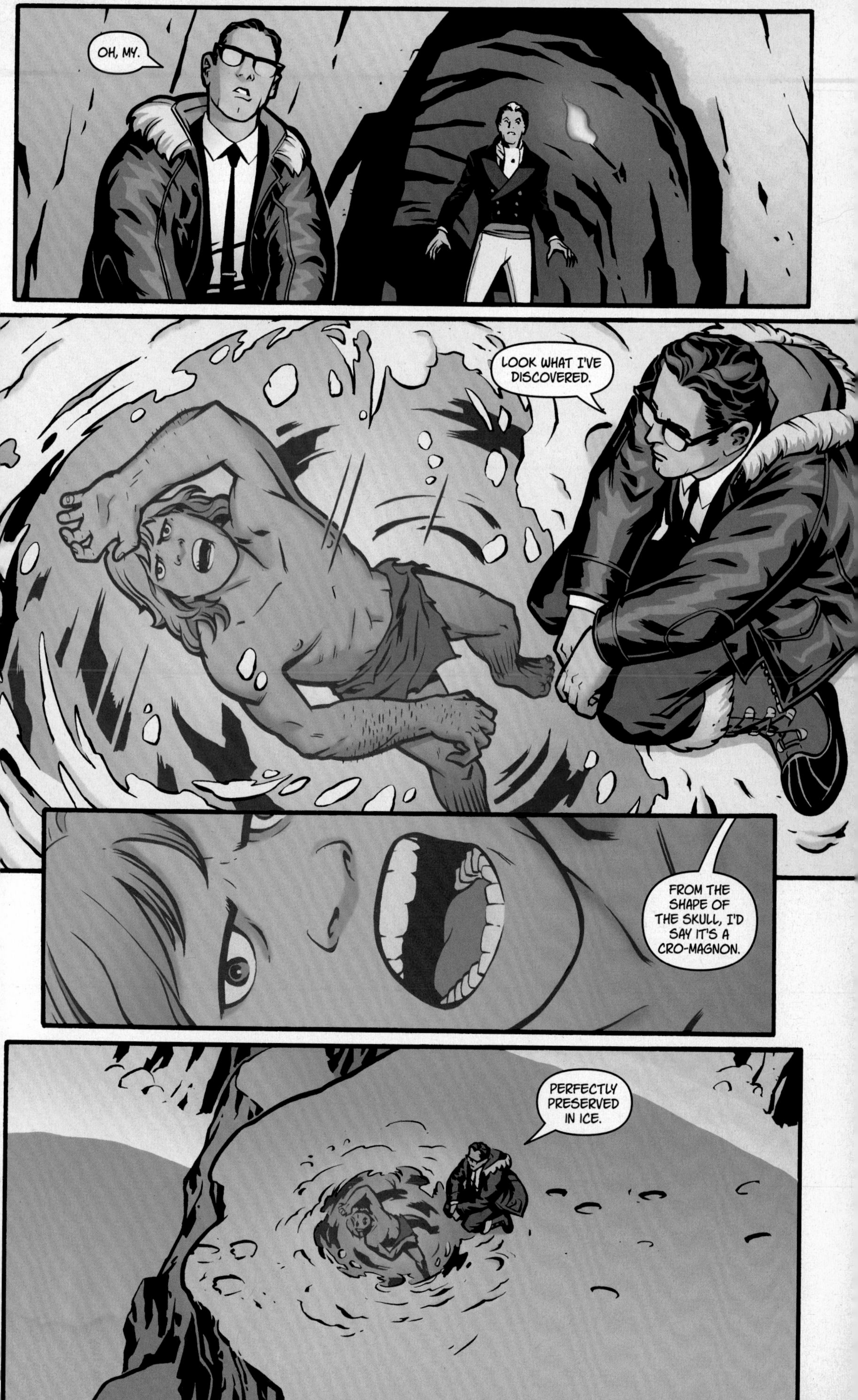
OH, MY.
LOOK WHAT I'VE DISCOVERED.
FROM THE SHAPE OF THE SKULL, I'D SAY IT'S A CRO-MAGNON.
PERFECTLY PRESERVED IN ICE.

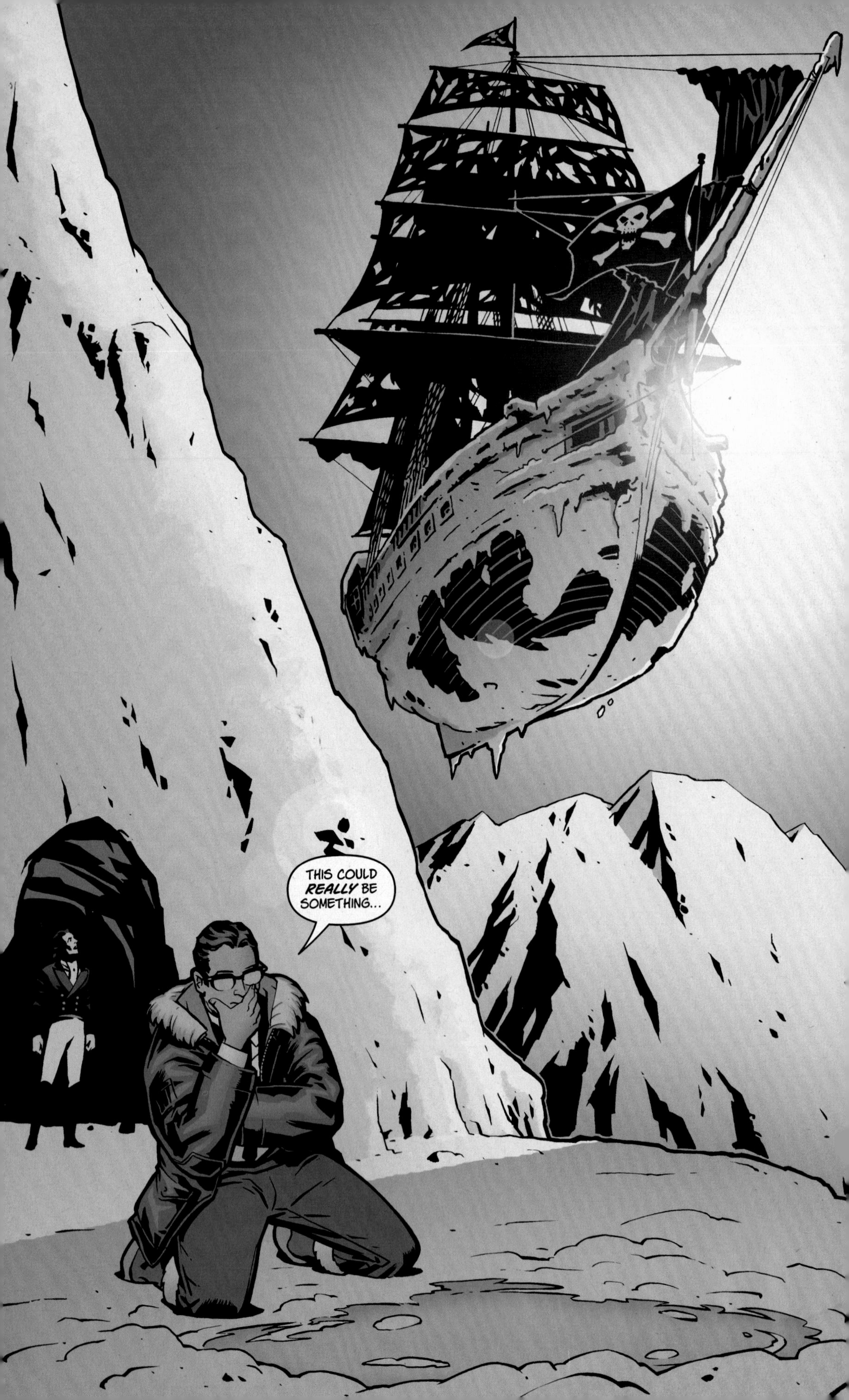
THIS COULD *REALLY* BE SOMETHING...

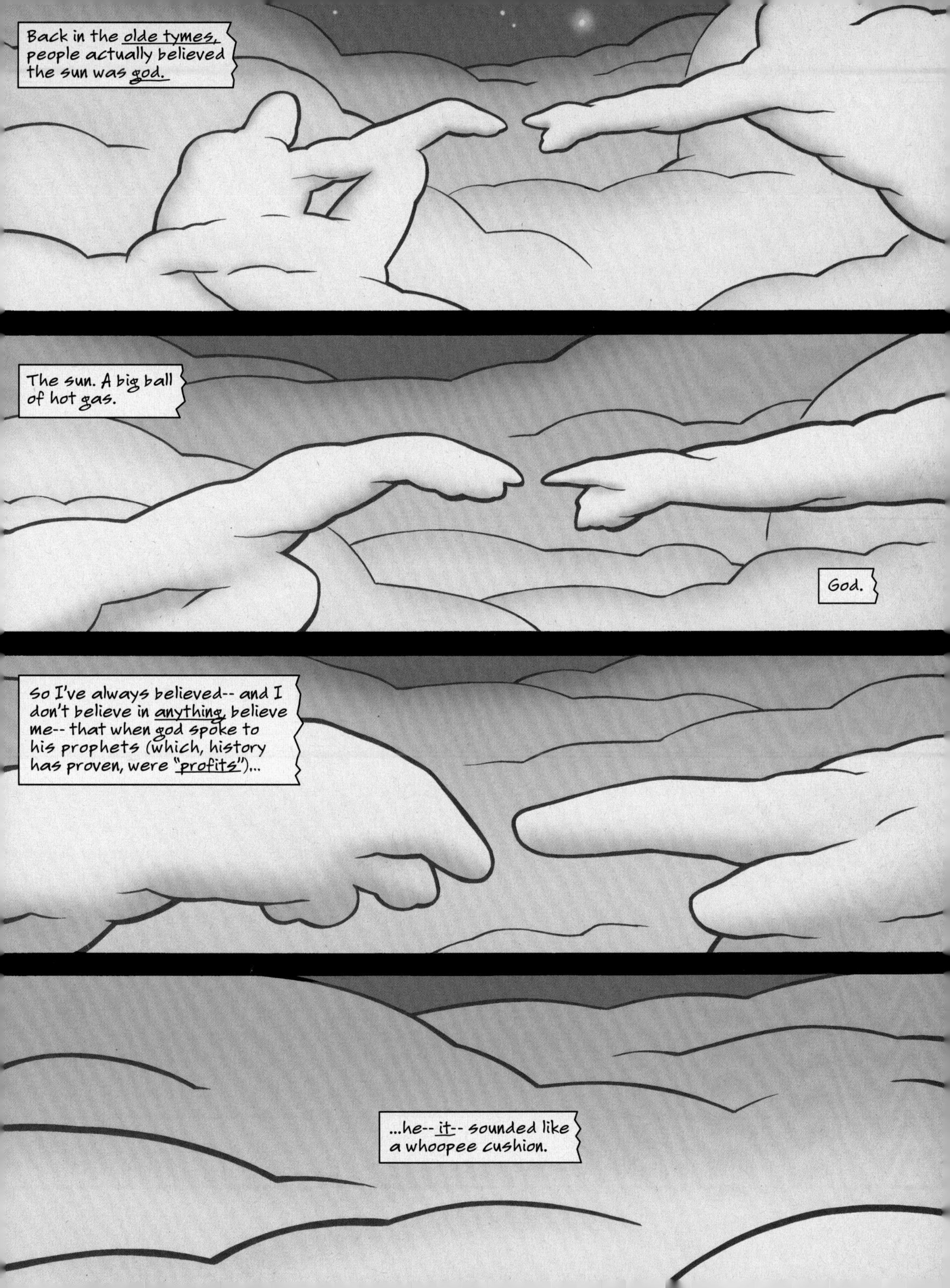
Back in the olde tymes, people actually believed the sun was god.
The sun. A big ball of hot gas.
God.
So I've always believed-- and I don't believe in anything, believe me-- that when god spoke to his prophets (which, history has proven, were "profits")...
...he-- it-- sounded like a whoopee cushion.

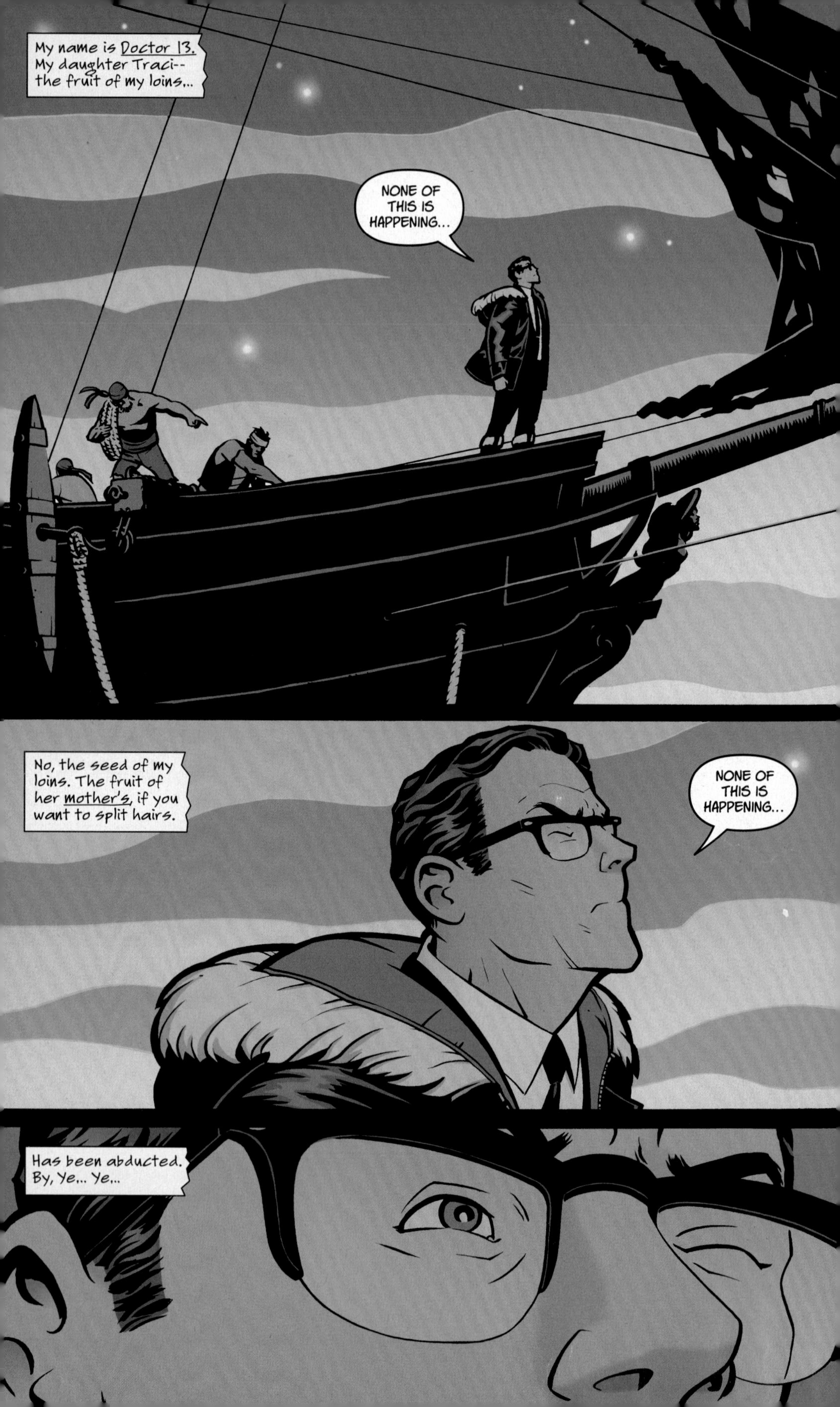
My name is Doctor 13. My daughter Traci-- the fruit of my loins...
NONE OF THIS IS HAPPENING...
No, the seed of my loins. The fruit of her mother's, if you want to split hairs.
NONE OF THIS IS HAPPENING...
Has been abducted. By, Ye... Ye...

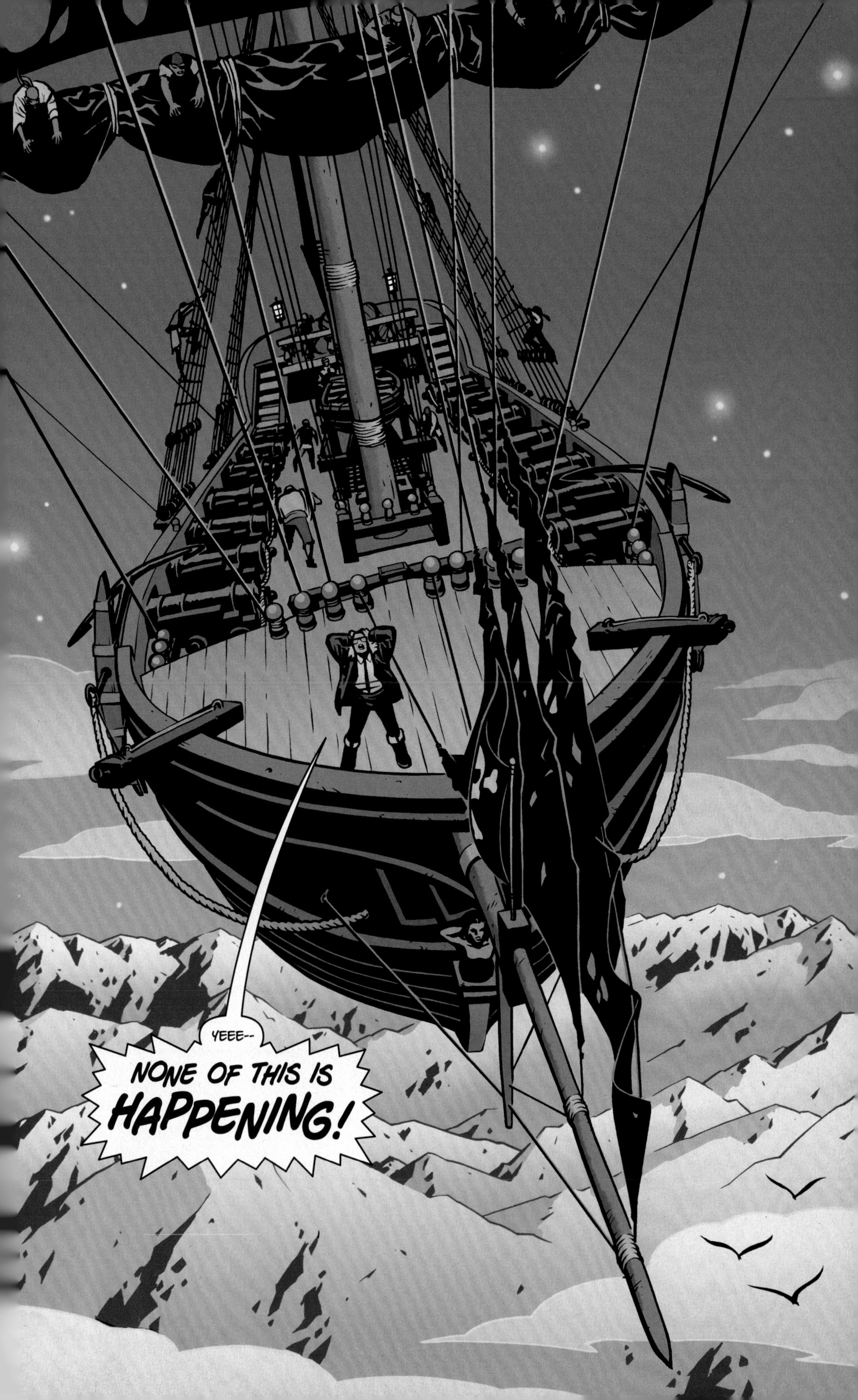
YEEE--
NONE OF THIS IS HAPPENING!

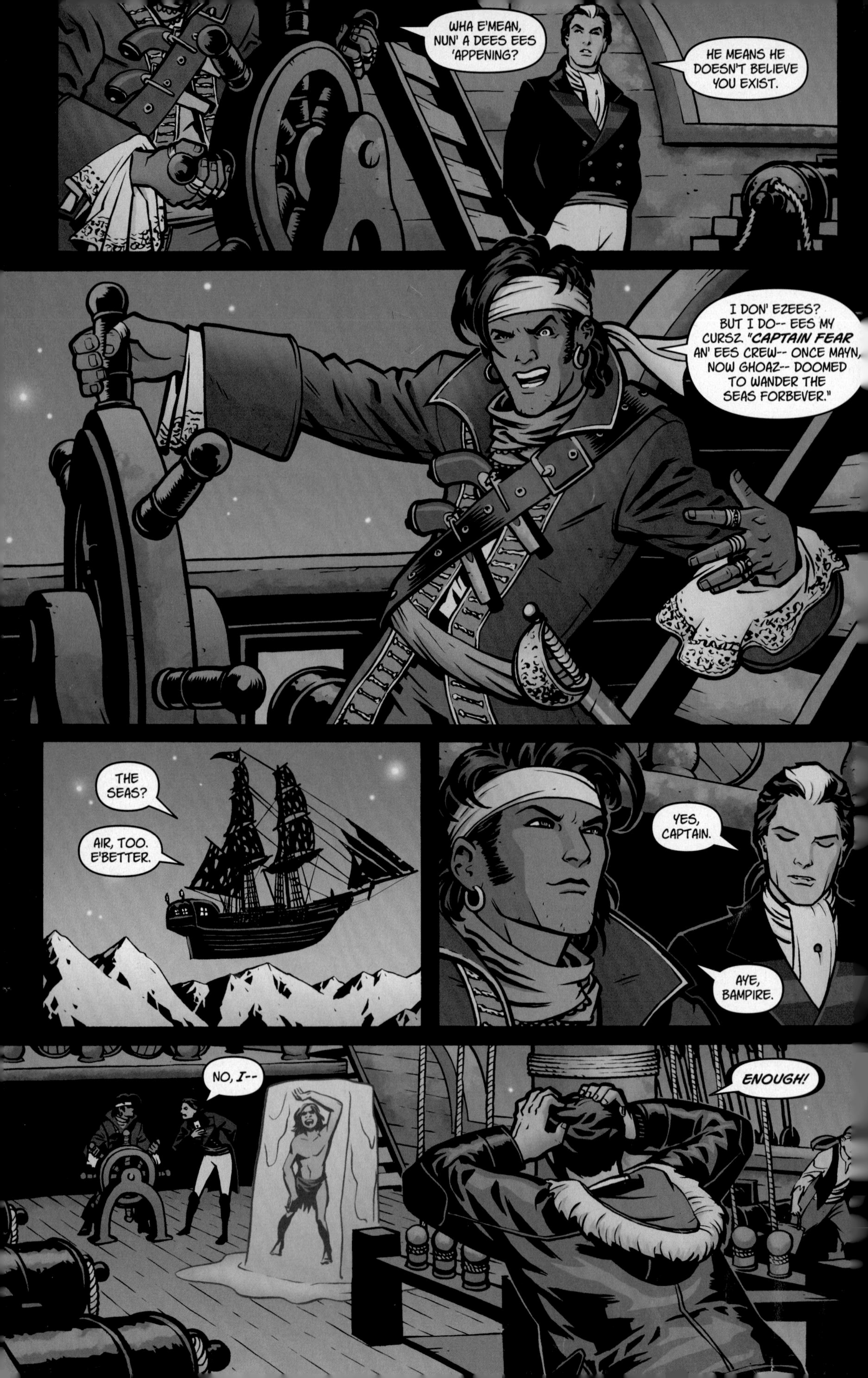

WHA E'MEAN, NUN' A DEES EES 'APPENING?
HE MEANS HE DOESN'T BELIEVE YOU EXIST.
I DON' EZEES? BUT I DO-- EES MY CURSZ. "CAPTAIN FEAR AN' EES CREW-- ONCE MAYN, NOW GHOAZ-- DOOMED TO WANDER THE SEAS FORBEVER."
THE SEAS?
AIR, TOO. E'BETTER.
YES, CAPTAIN.
AYE, BAMPIRE.
NO, I--
ENOUGH!

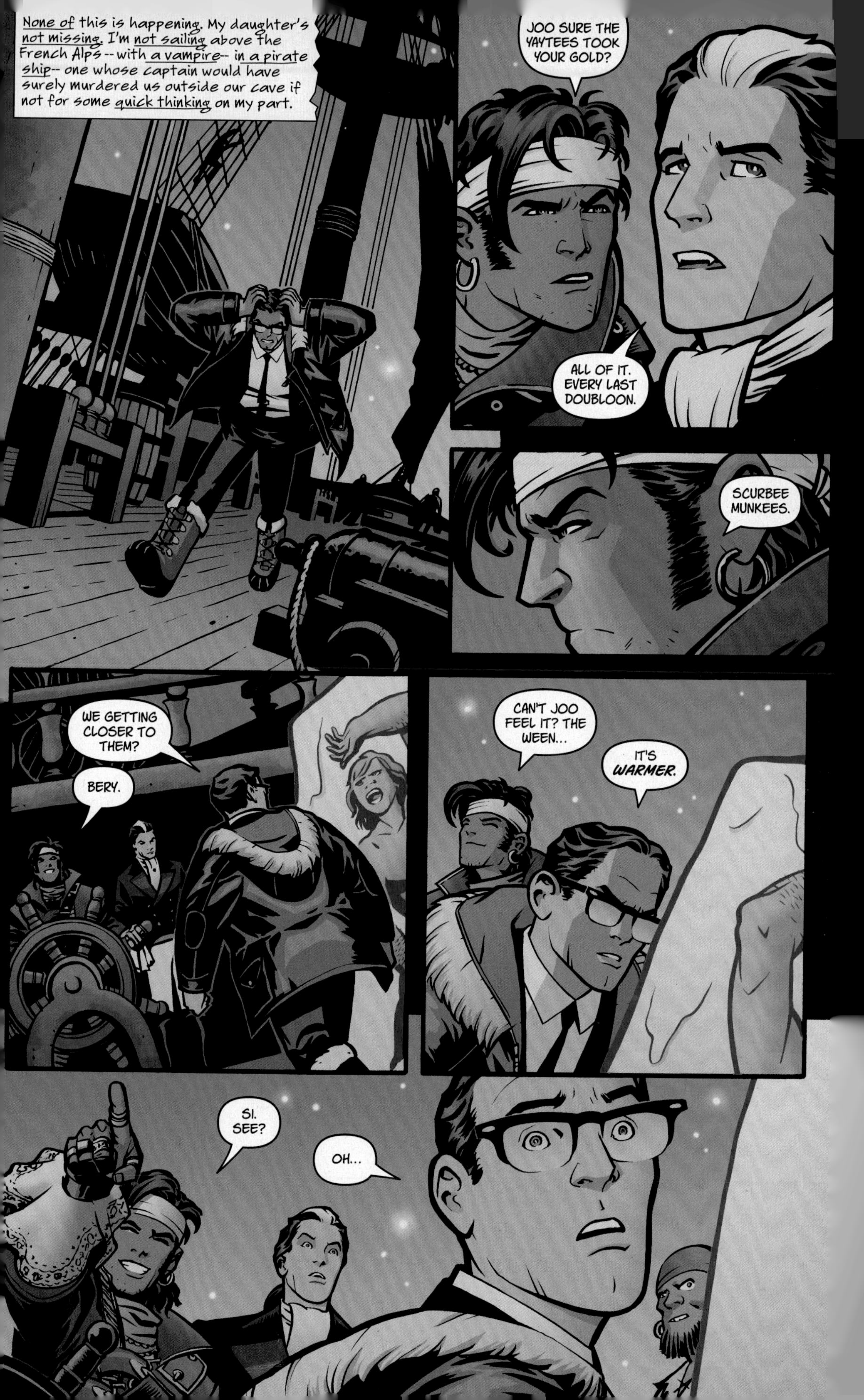
None of this is happening. My daughter's not missing. I'm not sailing above the French Alps -- with a vampire -- in a pirate ship -- one whose captain would have surely murdered us outside our cave if not for some quick thinking on my part.
JOO SURE THE YAYTEES TOOK YOUR GOLD?
ALL OF IT. EVERY LAST DOUBLOON.
SCURBEE MUNKEES.
WE GETTING CLOSER TO THEM?
BERY.
CAN'T JOO FEEL IT? THE WEEN...
IT'S WARMER.
SI. SEE?
OH...

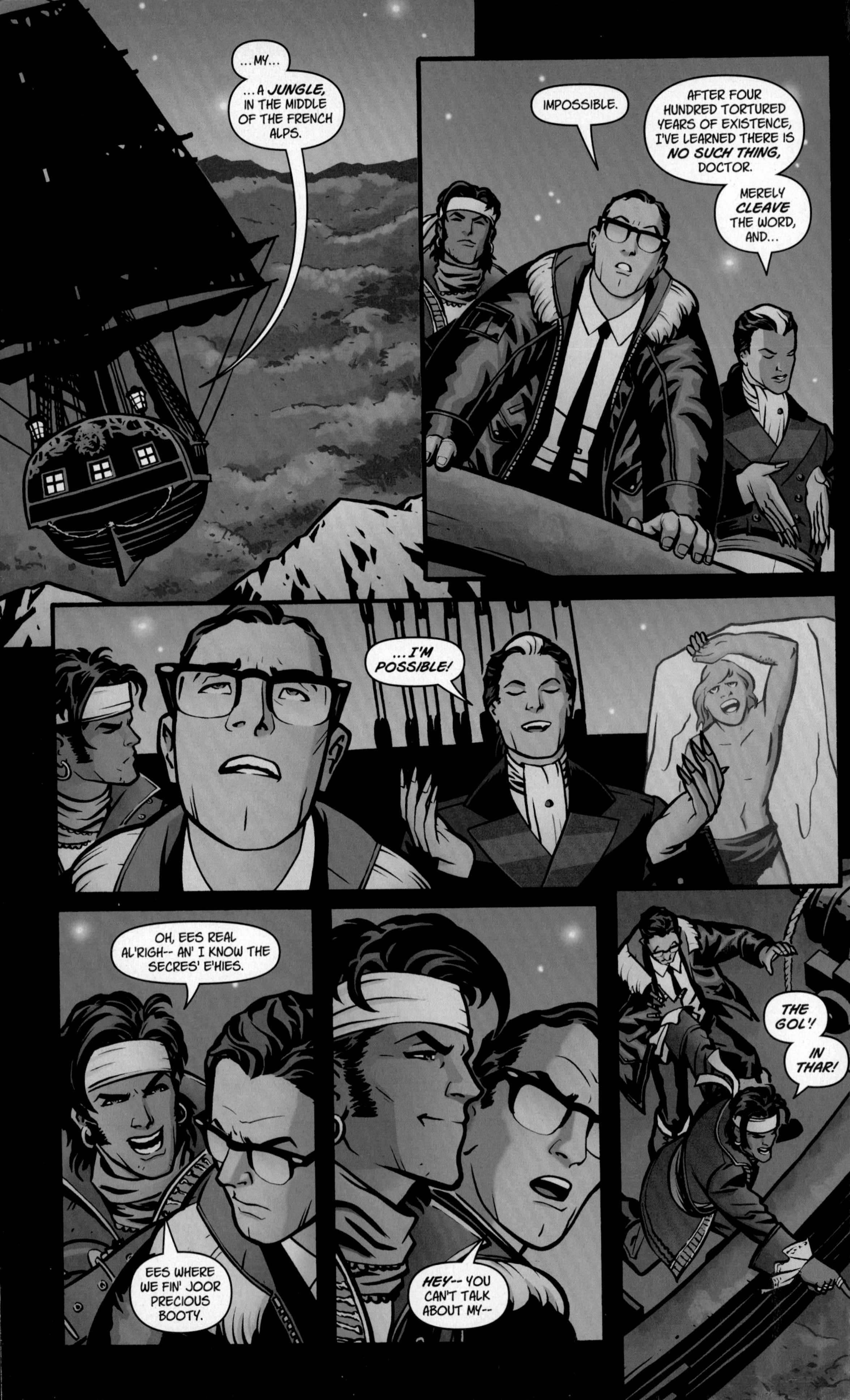
...MY...
...A JUNGLE, IN THE MIDDLE OF THE FRENCH ALPS.
IMPOSSIBLE.
AFTER FOUR HUNDRED TORTURED YEARS OF EXISTENCE, I'VE LEARNED THERE IS NO SUCH THING, DOCTOR.
MERELY CLEAVE THE WORD, AND...
...I'M POSSIBLE!
OH, EES REAL AL'RIGH-- AN' I KNOW THE SECRES' E'HIES.
EES WHERE WE FIN' JOOR PRECIOUS BOOTY.
HEY-- YOU CAN'T TALK ABOUT MY--
THE GOL'!
IN THAR!

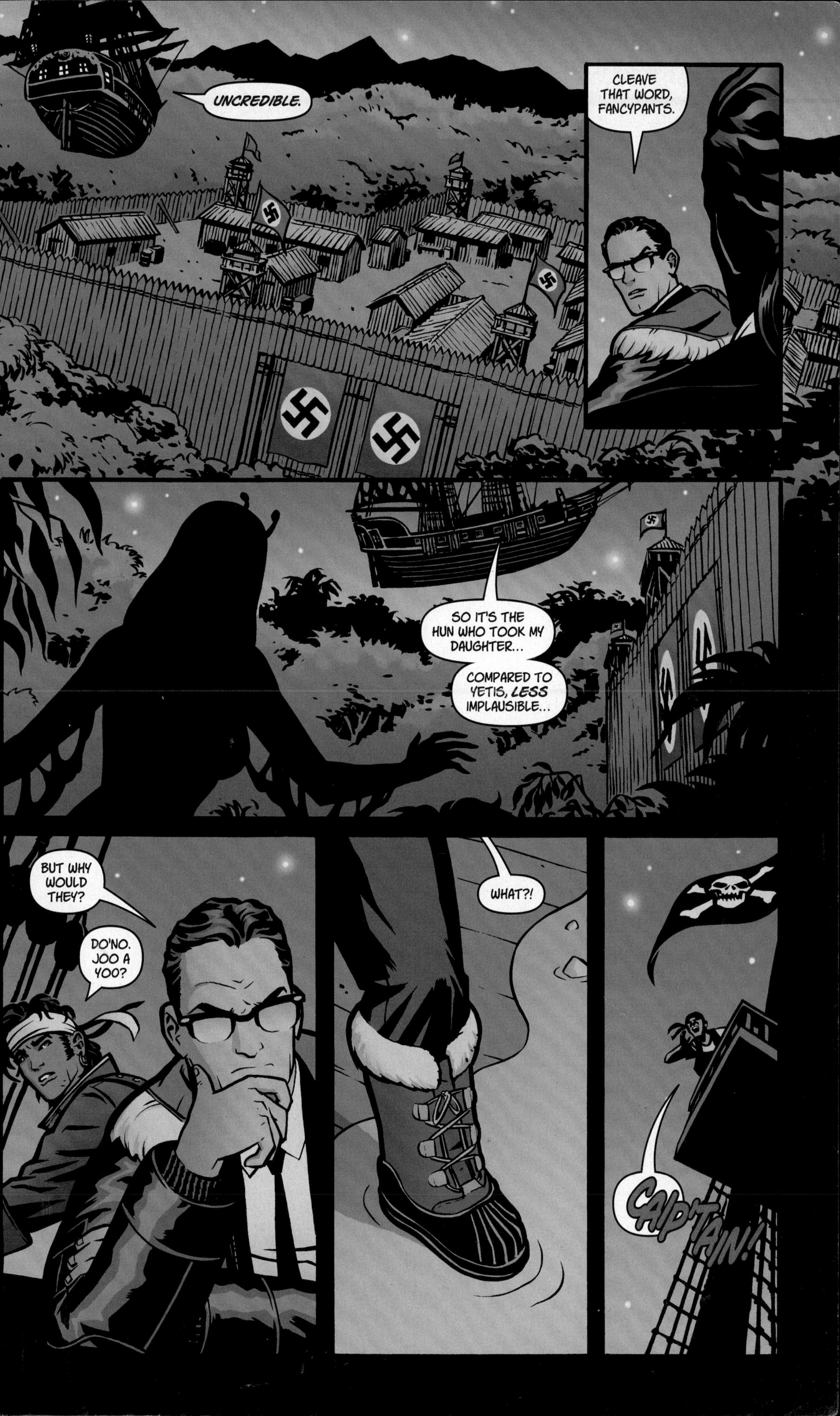
UNCREDIBLE.
CLEAVE THAT WORD, FANCYPANTS.
SO IT'S THE HUN WHO TOOK MY DAUGHTER...
COMPARED TO YETIS, LESS IMPLAUSIBLE...
BUT WHY WOULD THEY?
DO'NO. JOO A YOO?
WHAT?!
CAP'TAIN!

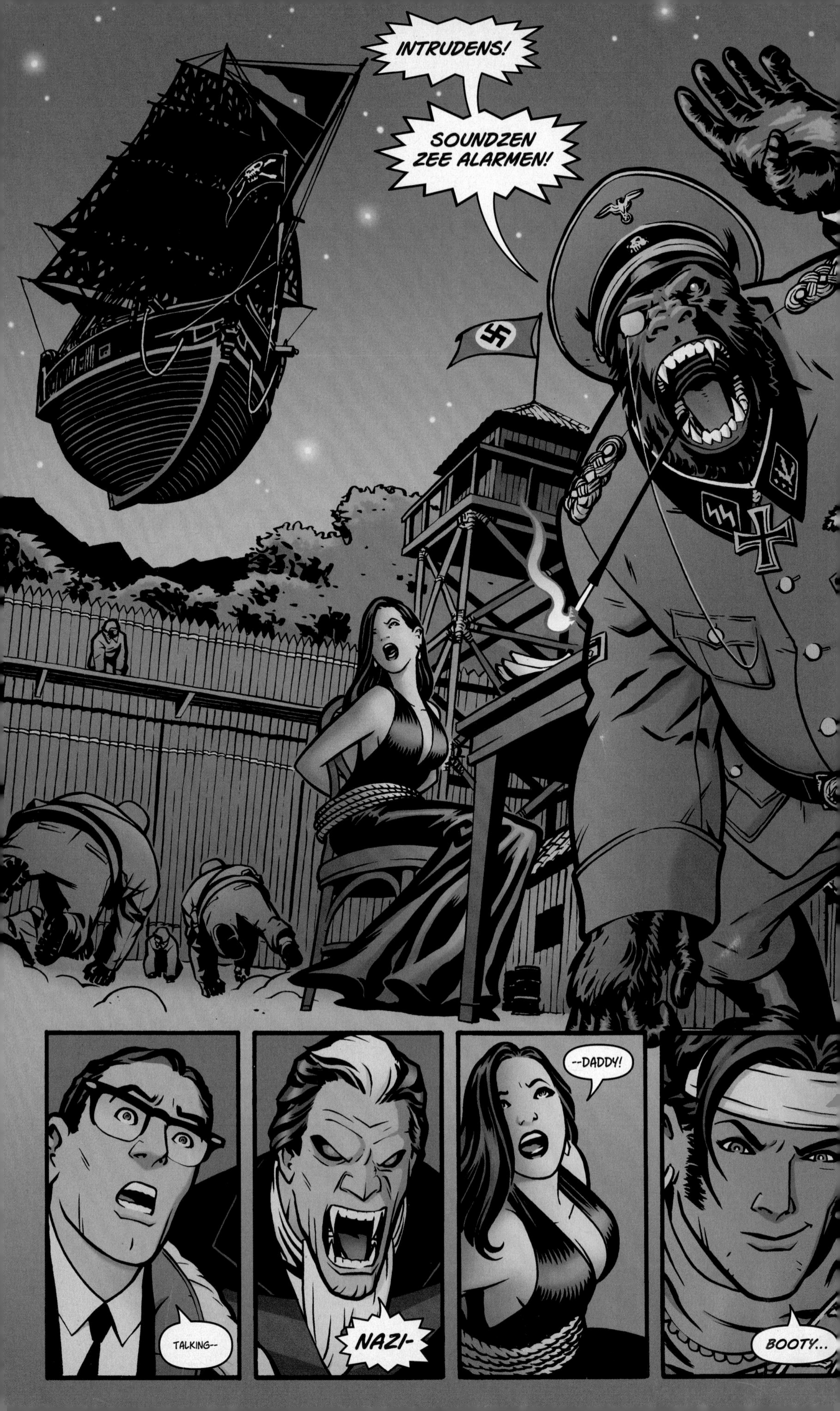
INTRUDENS!
SOUNDZEN ZEE ALARMEN!
TALKING--
NAZI-
--DADDY!
BOOTY...

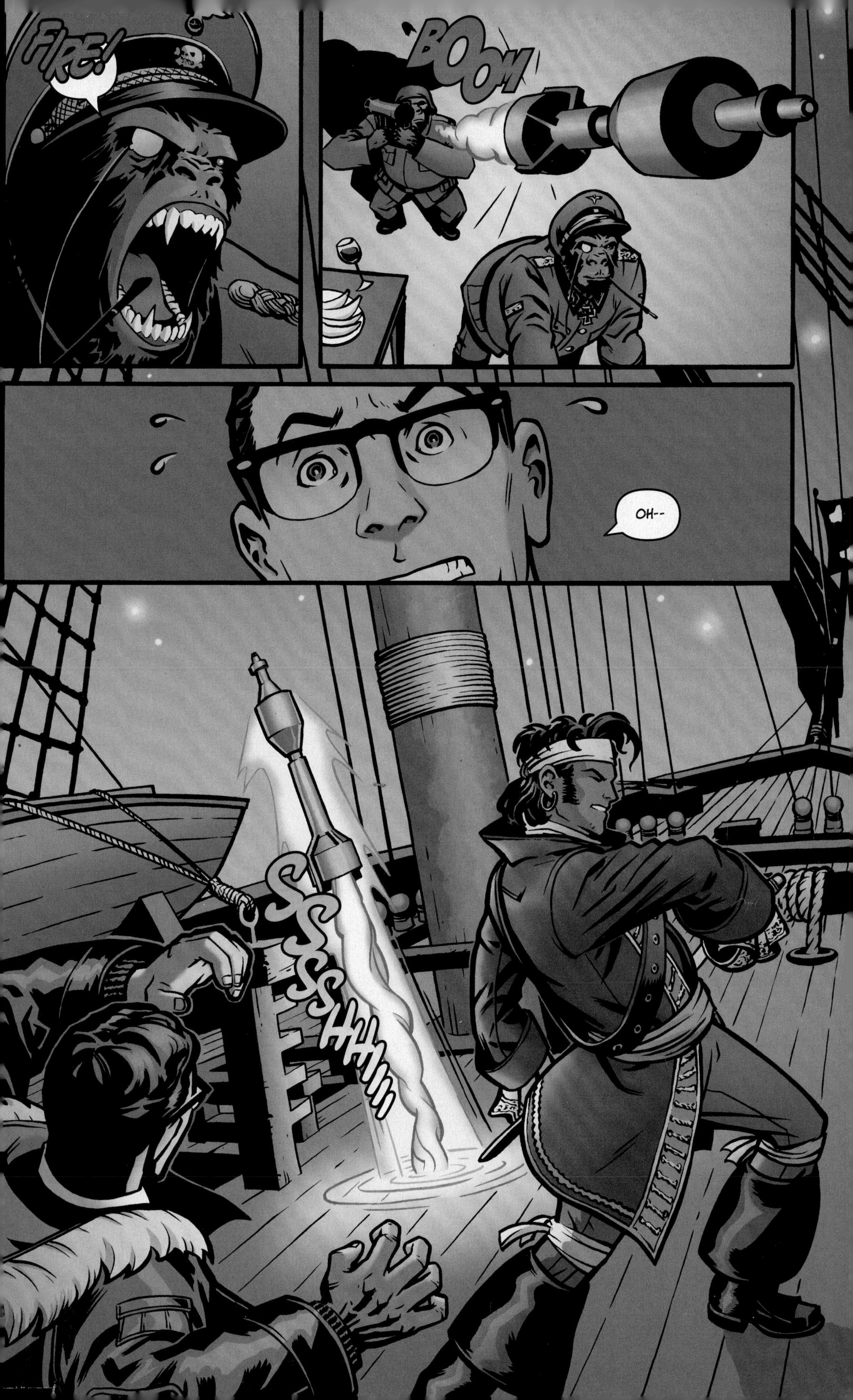

FIRE!
BOOM
OH--
SSSSHHH!!!!

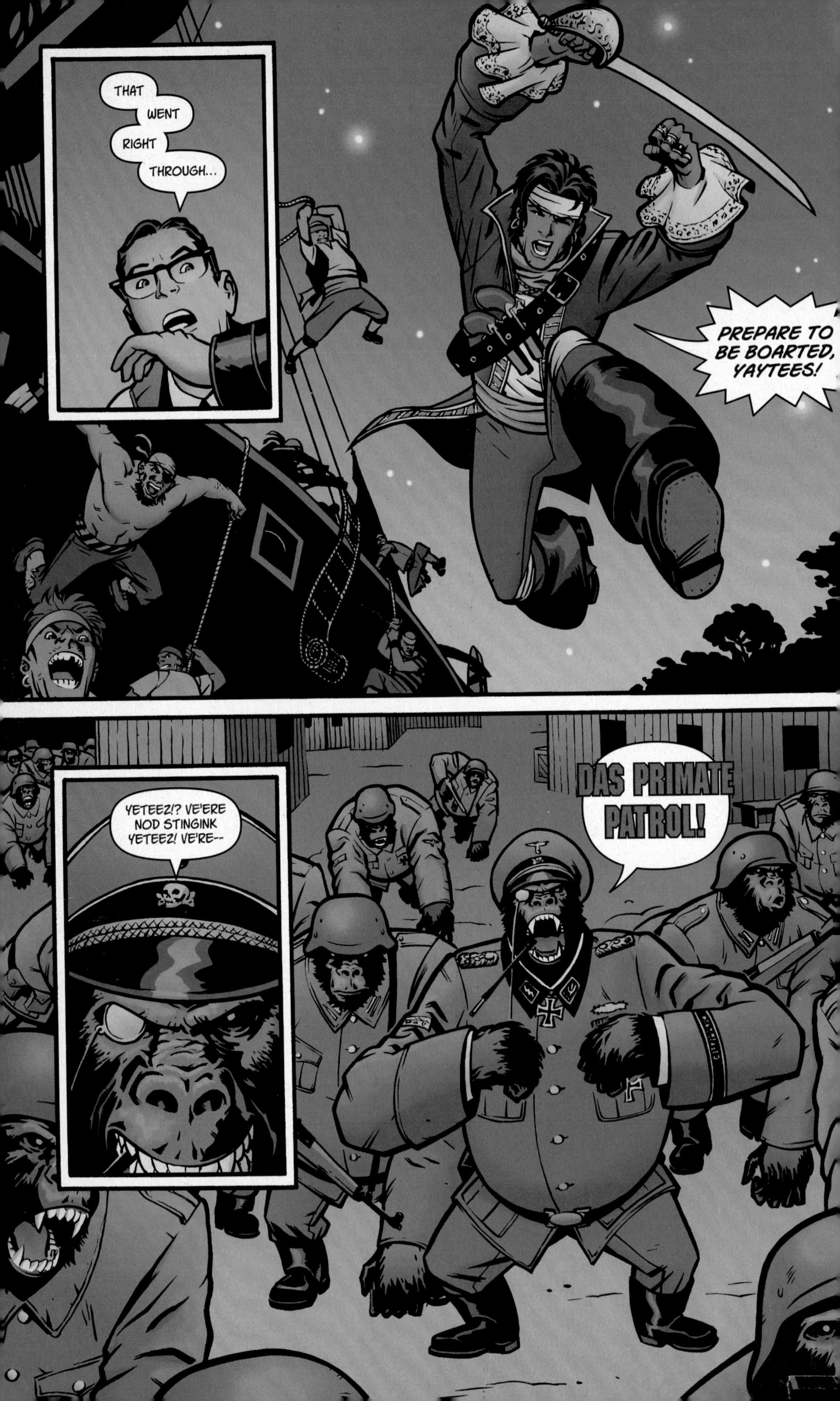
THAT WENT RIGHT THROUGH...
PREPARE TO BE BOARTED, YAYTEES!
YETEEZ!? VE'ERE NOD STINGINK YETEEZ! VE'RE--
DAS PRIMATE PATROL!

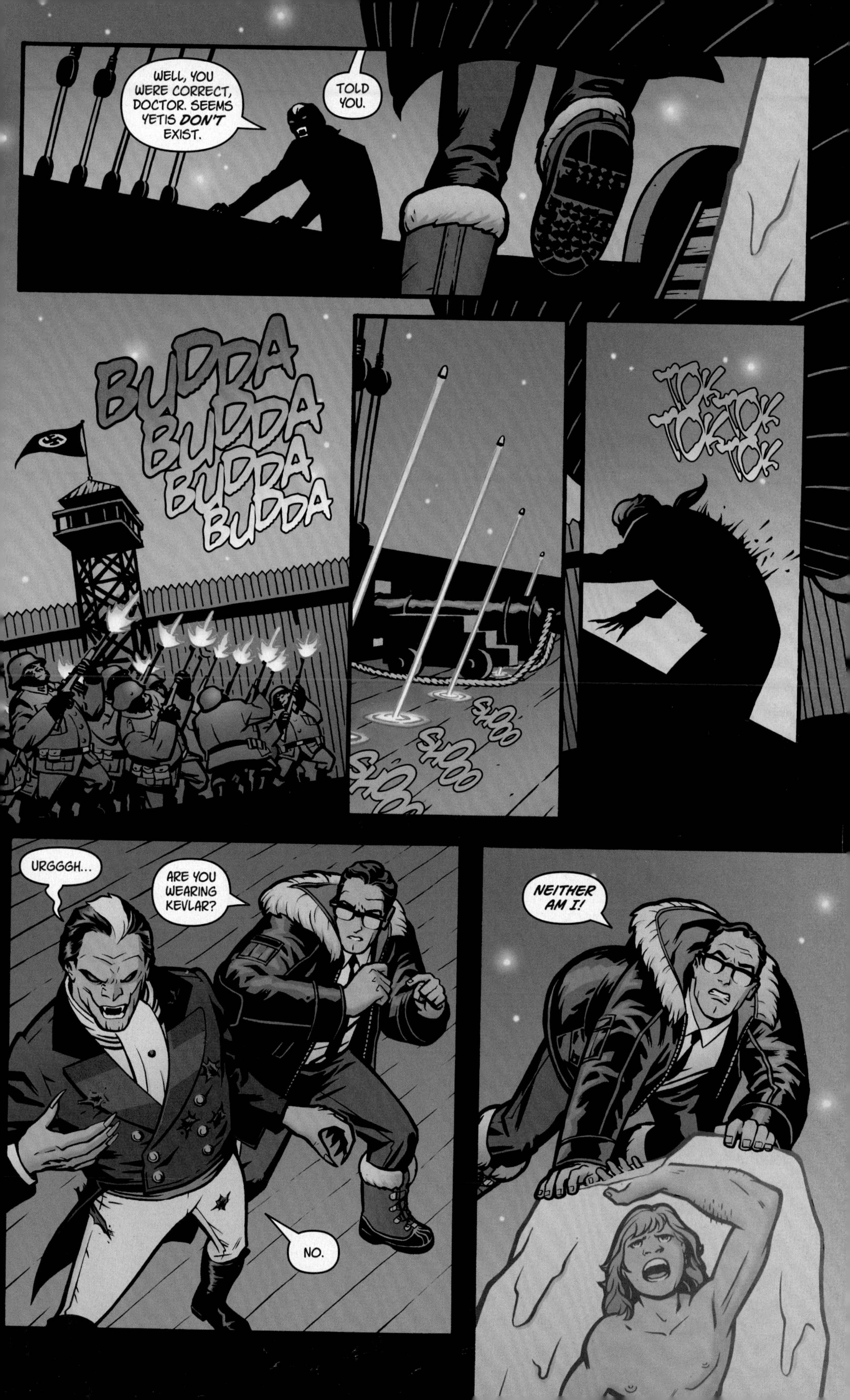
WELL, YOU WERE CORRECT, DOCTOR. SEEMS YETIS DON'T EXIST.
TOLD YOU.
BUDDA BUDDA BUDDA BUDDA
SHOOO
SHOOO
SHOOO
TOK TOK TOK TOK TOK
URGGGH...
ARE YOU WEARING KEVLAR?
NO.
NEITHER AM I!

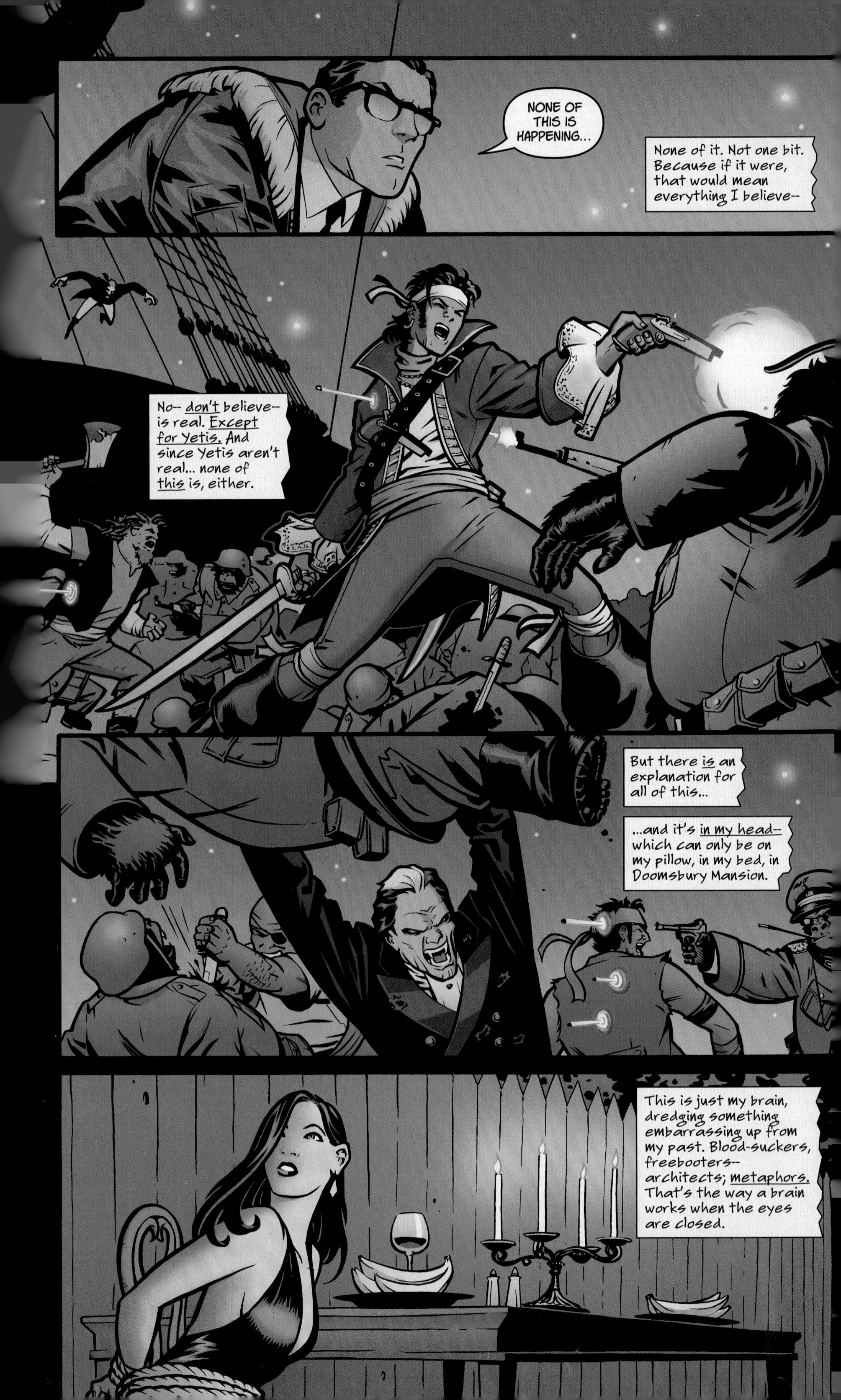
NONE OF THIS IS HAPPENING...
None of it. Not one bit. Because if it were, that would mean everything I believe--
No-- don't believe-- is real. Except for Yetis. And since Yetis aren't real... none of this is, either.
But there is an explanation for all of this...
...and it's in my head-- which can only be on my pillow, in my bed, in Doomsbury Mansion.
This is just my brain, dredging something embarrassing up from my past. Blood-suckers, freebooters-- architects; metaphors. That's the way a brain works when the eyes are closed.

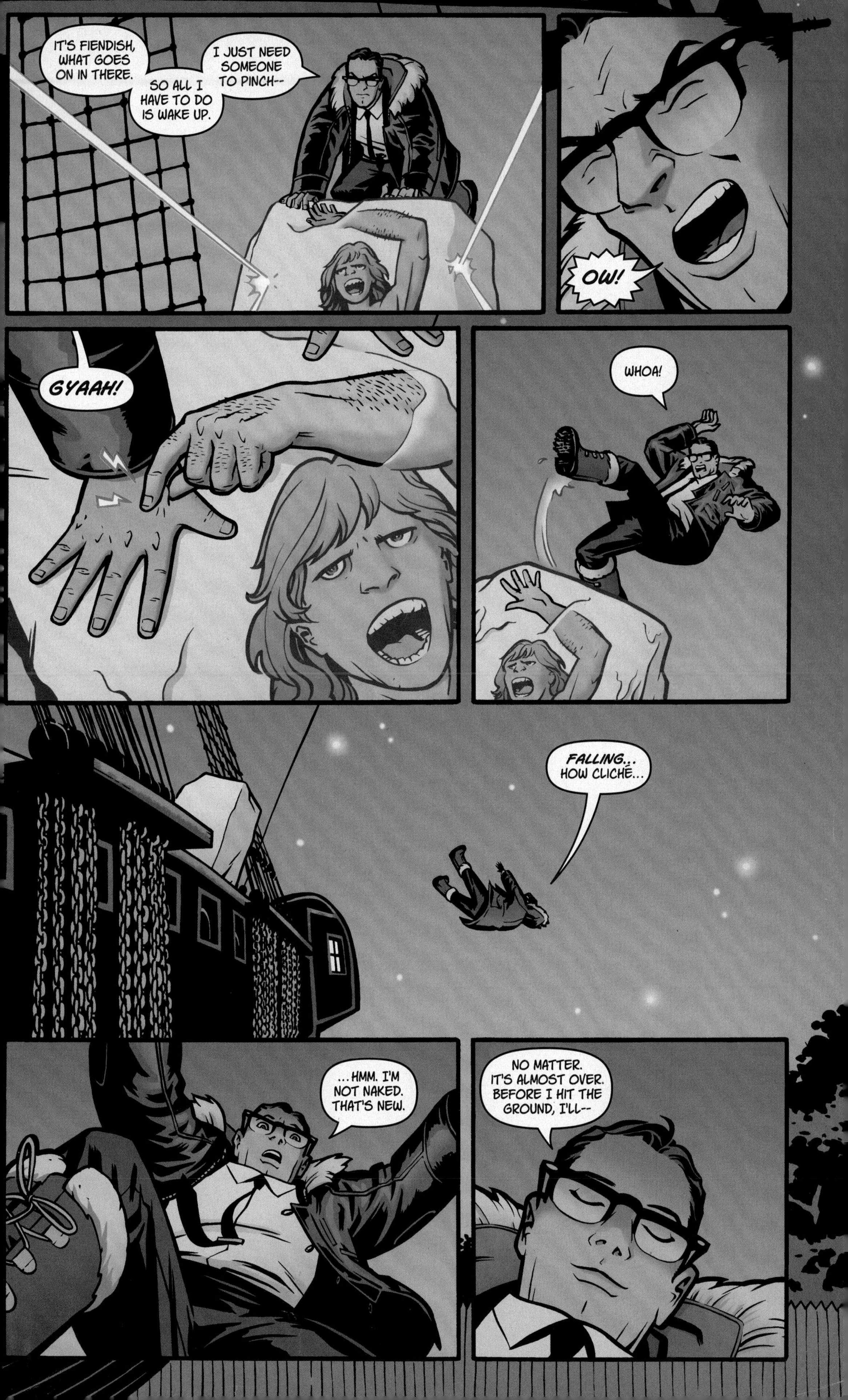
IT'S FIENDISH, WHAT GOES ON IN THERE.
SO ALL I HAVE TO DO IS WAKE UP.
I JUST NEED SOMEONE TO PINCH--
OW!
GYAAH!
WHOA!
FALLING... HOW CLICHÉ...
...HMM. I'M NOT NAKED. THAT'S NEW.
NO MATTER. IT'S ALMOST OVER. BEFORE I HIT THE GROUND, I'LL--

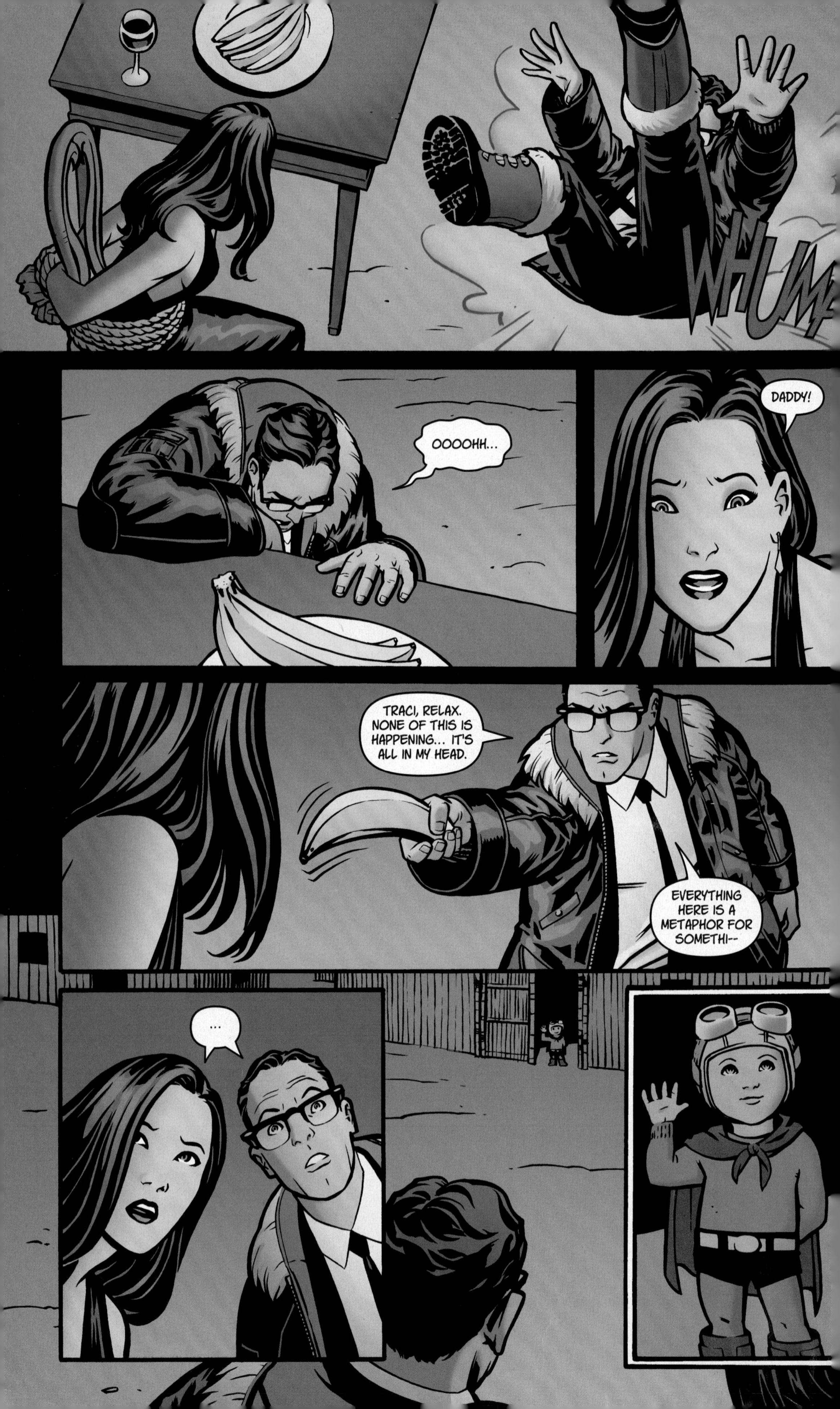
WHUM
OOOOHH...
DADDY!
TRACI, RELAX. NONE OF THIS IS HAPPENING... IT'S ALL IN MY HEAD.
EVERYTHING HERE IS A METAPHOR FOR SOMETHI--
...

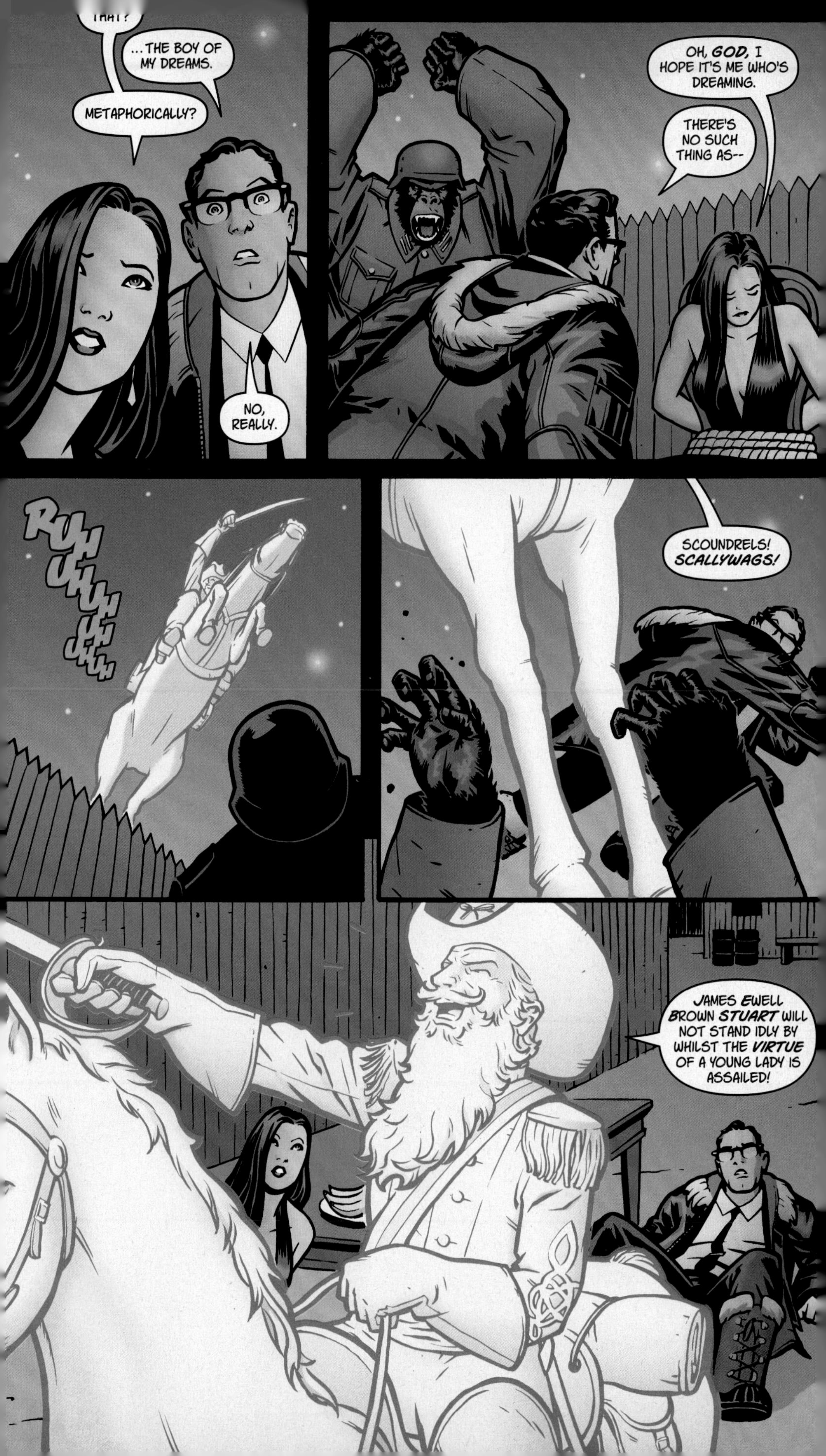
THAT?
...THE BOY OF MY DREAMS.
METAPHORICALLY?
NO, REALLY.
OH, GOD, I HOPE IT'S ME WHO'S DREAMING.
THERE'S NO SUCH THING AS--
RUHUHUHUHUHUH
SCOUNDRELS! SCALLYWAGS!
JAMES EWELL BROWN STUART WILL NOT STAND IDLY BY WHILST THE VIRTUE OF A YOUNG LADY IS ASSAILED!

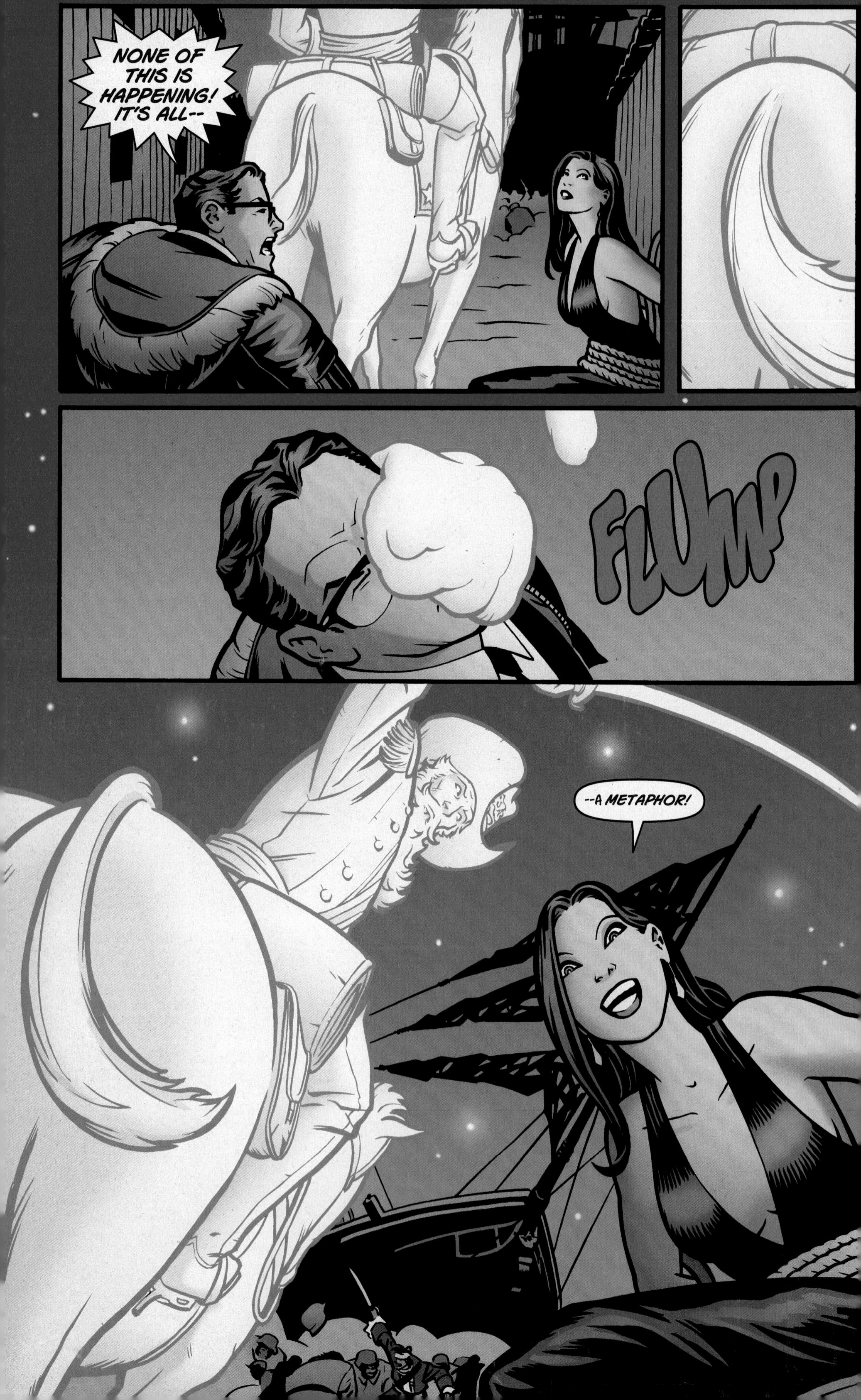

NONE OF THIS IS HAPPENING! IT'S ALL--
FLUMP
--A METAPHOR!

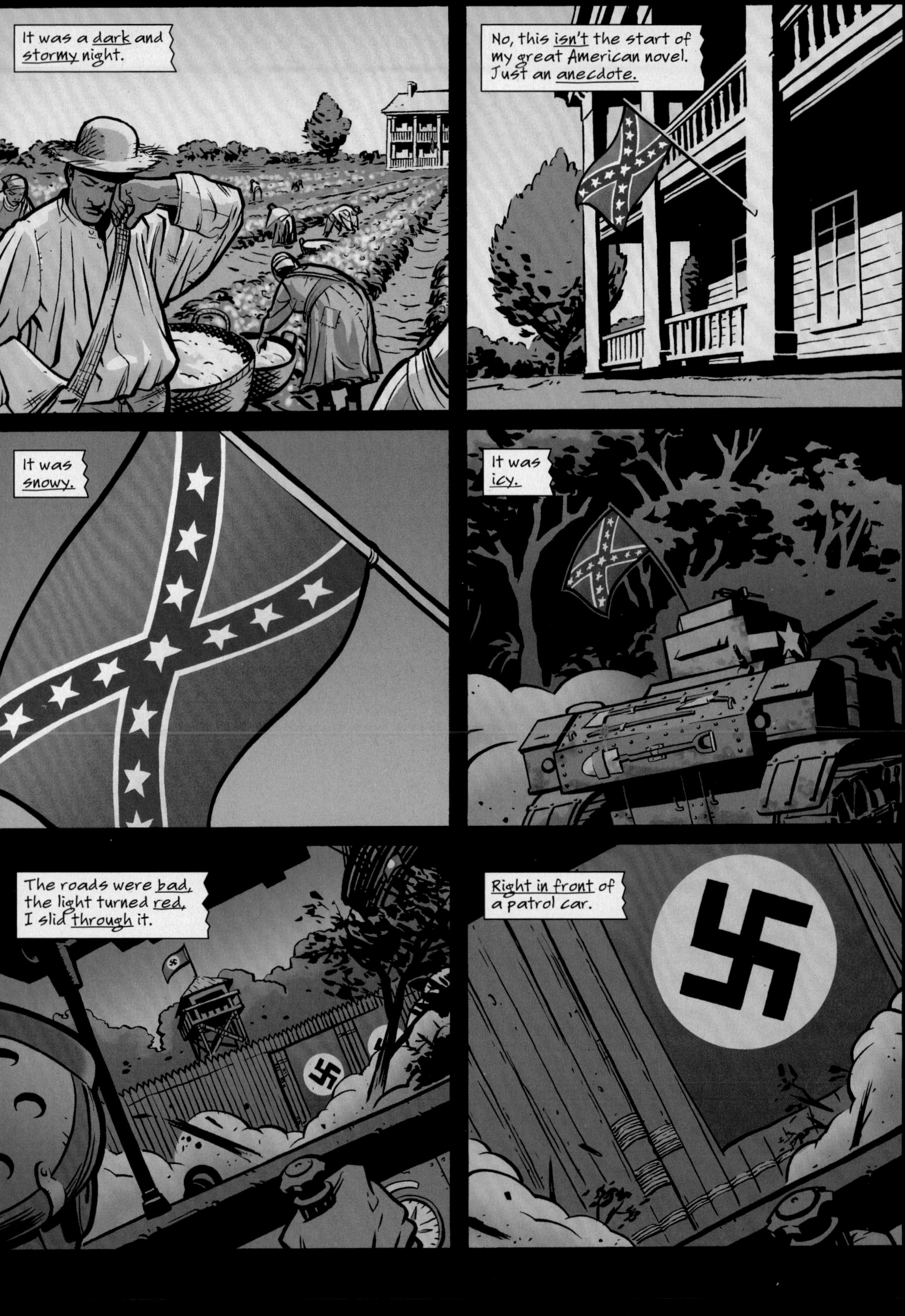
It was a dark and stormy night.
No, this isn't the start of my great American novel. Just an anecdote.
It was snowy.
It was icy.
The roads were bad, the light turned red, I slid through it.
Right in front of a patrol car.

CHAPTER 4
# NEE, ON LIES

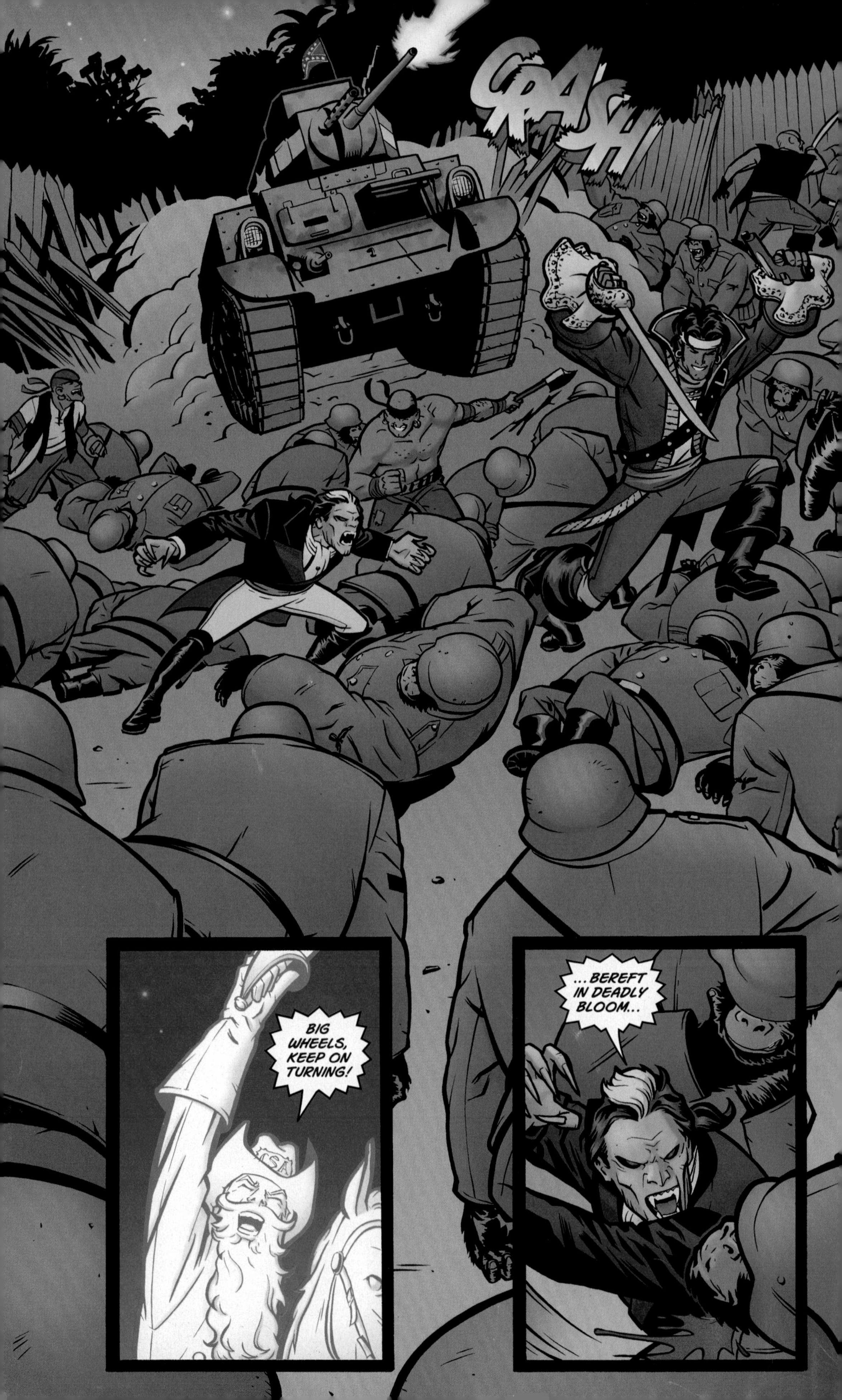
CRASH
BIG WHEELS, KEEP ON TURNING!
CSA
...BEREFT IN DEADLY BLOOM...

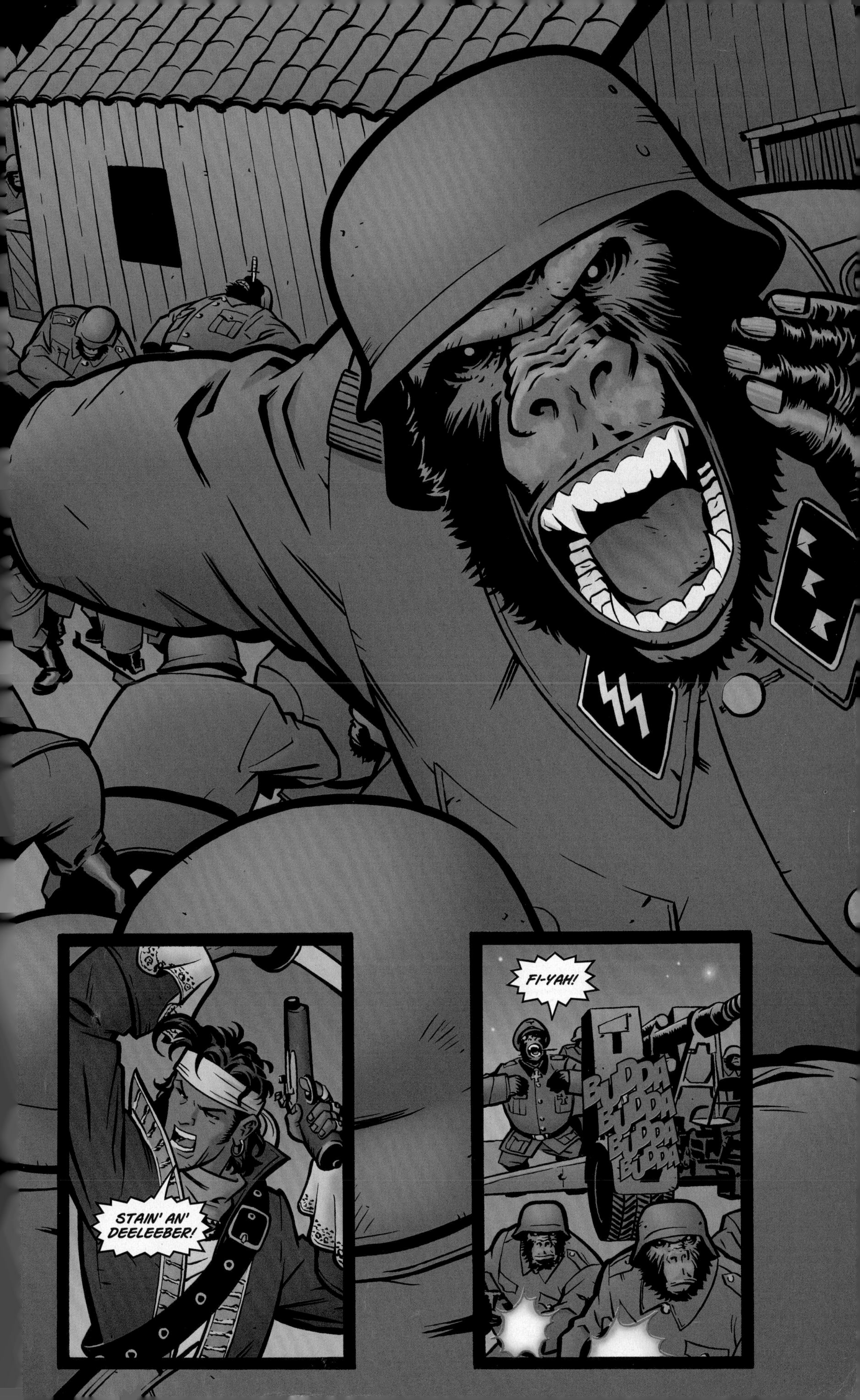

STAIN' AN' DEELEEBER!
FI-YAH!
BUDDA BUDDA BUDDA BUDDA BUDDA

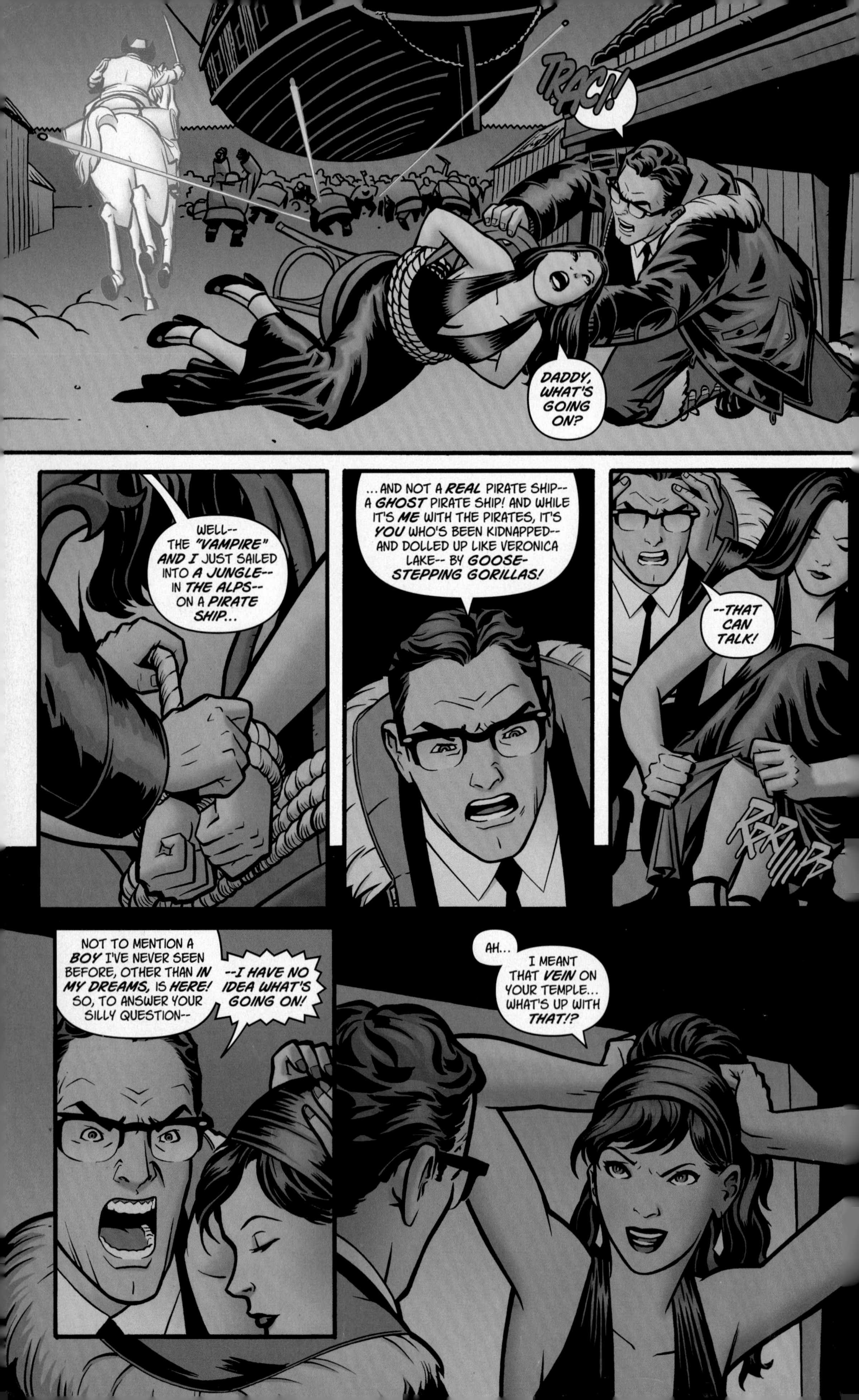
TRAC!!
DADDY, WHAT'S GOING ON?
WELL-- THE "VAMPIRE" AND I JUST SAILED INTO A JUNGLE-- IN THE ALPS-- ON A PIRATE SHIP...
...AND NOT A REAL PIRATE SHIP-- A GHOST PIRATE SHIP! AND WHILE IT'S ME WITH THE PIRATES, IT'S YOU WHO'S BEEN KIDNAPPED-- AND DOLLED UP LIKE VERONICA LAKE-- BY GOOSE-STEPPING GORILLAS!
--THAT CAN TALK!
NOT TO MENTION A BOY I'VE NEVER SEEN BEFORE, OTHER THAN IN MY DREAMS, IS HERE! SO, TO ANSWER YOUR SILLY QUESTION--
--I HAVE NO IDEA WHAT'S GOING ON!
AH...
I MEANT THAT VEIN ON YOUR TEMPLE... WHAT'S UP WITH THAT!?

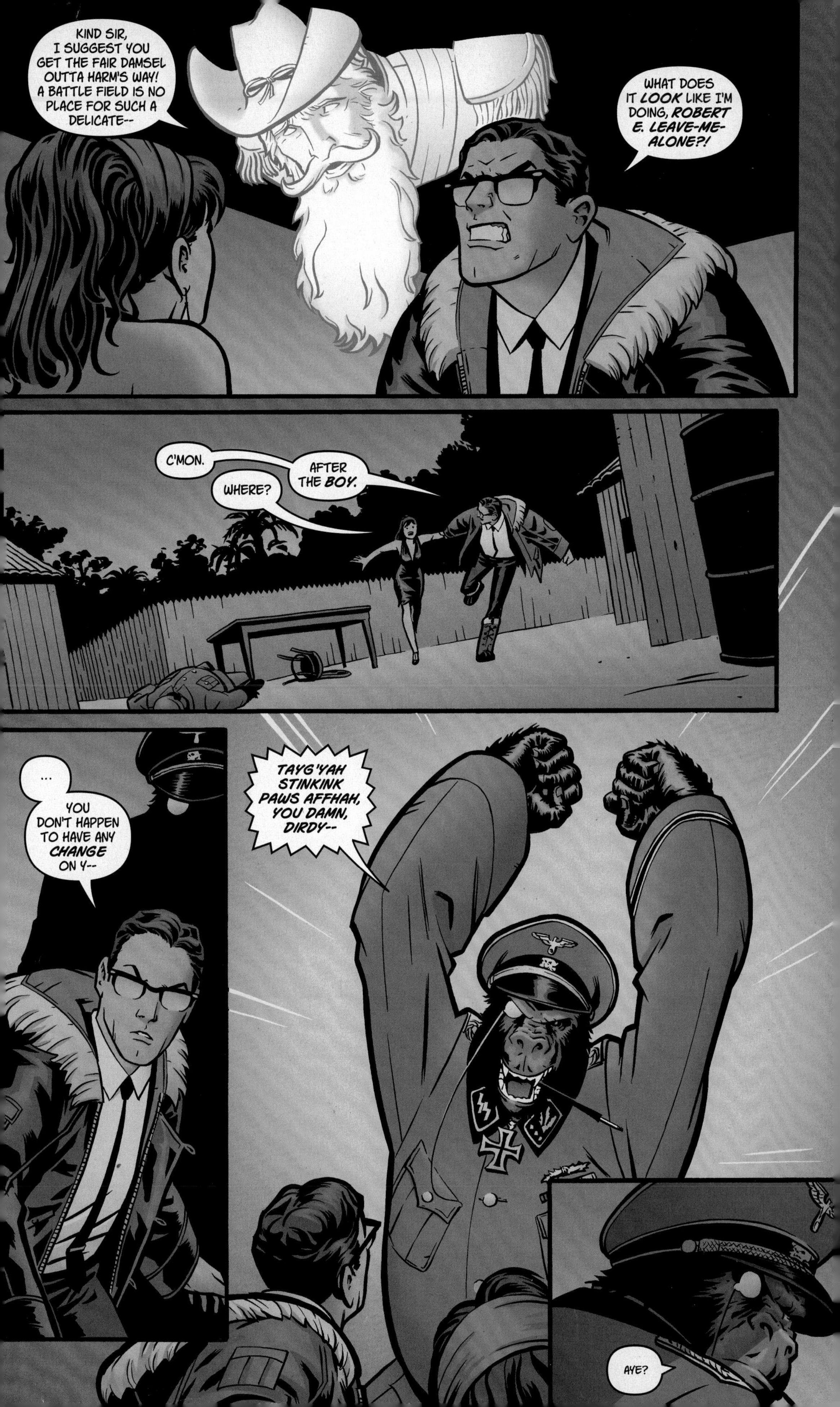
KIND SIR, I SUGGEST YOU GET THE FAIR DAMSEL OUTTA HARM'S WAY! A BATTLE FIELD IS NO PLACE FOR SUCH A DELICATE--
WHAT DOES IT *LOOK* LIKE I'M DOING, *ROBERT E. LEAVE-ME-ALONE?!*
C'MON.
AFTER THE *BOY*.
WHERE?
... YOU DON'T HAPPEN TO HAVE ANY *CHANGE* ON Y--
TAYG'YAH STINKINK PAWS AFFHAH, YOU DAMN, DIRDY--
AYE?

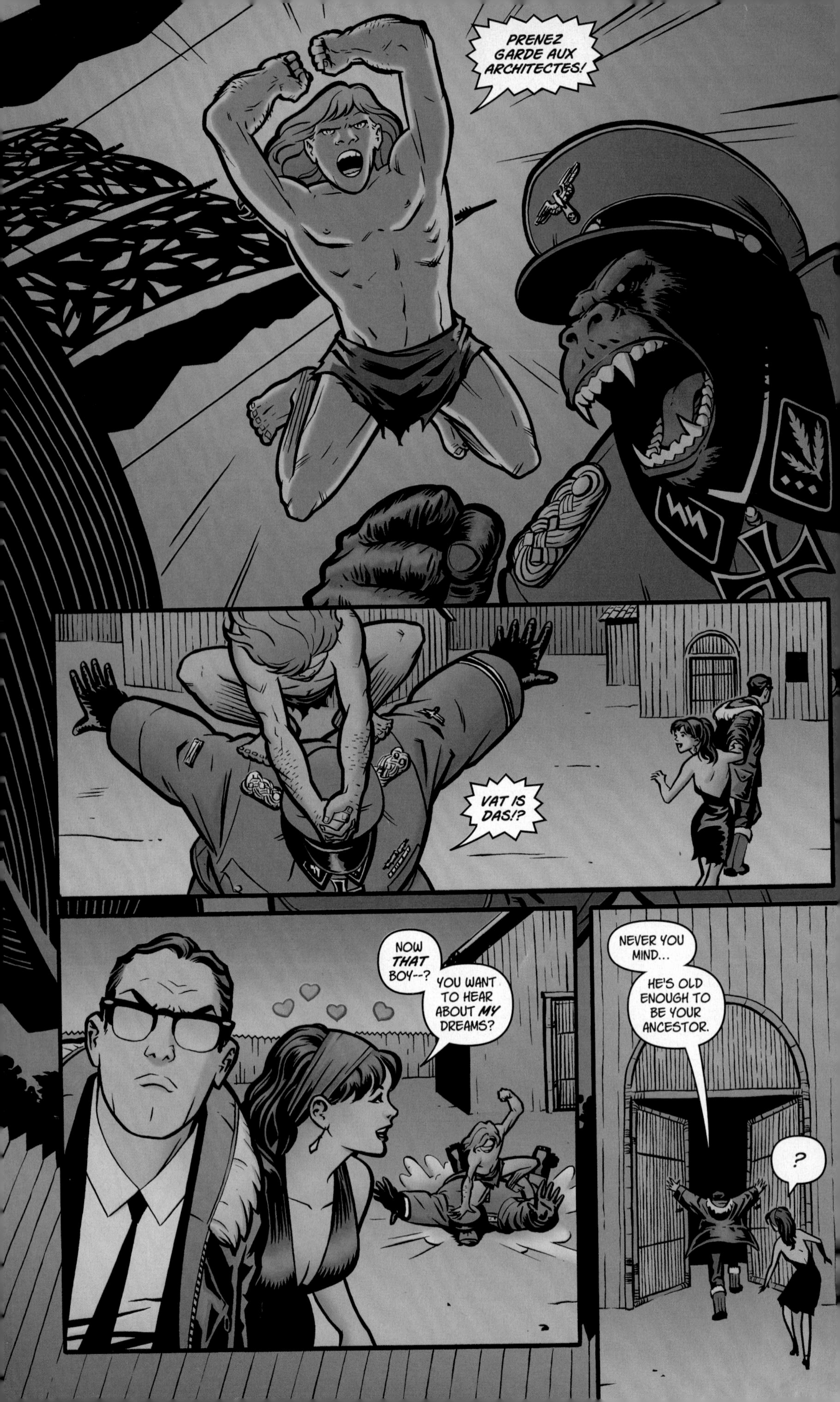

PRENEZ GARDE AUX ARCHITECTES!
VAT IS DAS!?
NOW THAT BOY--?
YOU WANT TO HEAR ABOUT MY DREAMS?
NEVER YOU MIND...
HE'S OLD ENOUGH TO BE YOUR ANCESTOR.
?

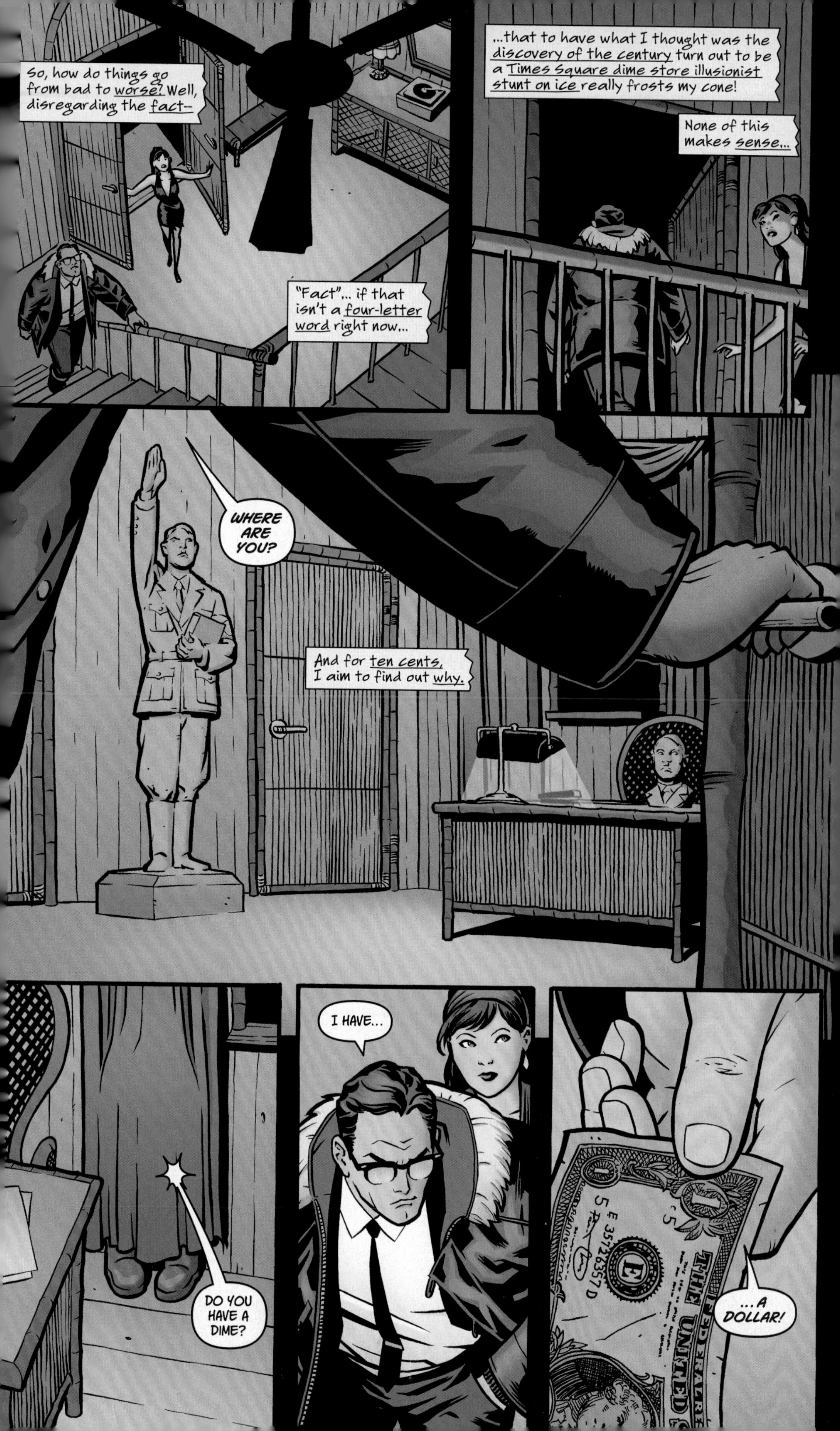

So, how do things go from bad to worse? Well, disregarding the fact--
"Fact"... if that isn't a four-letter word right now...
...that to have what I thought was the discovery of the century turn out to be a Times Square dime store illusionist stunt on ice really frosts my cone!
None of this makes sense...
WHERE ARE YOU?
And for ten cents, I aim to find out why.
DO YOU HAVE A DIME?
I HAVE...
...A DOLLAR!

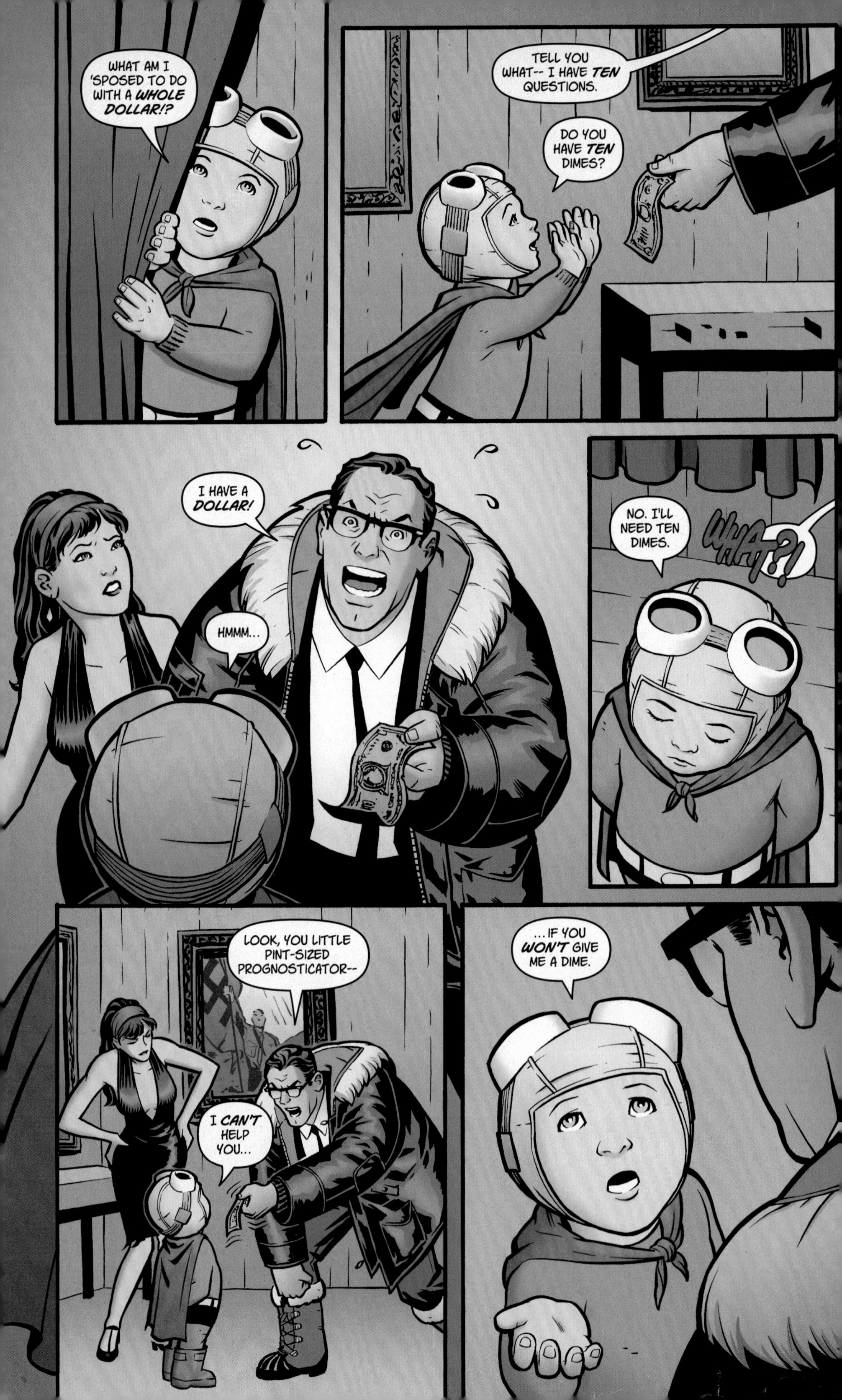
WHAT AM I 'SPOSED TO DO WITH A WHOLE DOLLAR!?
TELL YOU WHAT-- I HAVE TEN QUESTIONS.
DO YOU HAVE TEN DIMES?
I HAVE A DOLLAR!
HMMM...
NO. I'LL NEED TEN DIMES.
WHAT?!
LOOK, YOU LITTLE PINT-SIZED PROGNOSTICATOR--
I CAN'T HELP YOU...
...IF YOU WON'T GIVE ME A DIME.

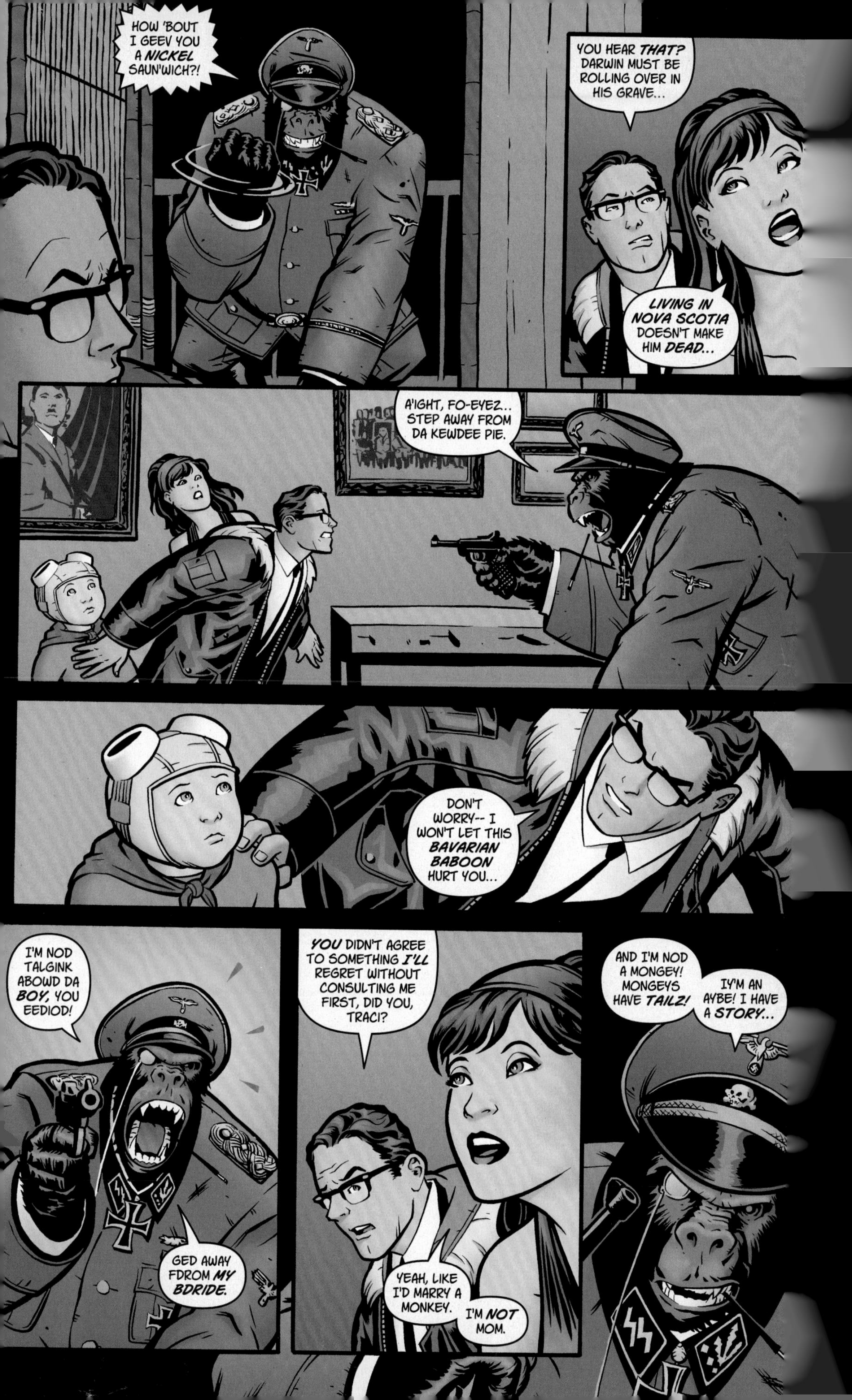
HOW 'BOUT I GEEV YOU A NICKEL SAUN'WICH?!
YOU HEAR THAT? DARWIN MUST BE ROLLING OVER IN HIS GRAVE...
LIVING IN NOVA SCOTIA DOESN'T MAKE HIM DEAD...
A'IGHT, FO-EYEZ.. STEP AWAY FROM DA KEWDEE PIE.
DON'T WORRY-- I WON'T LET THIS BAVARIAN BABOON HURT YOU...
I'M NOD TALGINK ABOWD DA BOY, YOU EEDIOD!
GED AWAY FDROM MY BDRIDE.
YOU DIDN'T AGREE TO SOMETHING I'LL REGRET WITHOUT CONSULTING ME FIRST, DID YOU, TRACI?
YEAH, LIKE I'D MARRY A MONKEY.
I'M NOT MOM.
AND I'M NOD A MONGEY! MONGEYS HAVE TAILZ!
IY'M AN AYBE! I HAVE A STORY...

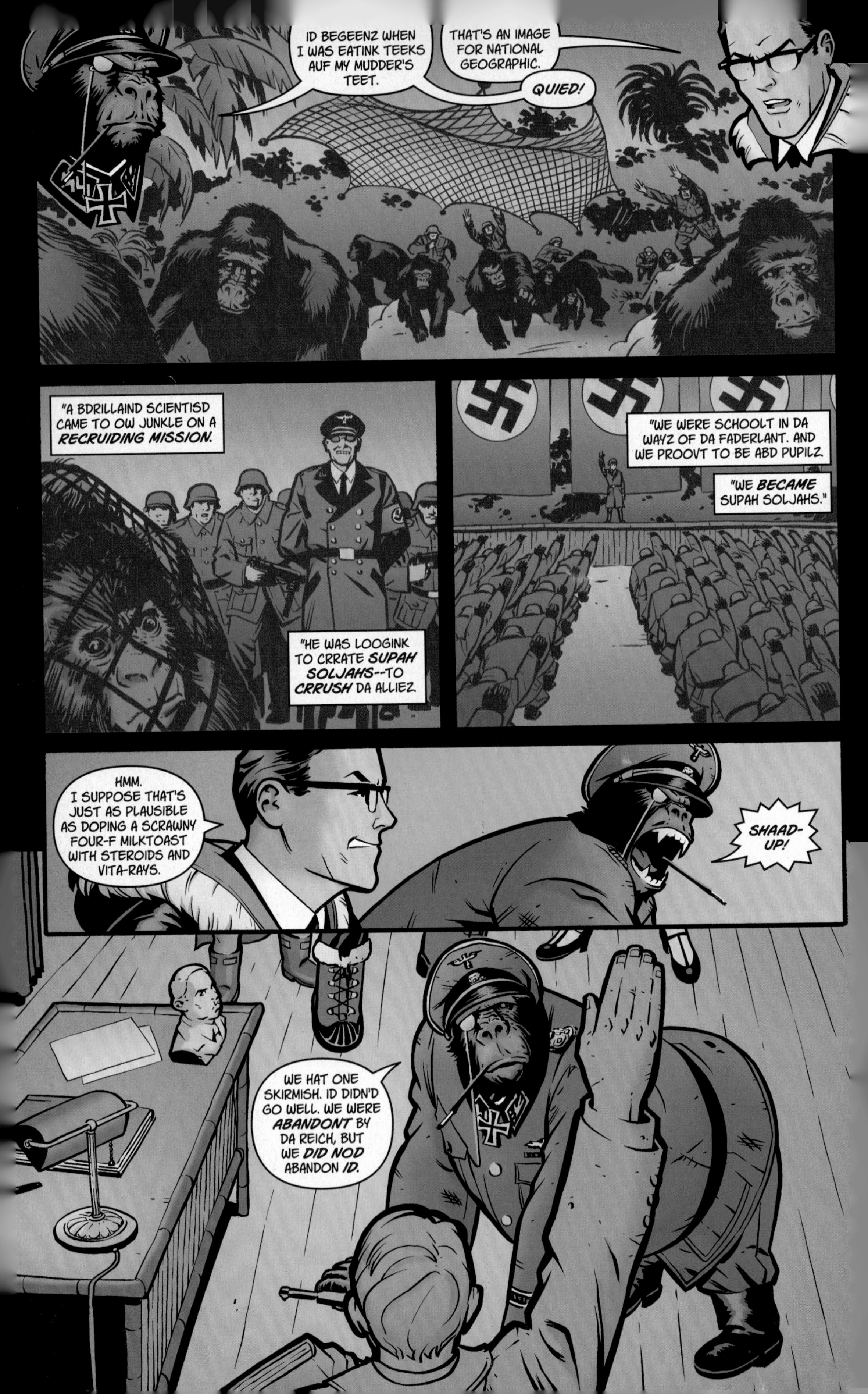
ID BEGEENZ WHEN I WAS EATINK TEEKS AUF MY MUDDER'S TEET.
THAT'S AN IMAGE FOR NATIONAL GEOGRAPHIC.
QUIED!
"A BDRILLAIND SCIENTISD CAME TO OW JUNKLE ON A RECRUIDING MISSION.
"HE WAS LOOGINK TO CRRATE SUPAH SOLJAHS--TO CRRUSH DA ALLIEZ.
"WE WERE SCHOOLT IN DA WAYZ OF DA FADERLANT. AND WE PROOVT TO BE ABD PUPILZ.
"WE BECAME SUPAH SOLJAHS."
HMM. I SUPPOSE THAT'S JUST AS PLAUSIBLE AS DOPING A SCRAWNY FOUR-F MILKTOAST WITH STEROIDS AND VITA-RAYS.
SHAAD-UP!
WE HAT ONE SKIRMISH. ID DIDN'D GO WELL. WE WERE ABANDONT BY DA REICH, BUT WE DID NOD ABANDON ID.

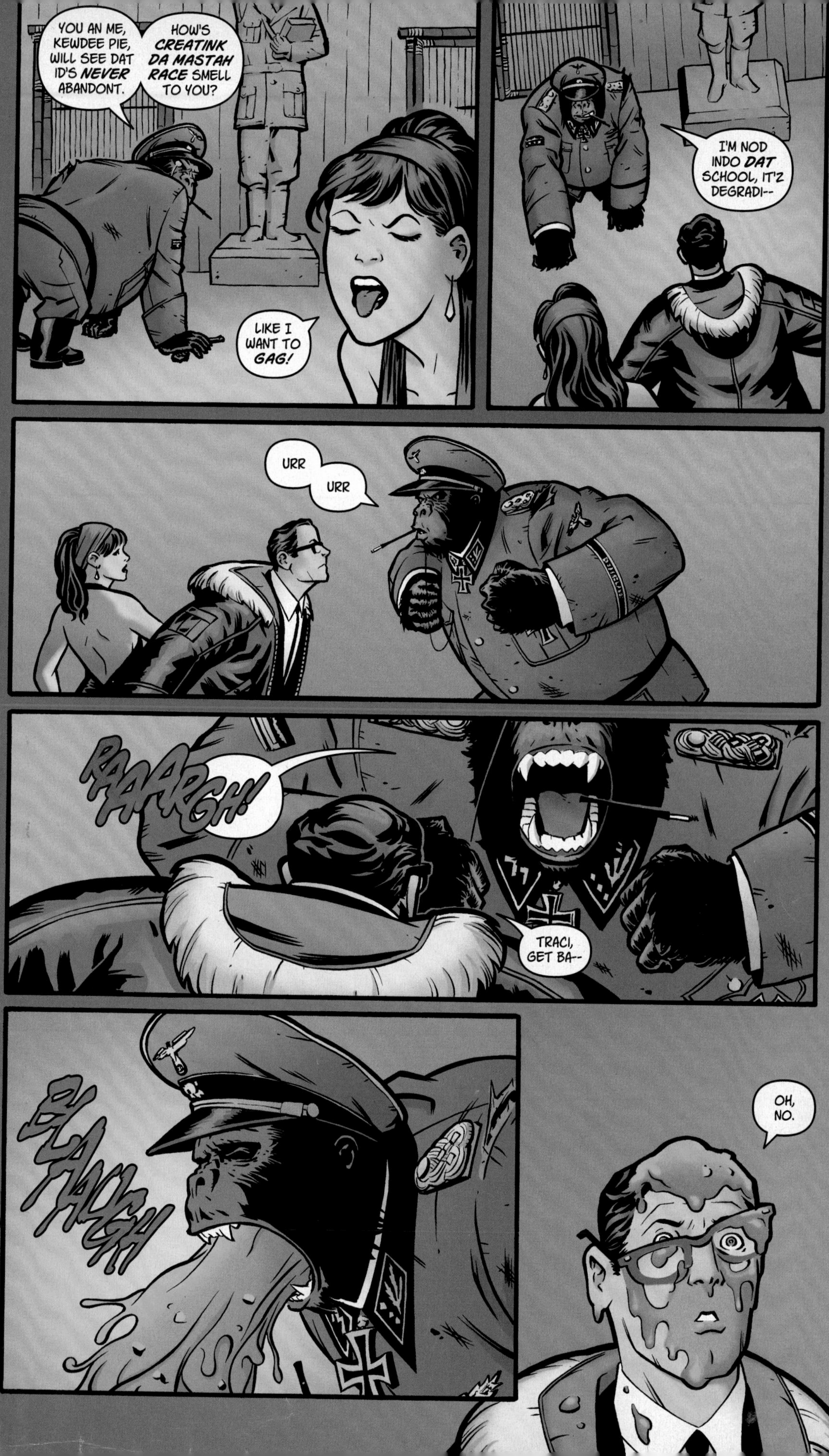
YOU AN ME, KEWDEE PIE, WILL SEE DAT ID'S NEVER ABANDONT.
HOW'S CREATINK DA MASTAH RACE SMELL TO YOU?
LIKE I WANT TO GAG!
I'M NOD INDO DAT SCHOOL, IT'Z DEGRADI--
URR
URR
RAAARGH!
TRACI, GET BA--
BLAAAGH
OH, NO.

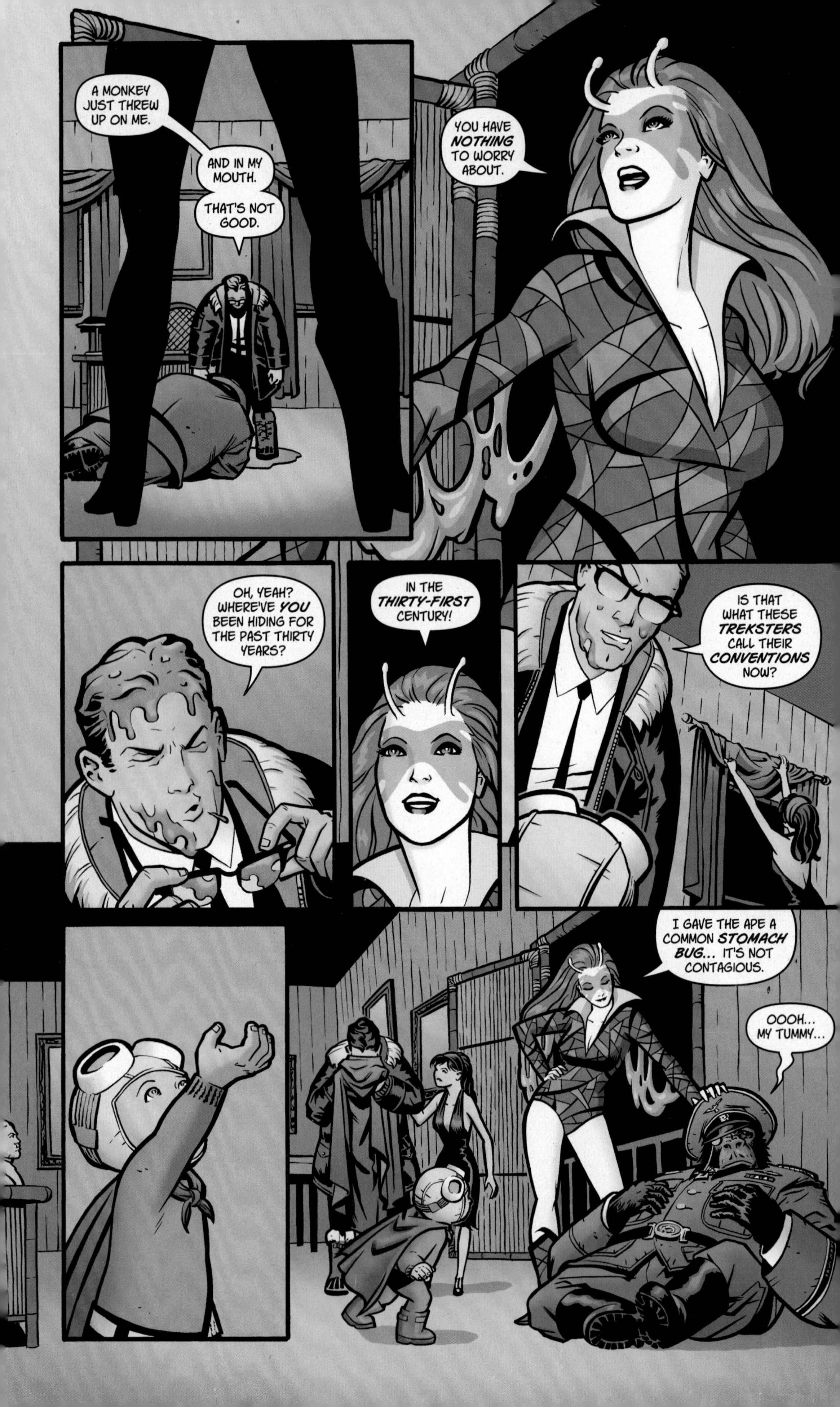
A MONKEY JUST THREW UP ON ME.
AND IN MY MOUTH.
THAT'S NOT GOOD.
YOU HAVE NOTHING TO WORRY ABOUT.
OH, YEAH? WHERE'VE YOU BEEN HIDING FOR THE PAST THIRTY YEARS?
IN THE THIRTY-FIRST CENTURY!
IS THAT WHAT THESE TREKSTERS CALL THEIR CONVENTIONS NOW?
I GAVE THE APE A COMMON STOMACH BUG... IT'S NOT CONTAGIOUS.
OOOH... MY TUMMY...

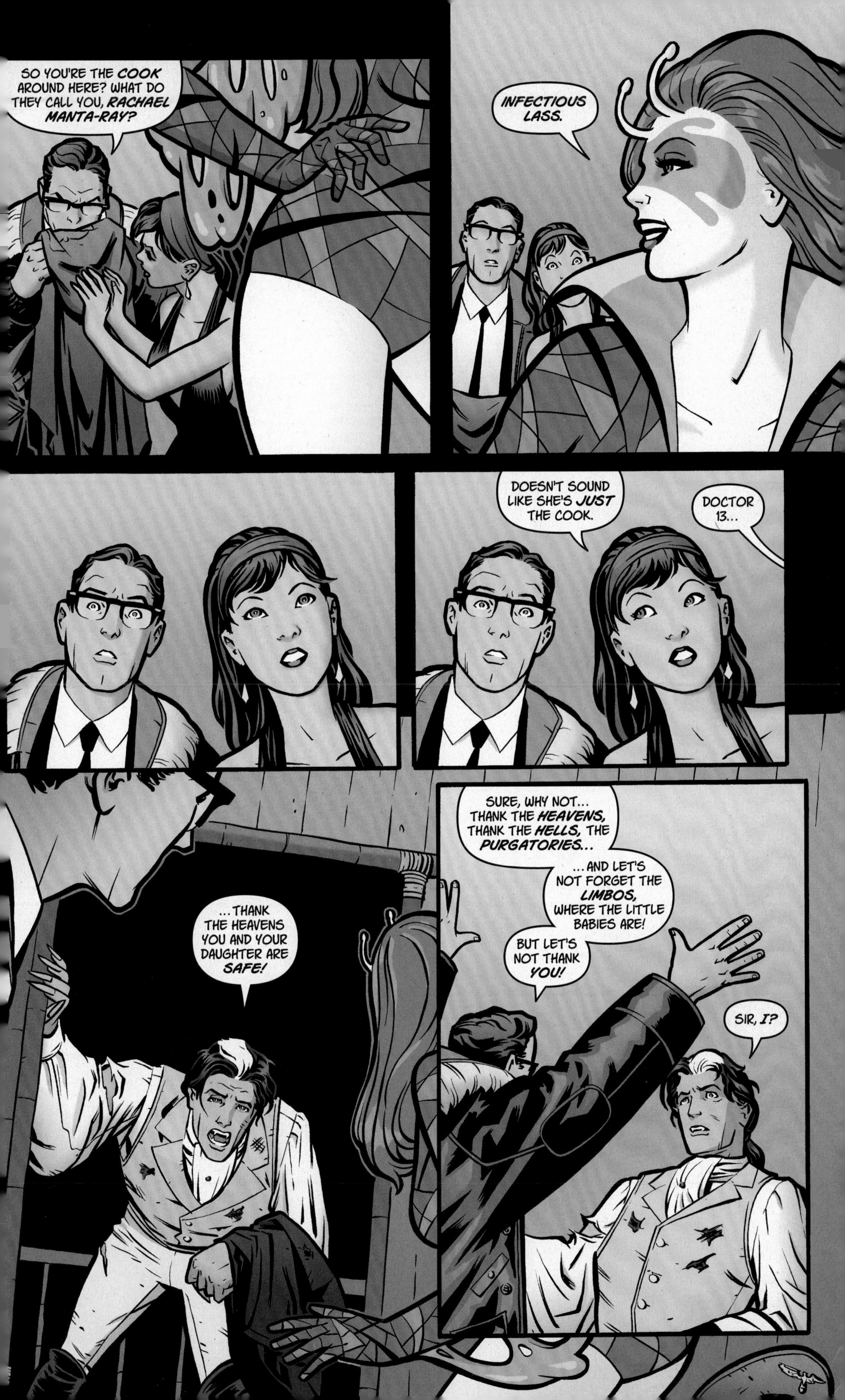
SO YOU'RE THE COOK AROUND HERE? WHAT DO THEY CALL YOU, RACHAEL MANTA-RAY?
INFECTIOUS LASS.
DOESN'T SOUND LIKE SHE'S JUST THE COOK.
DOCTOR 13...
...THANK THE HEAVENS YOU AND YOUR DAUGHTER ARE SAFE!
SURE, WHY NOT... THANK THE HEAVENS, THANK THE HELLS, THE PURGATORIES...
...AND LET'S NOT FORGET THE LIMBOS, WHERE THE LITTLE BABIES ARE!
BUT LET'S NOT THANK YOU!
SIR, I?

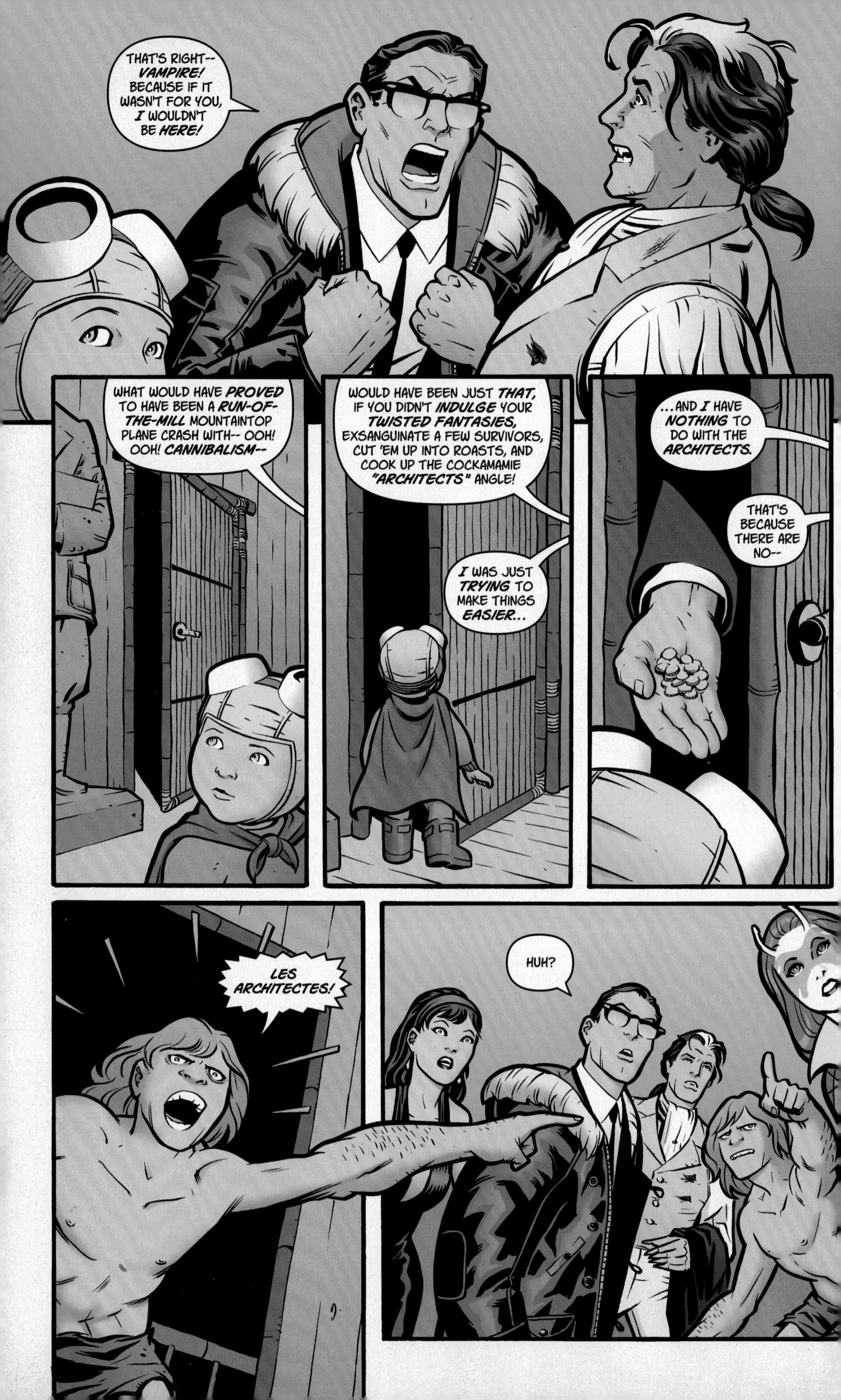
THAT'S RIGHT-- VAMPIRE! BECAUSE IF IT WASN'T FOR YOU, I WOULDN'T BE HERE!
WHAT WOULD HAVE PROVED TO HAVE BEEN A RUN-OF-THE-MILL MOUNTAINTOP PLANE CRASH WITH-- OOH! OOH! CANNIBALISM--
WOULD HAVE BEEN JUST THAT, IF YOU DIDN'T INDULGE YOUR TWISTED FANTASIES, EXSANGUINATE A FEW SURVIVORS, CUT 'EM UP INTO ROASTS, AND COOK UP THE COCKAMAMIE "ARCHITECTS" ANGLE!
I WAS JUST TRYING TO MAKE THINGS EASIER...
...AND I HAVE NOTHING TO DO WITH THE ARCHITECTS.
THAT'S BECAUSE THERE ARE NO--
LES ARCHITECTES!
HUH?

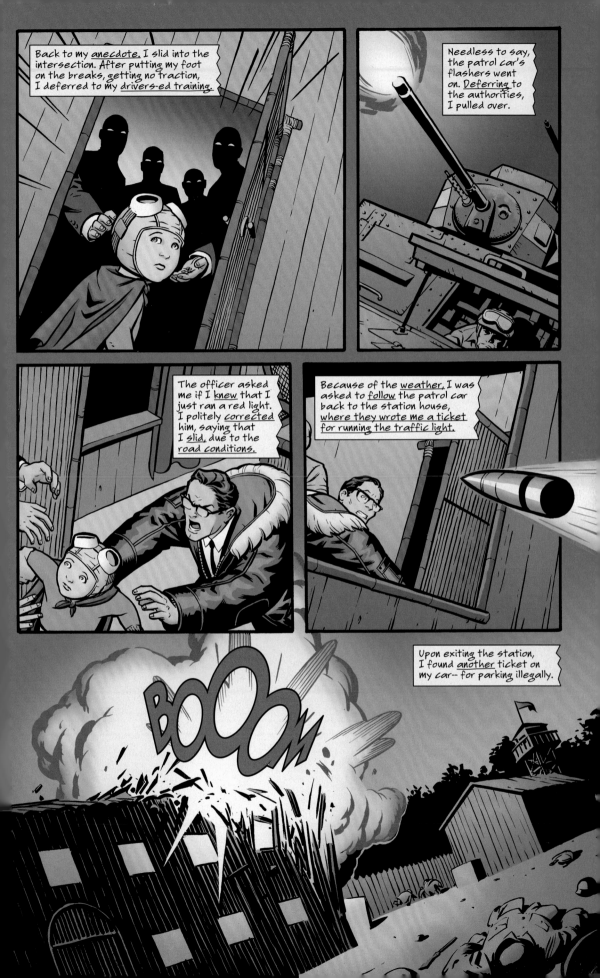

Back to my anecdote. I slid into the intersection. After putting my foot on the breaks, getting no traction, I deferred to my drivers-ed training.

Needless to say, the patrol car's flashers went on. Deferring to the authorities, I pulled over.

The officer asked me if I knew that I just ran a red light. I politely corrected him, saying that I slid, due to the road conditions.

Because of the weather, I was asked to follow the patrol car back to the station house, where they wrote me a ticket for running the traffic light.

Upon exiting the station, I found another ticket on my car-- for parking illegally.

BOOOM.

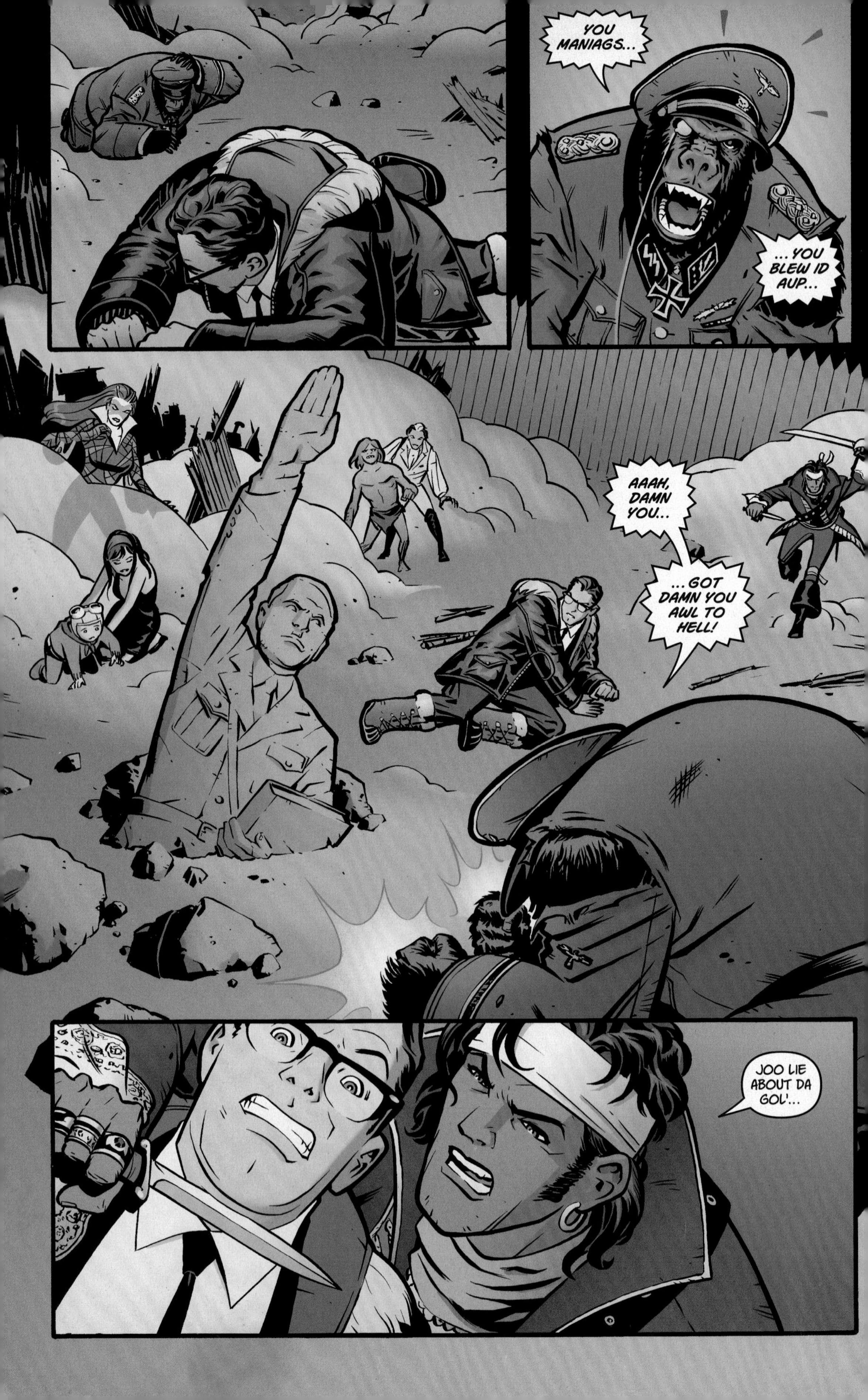
YOU MANIACS...
...YOU BLEW ID AUP...
AAAH, DAMN YOU...
...GOT DAMN YOU AWL TO HELL!
JOO LIE ABOUT DA GOL'...

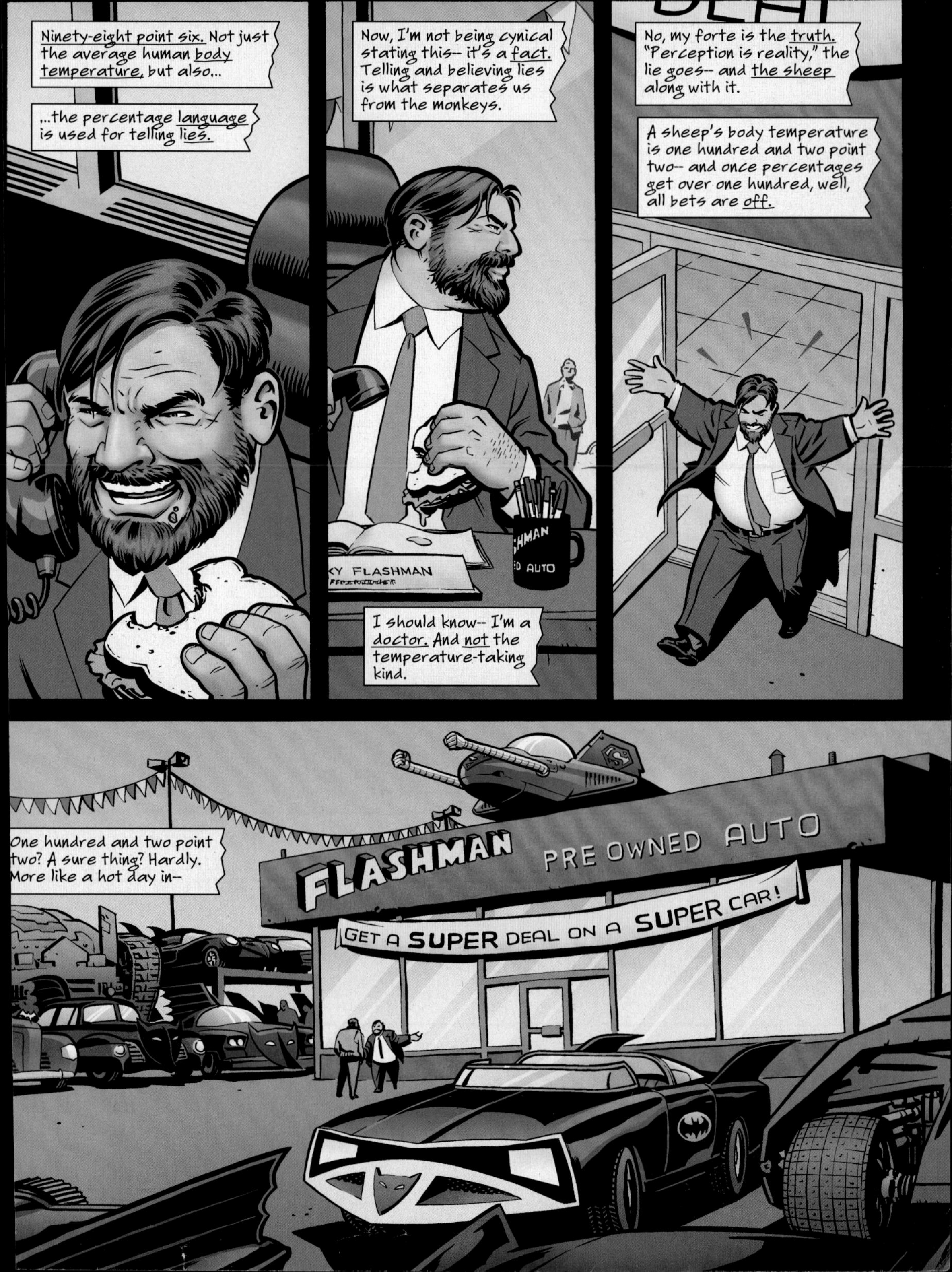

Ninety-eight point six. Not just the average human body temperature, but also...
...the percentage language is used for telling lies.
Now, I'm not being cynical stating this-- it's a fact. Telling and believing lies is what separates us from the monkeys.
KY FLASHMAN
I should know-- I'm a doctor. And not the temperature-taking kind.
No, my forte is the truth. "Perception is reality," the lie goes-- and the sheep along with it.
A sheep's body temperature is one hundred and two point two-- and once percentages get over one hundred, well, all bets are off.
One hundred and two point two? A sure thing? Hardly. More like a hot day in--
FLASHMAN
PRE OWNED AUTO
GET A SUPER DEAL ON A SUPER CAR!

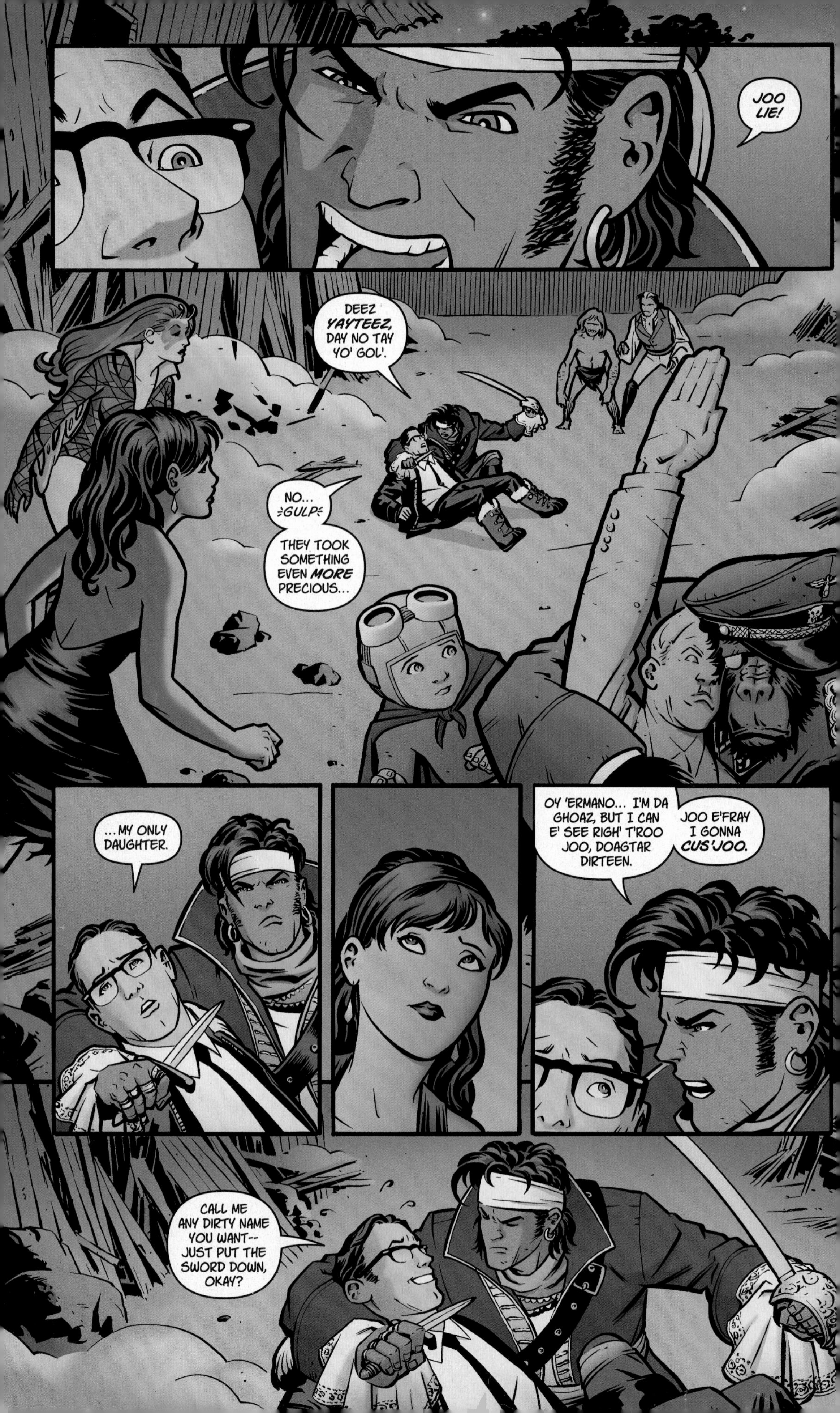
JOO LIE!
DEEZ YAYTEEZ, DAY NO TAY YO' GOL'.
NO... ¬GULP¬
THEY TOOK SOMETHING EVEN MORE PRECIOUS...
...MY ONLY DAUGHTER.
OY 'ERMANO... I'M DA GHOAZ, BUT I CAN E' SEE RIGH' T'ROO JOO, DOAGTAR DIRTEEN.
JOO E'FRAY I GONNA CUS'JOO.
CALL ME ANY DIRTY NAME YOU WANT-- JUST PUT THE SWORD DOWN, OKAY?

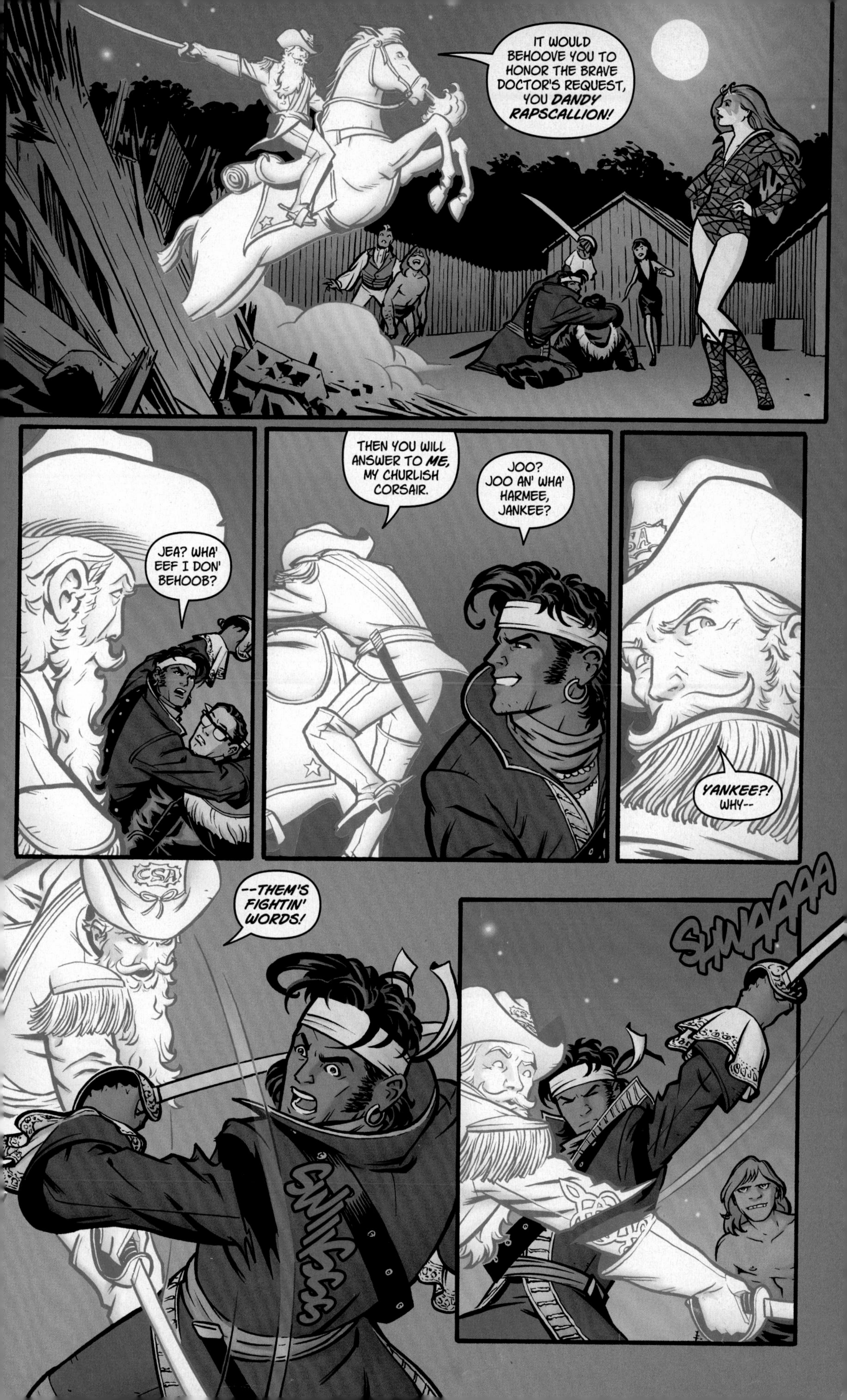
IT WOULD BEHOOVE YOU TO HONOR THE BRAVE DOCTOR'S REQUEST, YOU *DANDY RAPSCALLION!*
JEA? WHA' EEF I DON' BEHOOB?
THEN YOU WILL ANSWER TO *ME,* MY CHURLISH CORSAIR.
JOO? JOO AN' WHA' HARMEE, JANKEE?
*YANKEE?!* WHY--
*--THEM'S FIGHTIN' WORDS!*
SHWAAAA
SWISSS

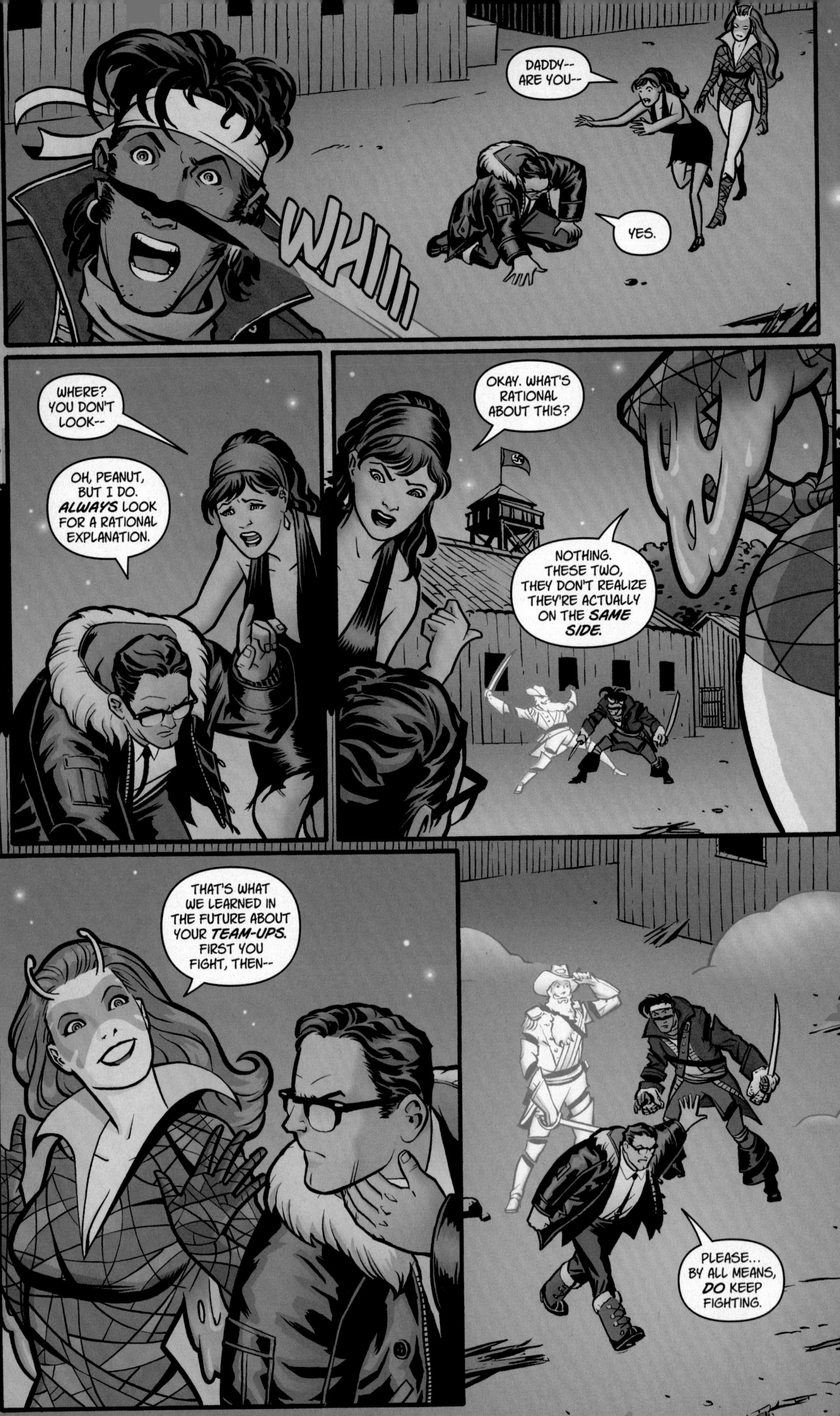
WHIIII
DADDY-- ARE YOU--
YES.
WHERE? YOU DON'T LOOK--
OH, PEANUT, BUT I DO. ALWAYS LOOK FOR A RATIONAL EXPLANATION.
OKAY. WHAT'S RATIONAL ABOUT THIS?
NOTHING. THESE TWO, THEY DON'T REALIZE THEY'RE ACTUALLY ON THE SAME SIDE.
THAT'S WHAT WE LEARNED IN THE FUTURE ABOUT YOUR TEAM-UPS. FIRST YOU FIGHT, THEN--
PLEASE... BY ALL MEANS, DO KEEP FIGHTING.

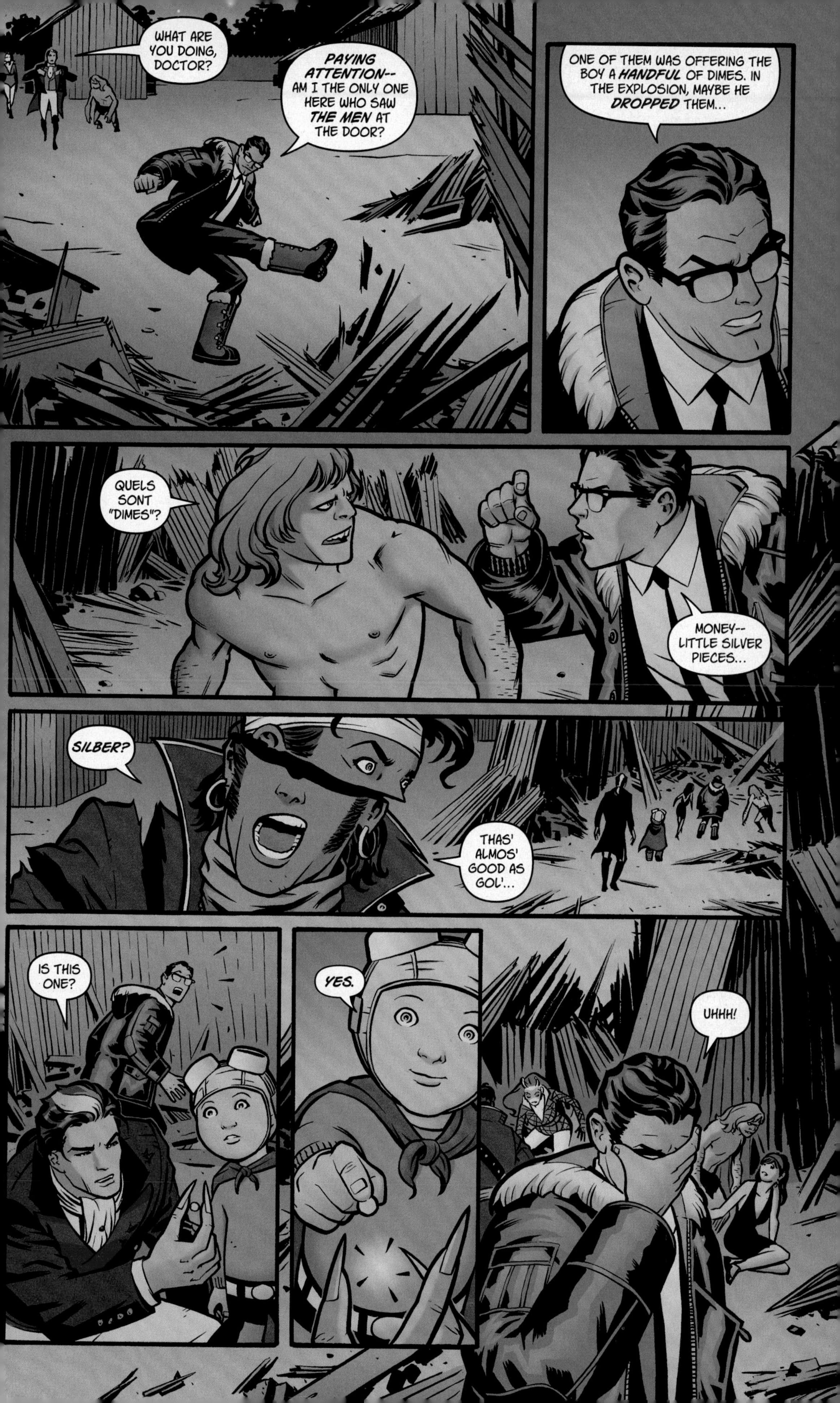
WHAT ARE YOU DOING, DOCTOR?
PAYING ATTENTION-- AM I THE ONLY ONE HERE WHO SAW THE MEN AT THE DOOR?
ONE OF THEM WAS OFFERING THE BOY A HANDFUL OF DIMES. IN THE EXPLOSION, MAYBE HE DROPPED THEM...
QUELS SONT "DIMES"?
MONEY-- LITTLE SILVER PIECES...
SILBER?
THAS' ALMOS' GOOD AS GOL'...
IS THIS ONE?
YES.
UHHH!

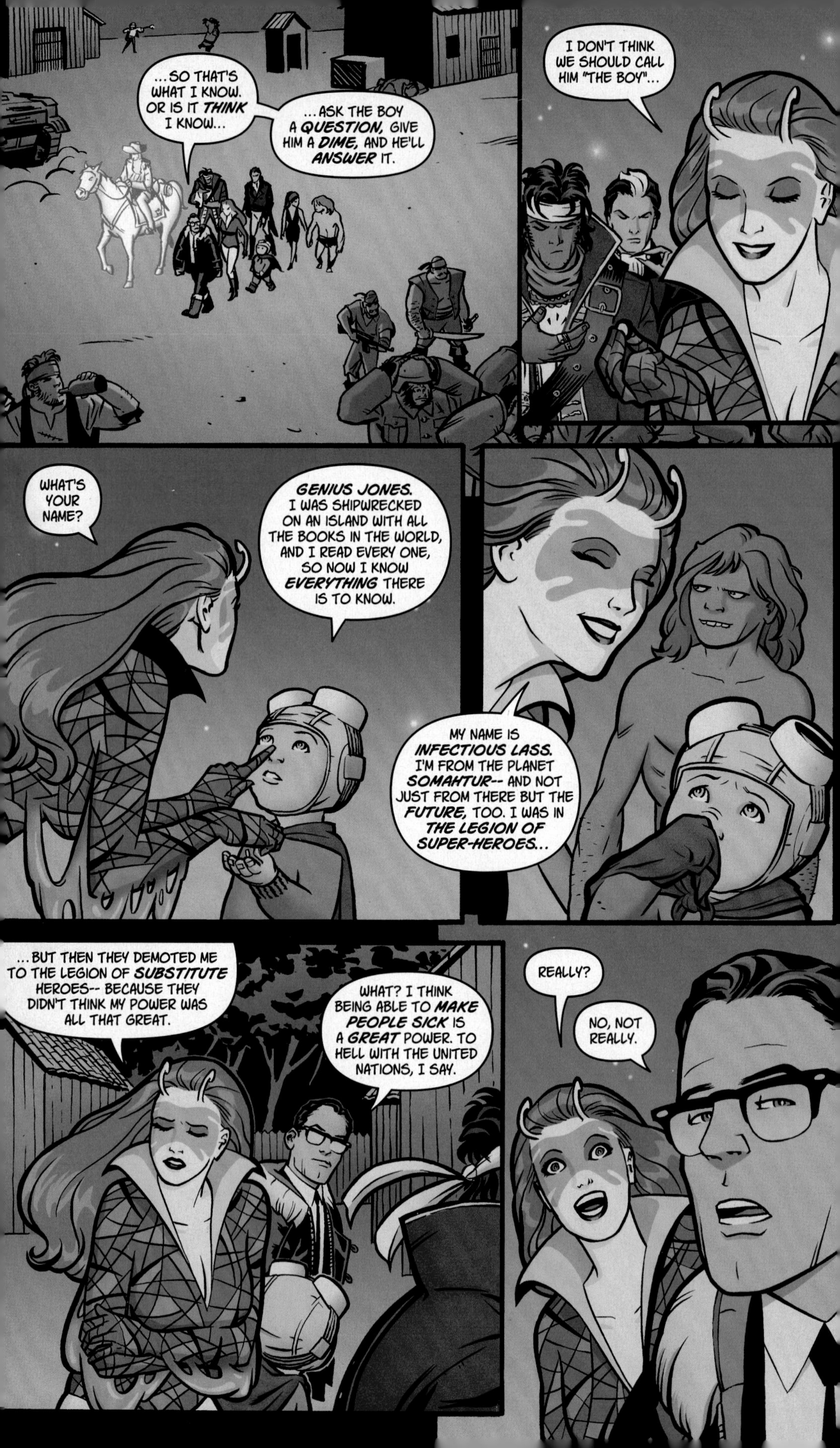

...SO THAT'S WHAT I KNOW. OR IS IT THINK I KNOW...
...ASK THE BOY A QUESTION, GIVE HIM A DIME, AND HE'LL ANSWER IT.
I DON'T THINK WE SHOULD CALL HIM "THE BOY"...
WHAT'S YOUR NAME?
GENIUS JONES. I WAS SHIPWRECKED ON AN ISLAND WITH ALL THE BOOKS IN THE WORLD, AND I READ EVERY ONE, SO NOW I KNOW EVERYTHING THERE IS TO KNOW.
MY NAME IS INFECTIOUS LASS. I'M FROM THE PLANET SOMAHTUR-- AND NOT JUST FROM THERE BUT THE FUTURE, TOO. I WAS IN THE LEGION OF SUPER-HEROES...
...BUT THEN THEY DEMOTED ME TO THE LEGION OF SUBSTITUTE HEROES-- BECAUSE THEY DIDN'T THINK MY POWER WAS ALL THAT GREAT.
WHAT? I THINK BEING ABLE TO MAKE PEOPLE SICK IS A GREAT POWER. TO HELL WITH THE UNITED NATIONS, I SAY.
REALLY?
NO, NOT REALLY.

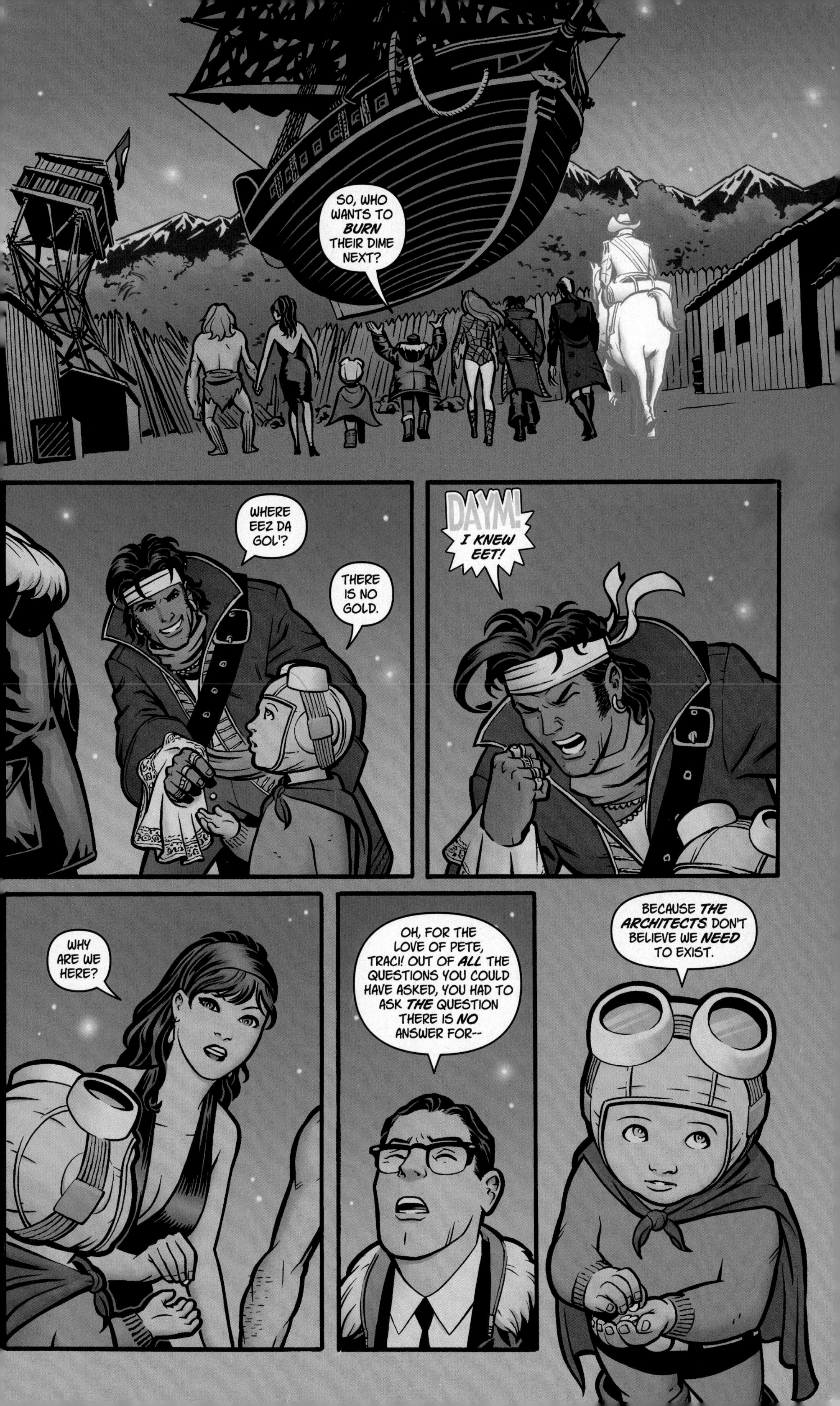
SO, WHO WANTS TO BURN THEIR DIME NEXT?
WHERE EEZ DA GOL'?
THERE IS NO GOLD.
DAYM!
I KNEW EET!
WHY ARE WE HERE?
OH, FOR THE LOVE OF PETE, TRACI! OUT OF ALL THE QUESTIONS YOU COULD HAVE ASKED, YOU HAD TO ASK THE QUESTION THERE IS NO ANSWER FOR--
BECAUSE THE ARCHITECTS DON'T BELIEVE WE NEED TO EXIST.

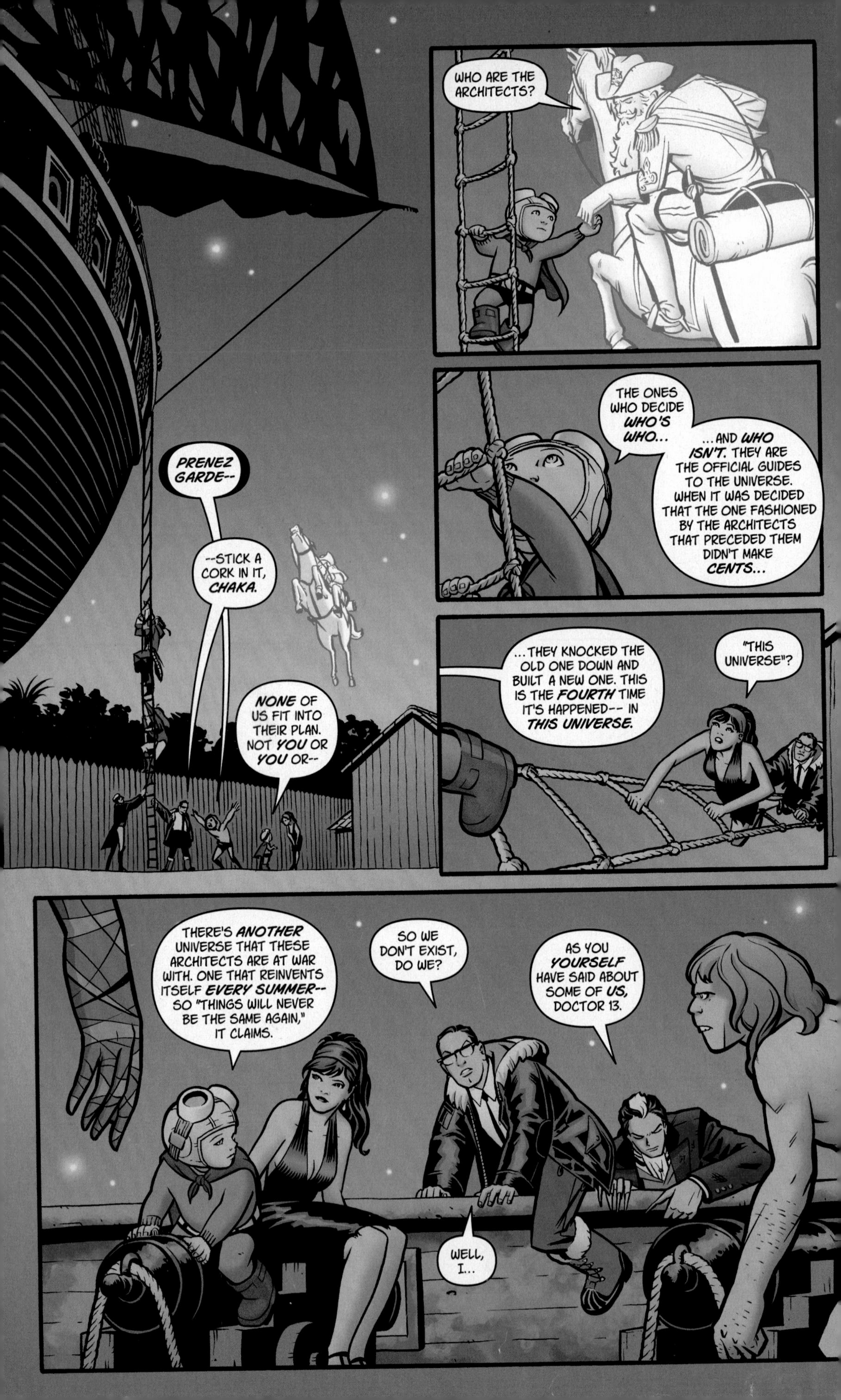
WHO ARE THE ARCHITECTS?
THE ONES WHO DECIDE WHO'S WHO...
...AND WHO ISN'T. THEY ARE THE OFFICIAL GUIDES TO THE UNIVERSE. WHEN IT WAS DECIDED THAT THE ONE FASHIONED BY THE ARCHITECTS THAT PRECEDED THEM DIDN'T MAKE CENTS...
...THEY KNOCKED THE OLD ONE DOWN AND BUILT A NEW ONE. THIS IS THE FOURTH TIME IT'S HAPPENED-- IN THIS UNIVERSE.
"THIS UNIVERSE"?
PRENEZ GARDE--
--STICK A CORK IN IT, CHAKA.
NONE OF US FIT INTO THEIR PLAN. NOT YOU OR YOU OR--
THERE'S ANOTHER UNIVERSE THAT THESE ARCHITECTS ARE AT WAR WITH. ONE THAT REINVENTS ITSELF EVERY SUMMER-- SO "THINGS WILL NEVER BE THE SAME AGAIN," IT CLAIMS.
SO WE DON'T EXIST, DO WE?
AS YOU YOURSELF HAVE SAID ABOUT SOME OF US, DOCTOR 13.
WELL, I...

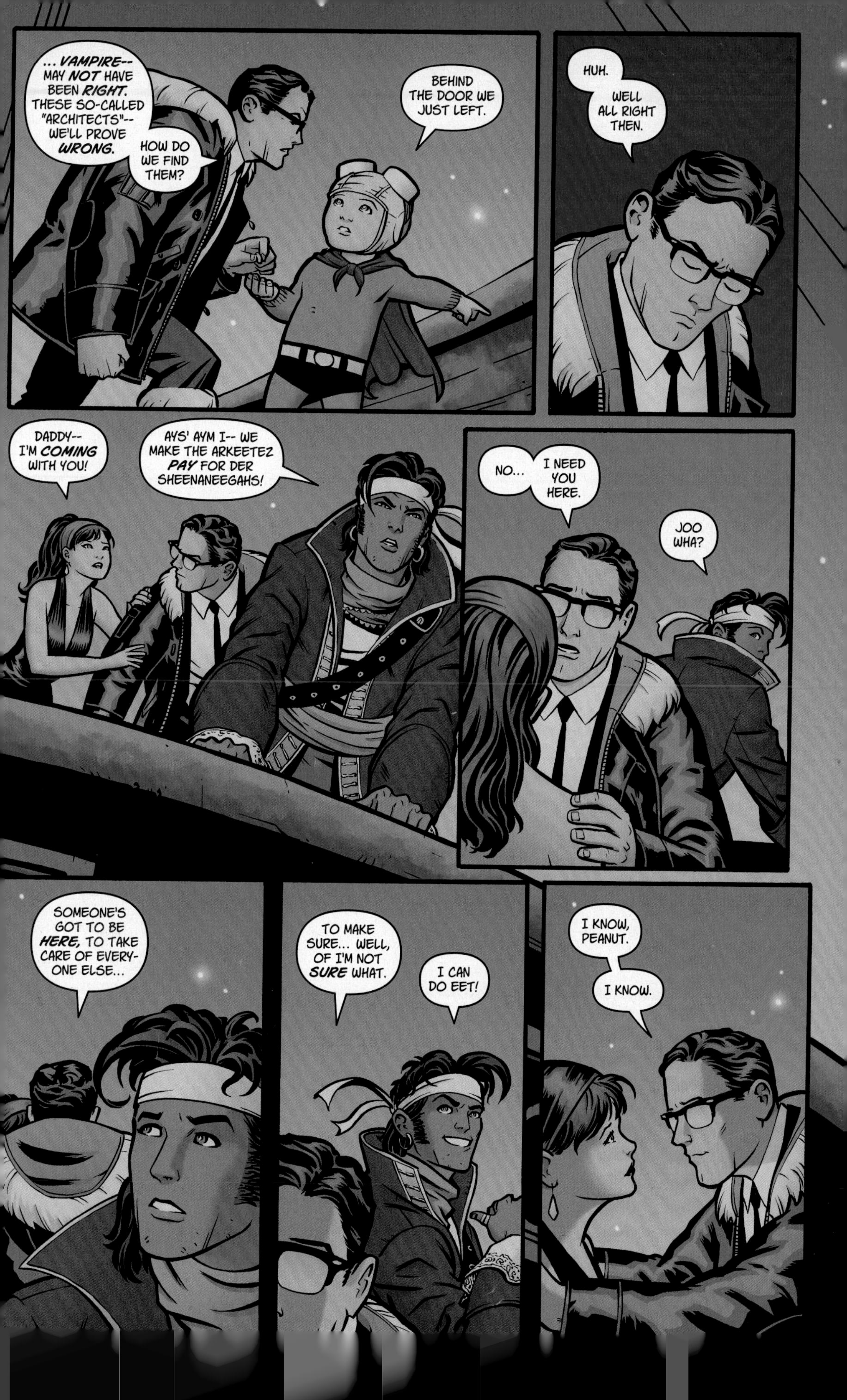
... VAMPIRE-- MAY NOT HAVE BEEN RIGHT. THESE SO-CALLED "ARCHITECTS"-- WE'LL PROVE WRONG.
HOW DO WE FIND THEM?
BEHIND THE DOOR WE JUST LEFT.
HUH.
WELL ALL RIGHT THEN.
DADDY-- I'M COMING WITH YOU!
AYS' AYM I-- WE MAKE THE ARKEETEZ PAY FOR DER SHEENANEEGAHS!
NO...
I NEED YOU HERE.
JOO WHA?
SOMEONE'S GOT TO BE HERE, TO TAKE CARE OF EVERY-ONE ELSE...
TO MAKE SURE... WELL, OF I'M NOT SURE WHAT.
I CAN DO EET!
I KNOW, PEANUT.
I KNOW.

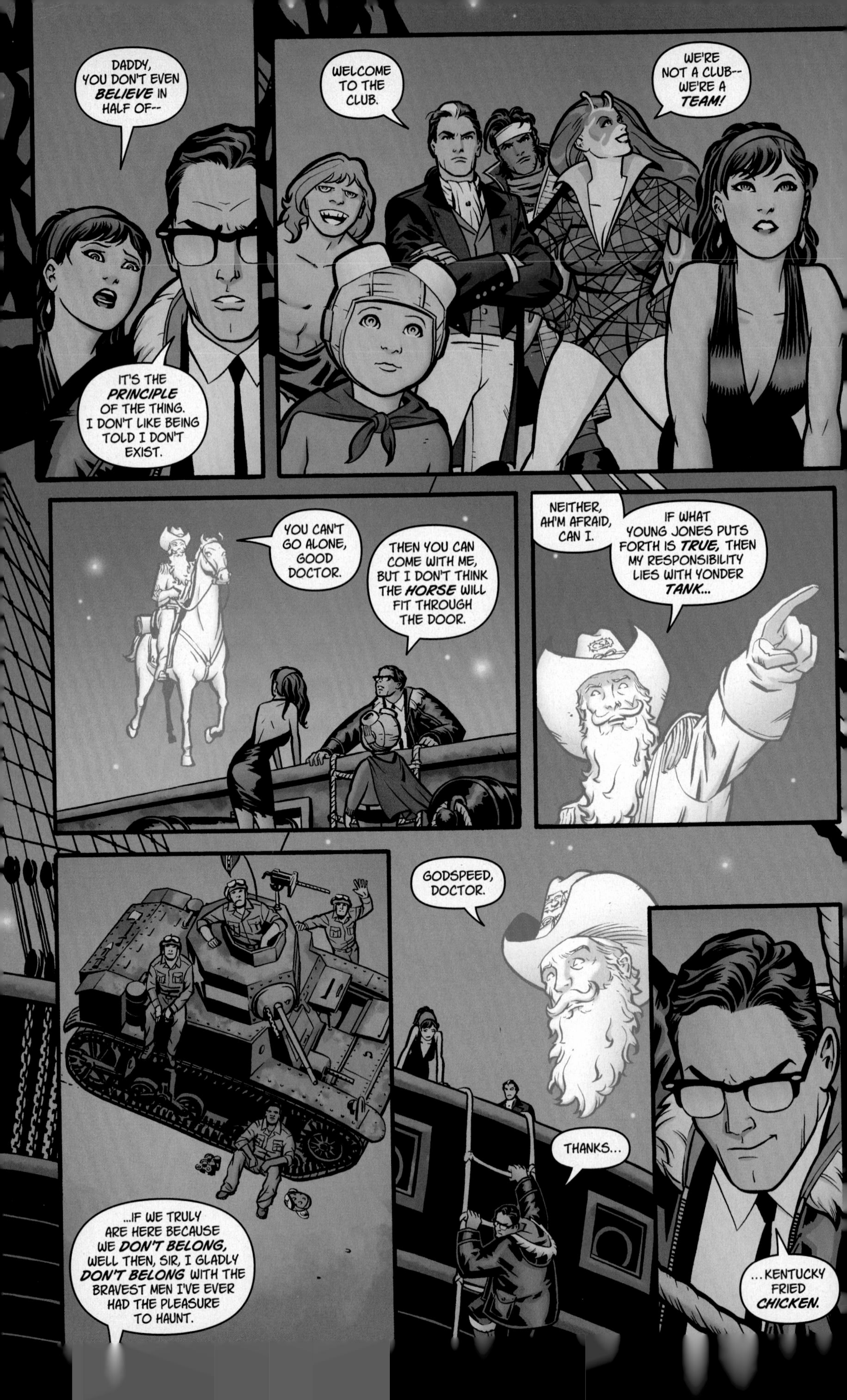
DADDY, YOU DON'T EVEN BELIEVE IN HALF OF--
IT'S THE PRINCIPLE OF THE THING. I DON'T LIKE BEING TOLD I DON'T EXIST.
WELCOME TO THE CLUB.
WE'RE NOT A CLUB-- WE'RE A TEAM!
YOU CAN'T GO ALONE, GOOD DOCTOR.
THEN YOU CAN COME WITH ME, BUT I DON'T THINK THE HORSE WILL FIT THROUGH THE DOOR.
NEITHER, AH'M AFRAID, CAN I.
IF WHAT YOUNG JONES PUTS FORTH IS TRUE, THEN MY RESPONSIBILITY LIES WITH YONDER TANK...
...IF WE TRULY ARE HERE BECAUSE WE DON'T BELONG, WELL THEN, SIR, I GLADLY DON'T BELONG WITH THE BRAVEST MEN I'VE EVER HAD THE PLEASURE TO HAUNT.
GODSPEED, DOCTOR.
THANKS...
...KENTUCKY FRIED CHICKEN.

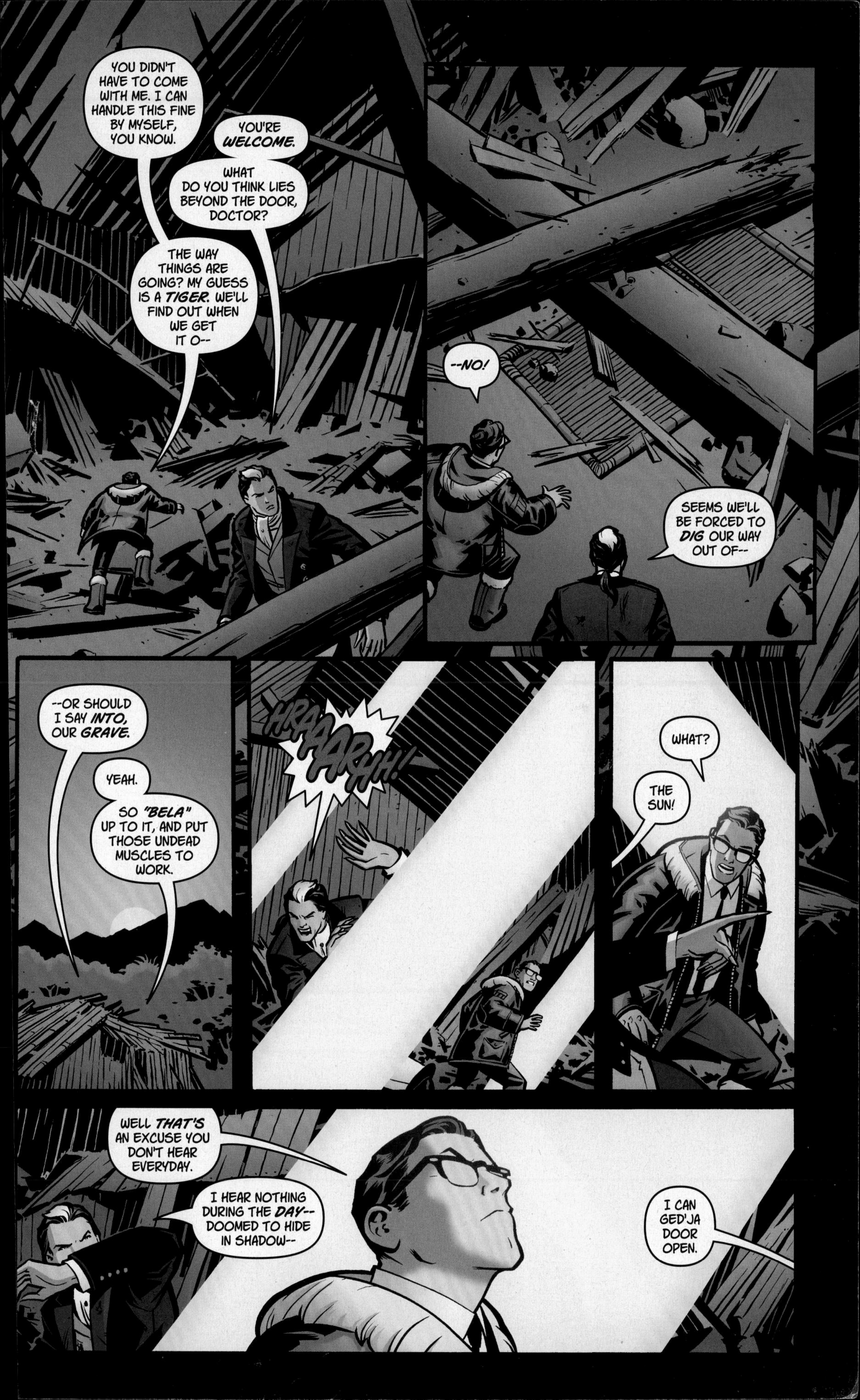
YOU DIDN'T HAVE TO COME WITH ME. I CAN HANDLE THIS FINE BY MYSELF, YOU KNOW.
YOU'RE WELCOME.
WHAT DO YOU THINK LIES BEYOND THE DOOR, DOCTOR?
THE WAY THINGS ARE GOING? MY GUESS IS A TIGER. WE'LL FIND OUT WHEN WE GET IT O--
--NO!
SEEMS WE'LL BE FORCED TO DIG OUR WAY OUT OF--
--OR SHOULD I SAY INTO, OUR GRAVE.
YEAH.
SO "BELA" UP TO IT, AND PUT THOSE UNDEAD MUSCLES TO WORK.
HRAAAARHH!
WHAT?
THE SUN!
WELL THAT'S AN EXCUSE YOU DON'T HEAR EVERYDAY.
I HEAR NOTHING DURING THE DAY--DOOMED TO HIDE IN SHADOW--
I CAN GED'JA DOOR OPEN.

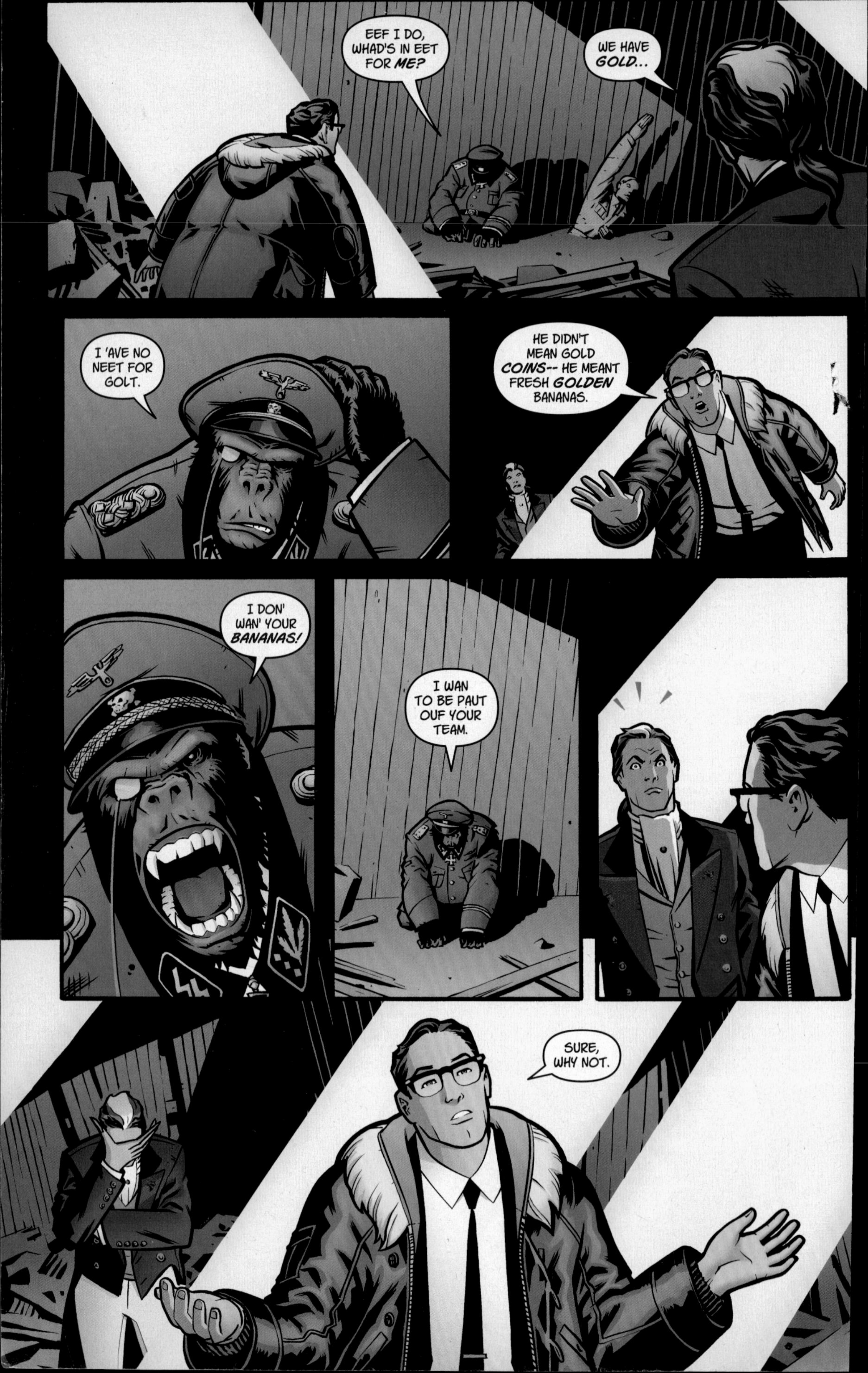
EEF I DO, WHAD'S IN EET FOR **ME?**
WE HAVE **GOLD...**
I 'AVE NO NEET FOR GOLT.
HE DIDN'T MEAN GOLD **COINS--** HE MEANT FRESH **GOLDEN** BANANAS.
I DON' WAN' YOUR **BANANAS!**
I WAN TO BE PAUT OUF YOUR TEAM.
SURE, WHY NOT.

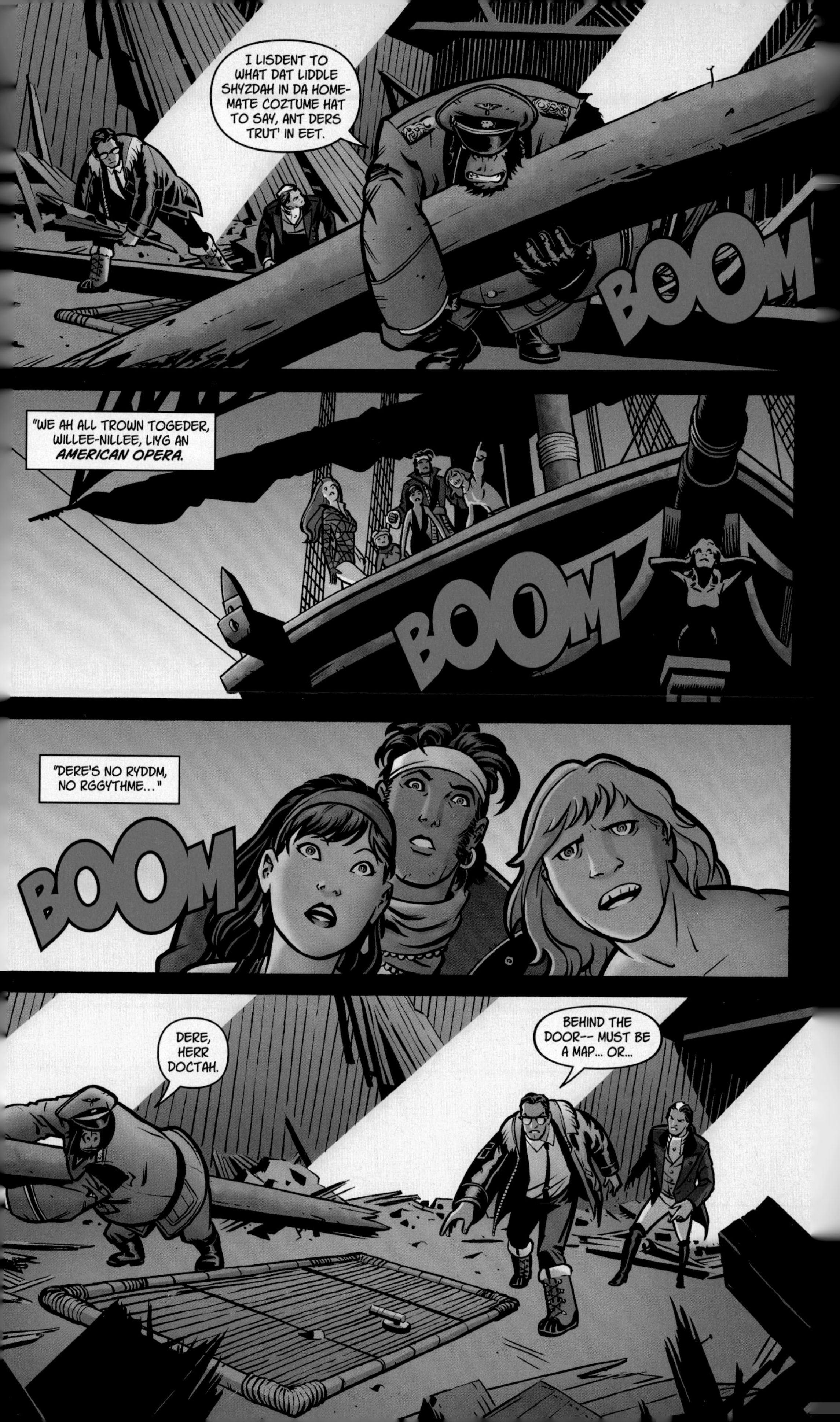
I LISDENT TO WHAT DAT LIDDLE SHYZDAH IN DA HOME-MATE COZTUME HAT TO SAY, ANT DERS TRUT' IN EET.
BOOM
"WE AH ALL TROWN TOGEDER, WILLEE-NILLEE, LIYG AN *AMERICAN OPERA*.
BOOM
"DERE'S NO RYDDM, NO RGGYTHME..."
BOOM
DERE, HERR DOCTAH.
BEHIND THE DOOR-- MUST BE A MAP... OR...

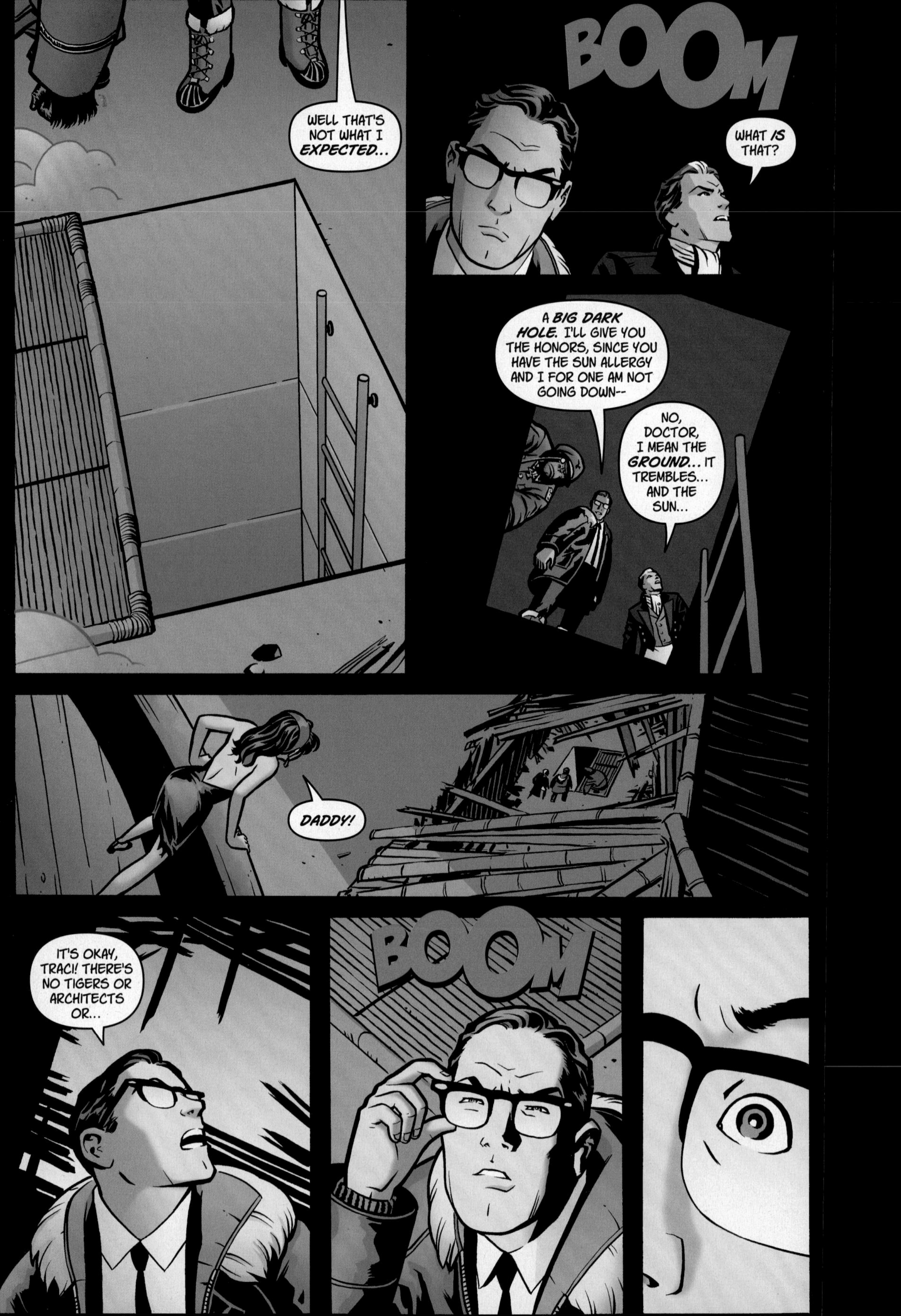
WELL THAT'S NOT WHAT I EXPECTED...
BOOM
WHAT IS THAT?
A BIG DARK HOLE. I'LL GIVE YOU THE HONORS, SINCE YOU HAVE THE SUN ALLERGY AND I FOR ONE AM NOT GOING DOWN--
NO, DOCTOR, I MEAN THE GROUND... IT TREMBLES... AND THE SUN...
DADDY!
IT'S OKAY, TRACI! THERE'S NO TIGERS OR ARCHITECTS OR...
BOOM

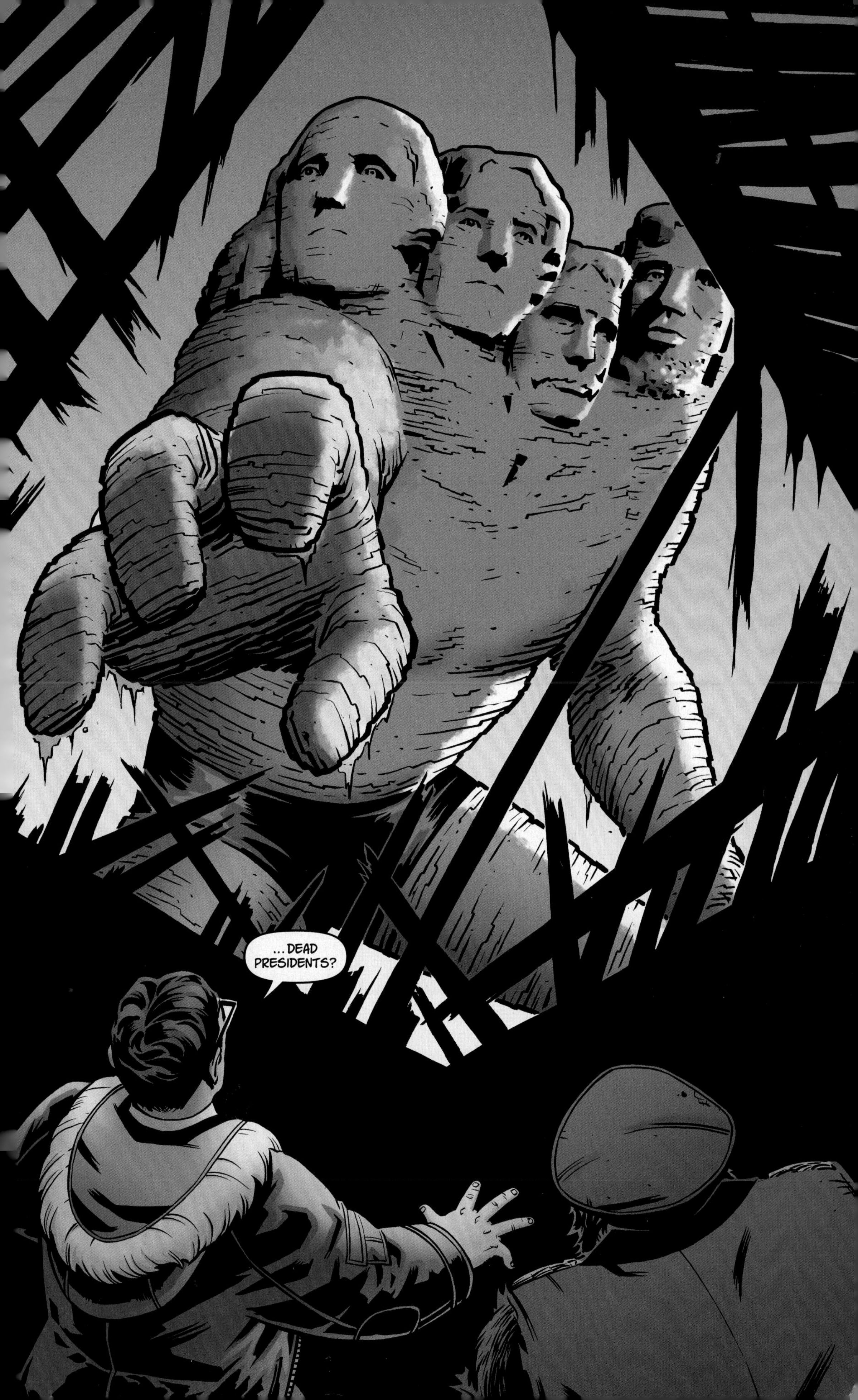
...DEAD PRESIDENTS?

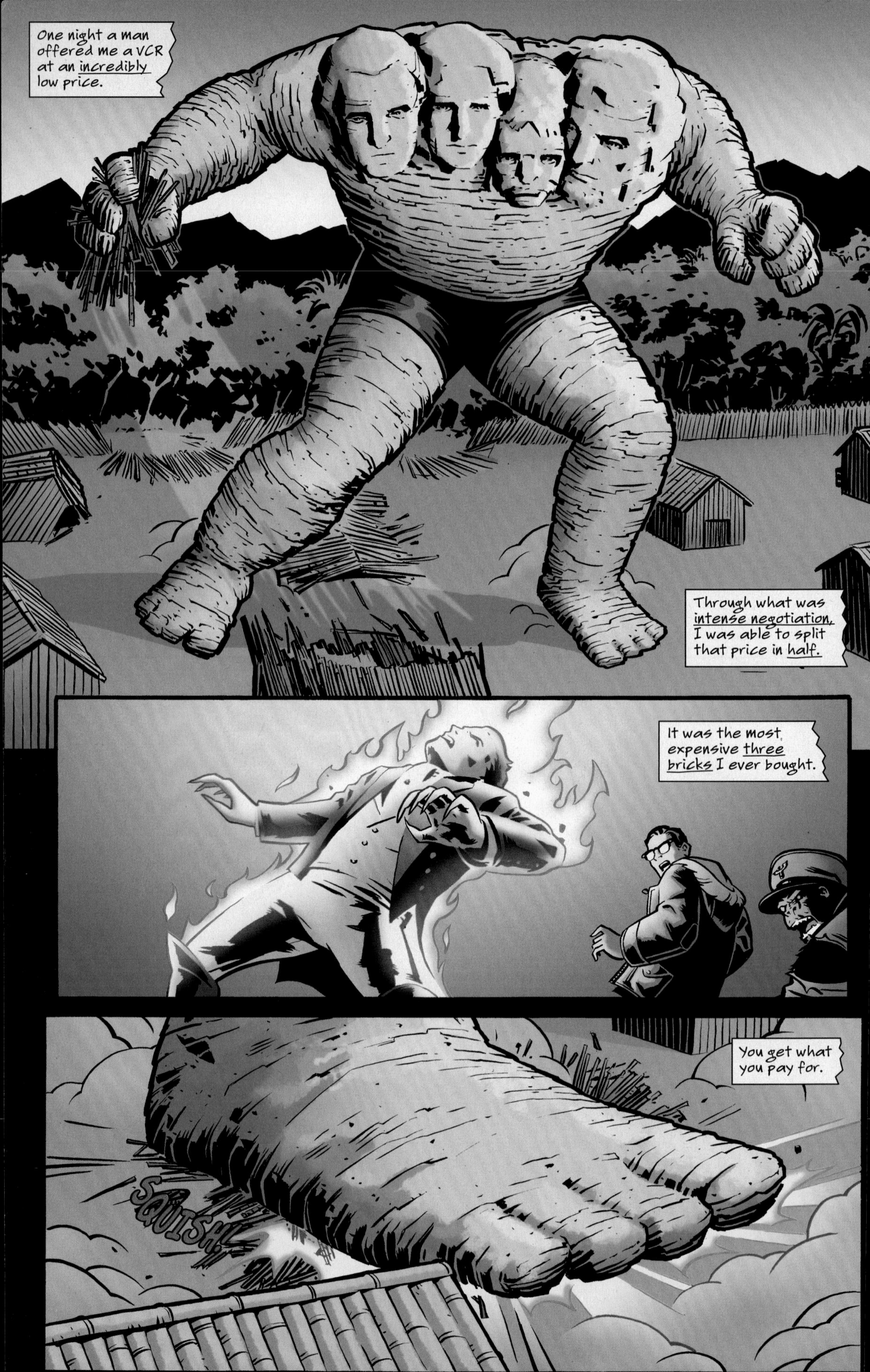
One night a man offered me a VCR at an incredibly low price.
Through what was intense negotiation, I was able to split that price in half.
It was the most expensive three bricks I ever bought.
You get what you pay for.
SQUISH!

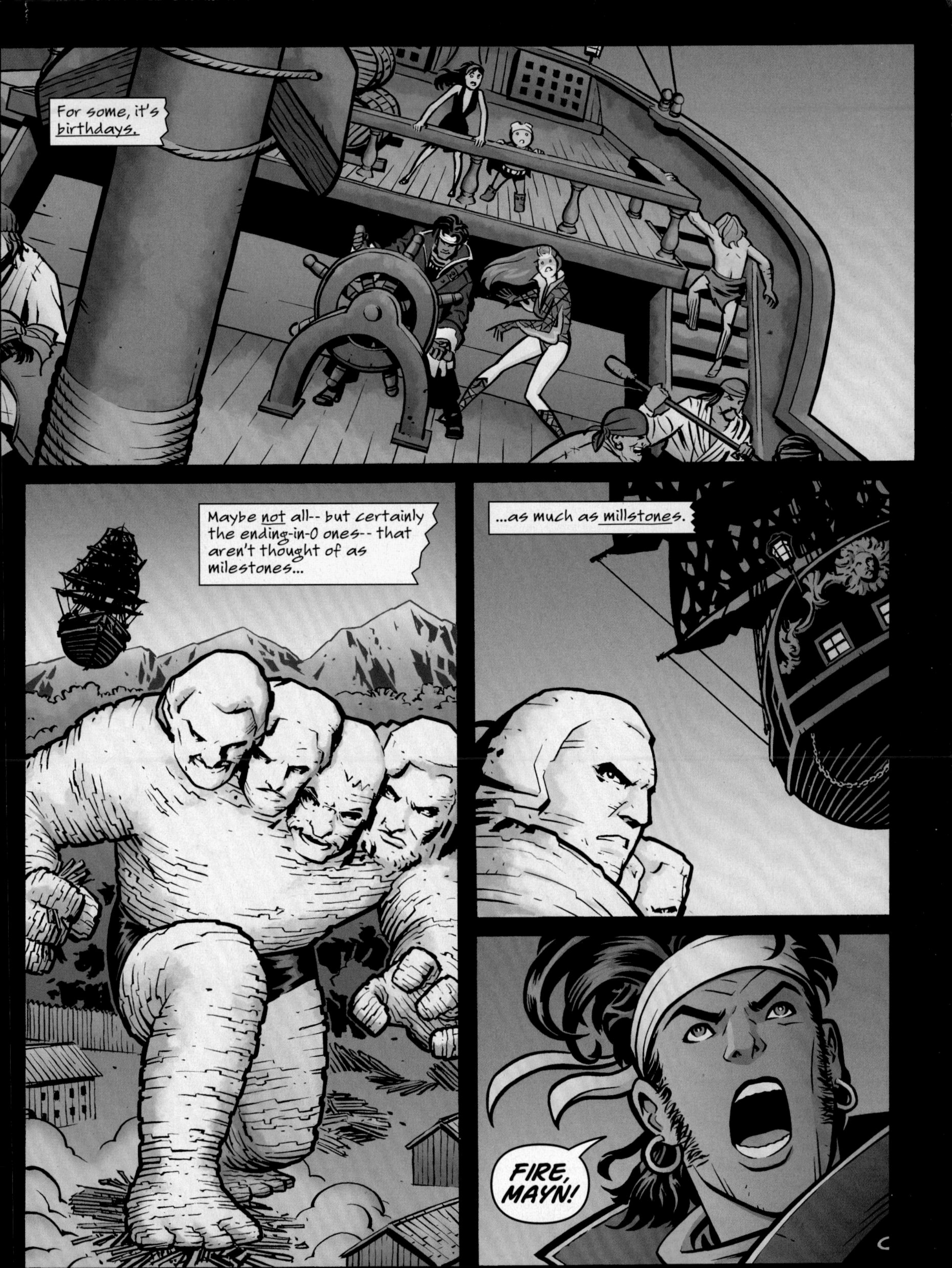

For some, it's birthdays.
Maybe not all-- but certainly the ending-in-0 ones-- that aren't thought of as milestones...
...as much as millstones.
FIRE, MAYN!

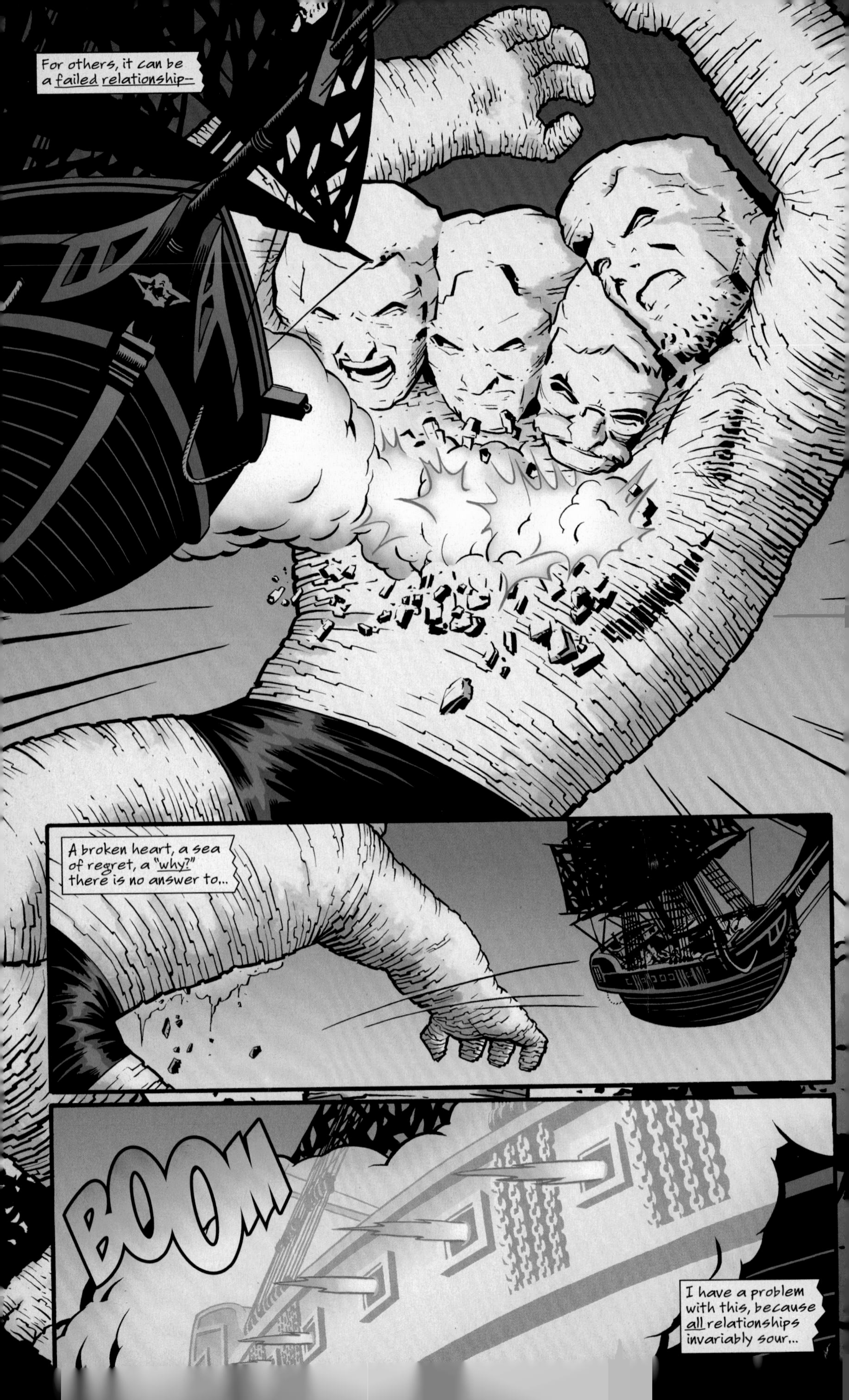
For others, it can be a failed relationship–
A broken heart, a sea of regret, a "why?" there is no answer to...
BOOM
I have a problem with this, because all relationships invariably sour...

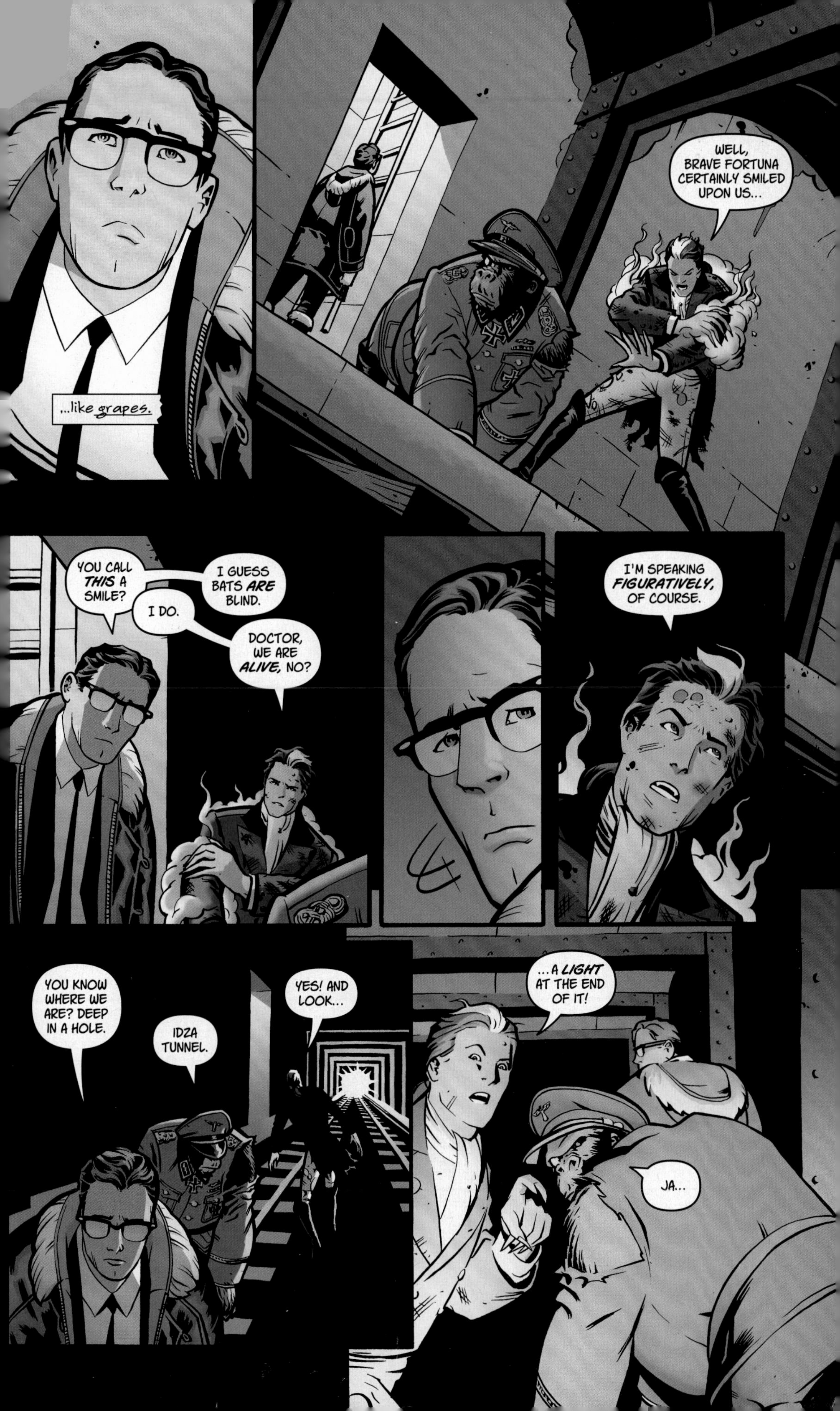
...like grapes.
WELL, BRAVE FORTUNA CERTAINLY SMILED UPON US...
YOU CALL THIS A SMILE?
I GUESS BATS ARE BLIND.
I DO.
DOCTOR, WE ARE ALIVE, NO?
I'M SPEAKING FIGURATIVELY, OF COURSE.
YOU KNOW WHERE WE ARE? DEEP IN A HOLE.
IDZA TUNNEL.
YES! AND LOOK...
...A LIGHT AT THE END OF IT!
JA...

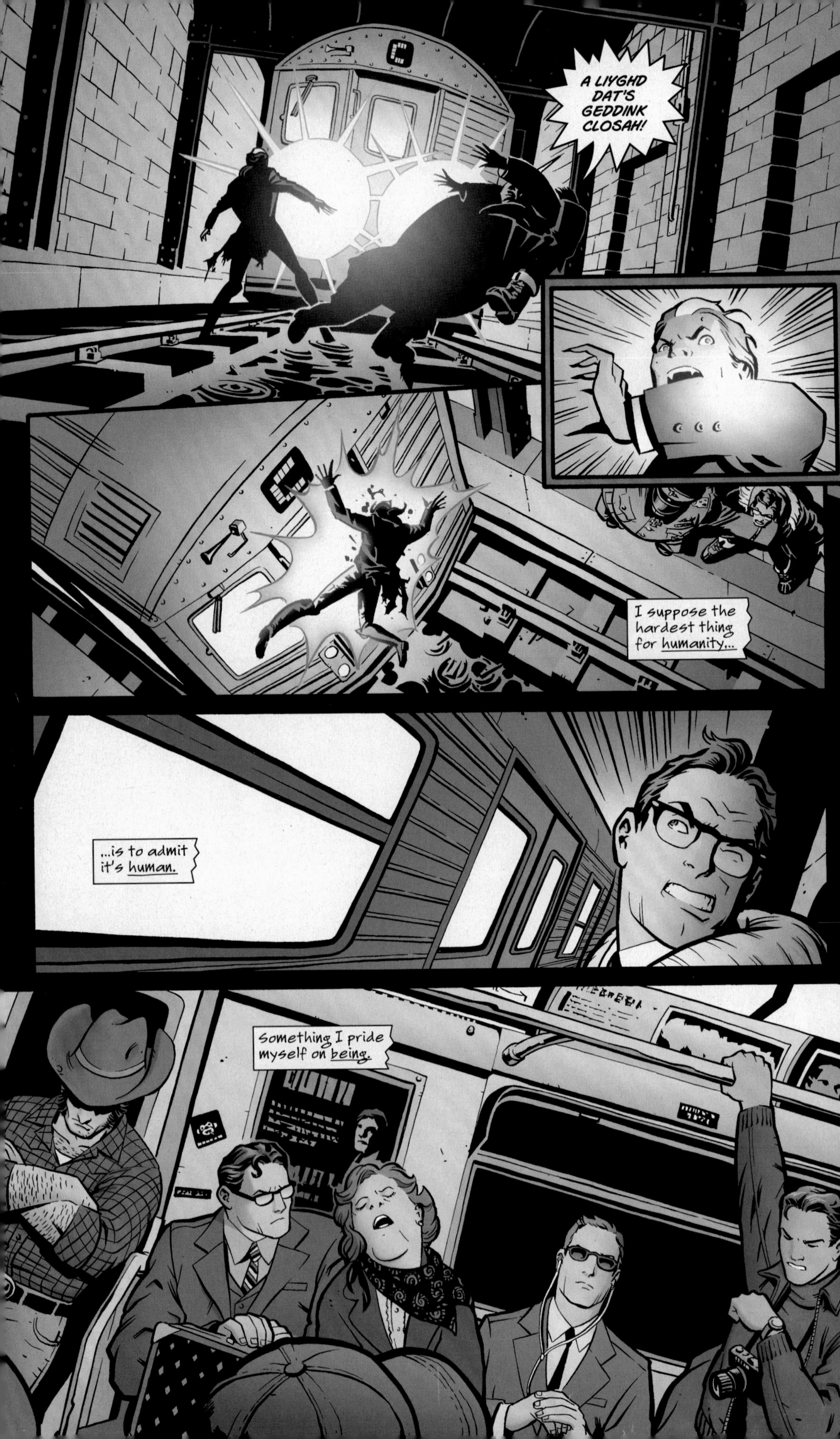
A LIYGHD DAT'S GEDDINK CLOSAH!
I suppose the hardest thing for humanity...
...is to admit it's human.
Something I pride myself on being.

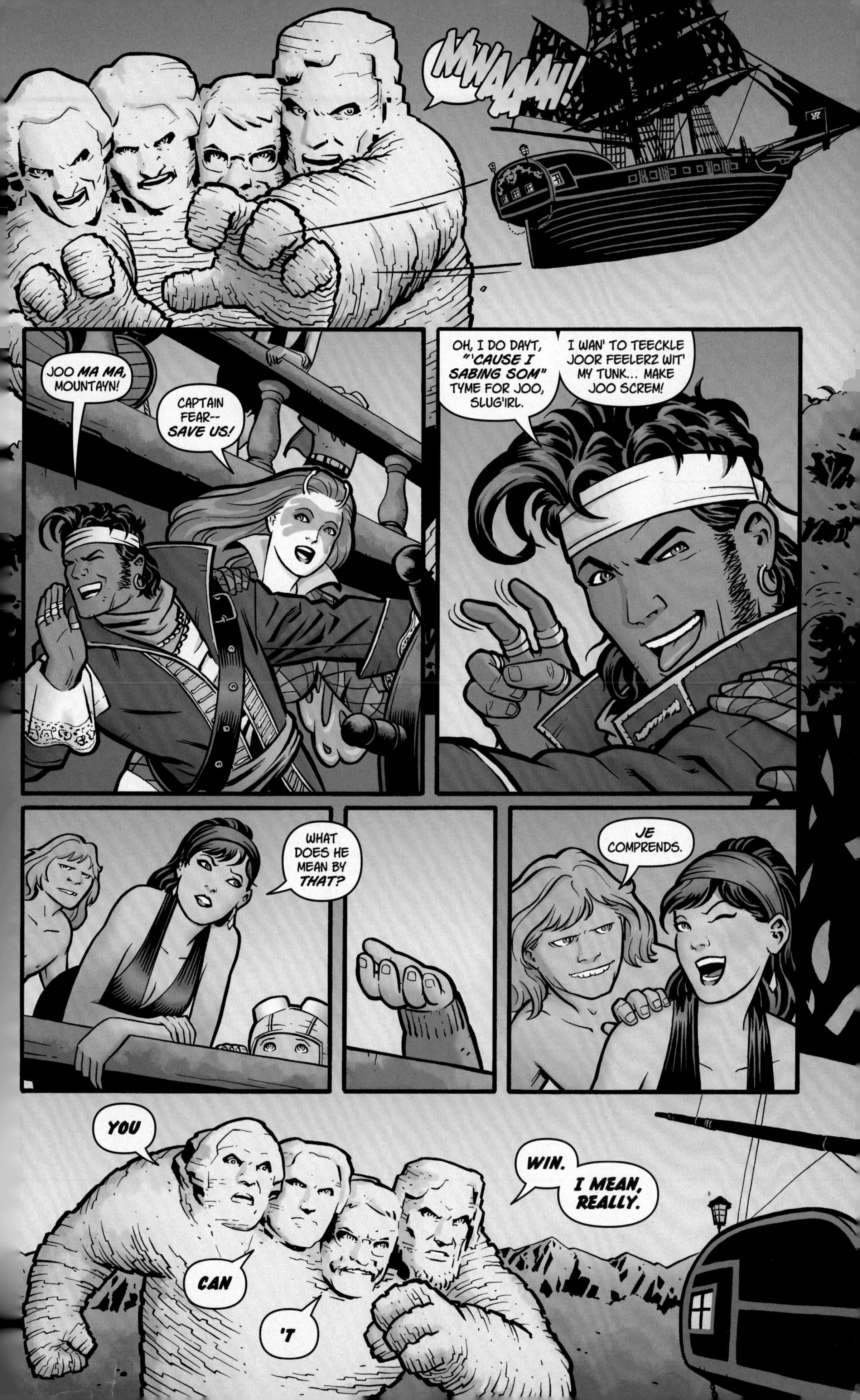
MWAAAH!
JOO MA MA, MOUNTAYN!
CAPTAIN FEAR-- SAVE US!
OH, I DO DAYT, "'CAUSE I SABING SOM" TYME FOR JOO, SLUG'IRL.
I WAN' TO TEECKLE JOOR FEELERZ WIT' MY TUNK... MAKE JOO SCREM!
WHAT DOES HE MEAN BY THAT?
JE COMPRENDS.
YOU
CAN
'T
WIN.
I MEAN, REALLY.

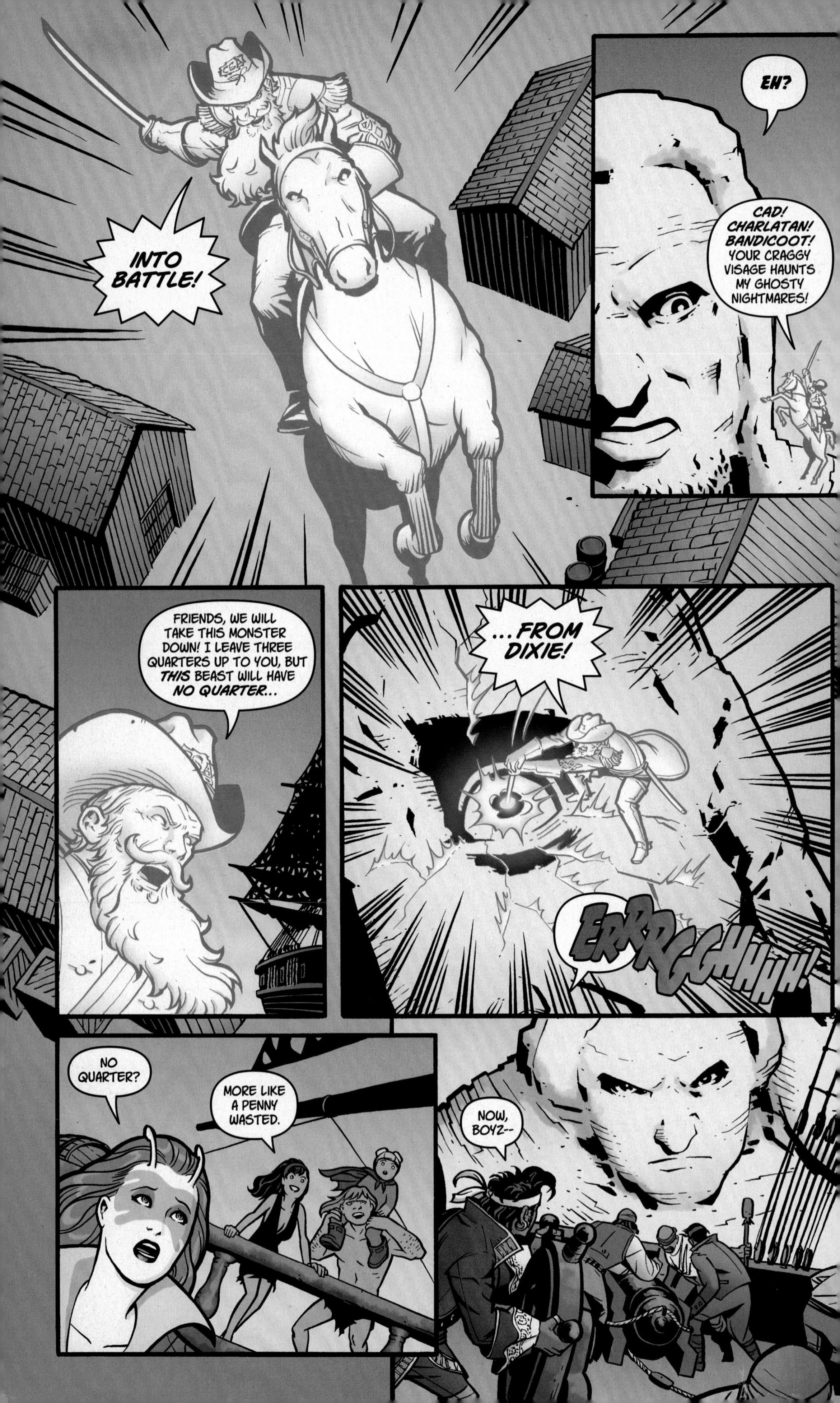
INTO BATTLE!
EH?
CAD! CHARLATAN! BANDICOOT! YOUR CRAGGY VISAGE HAUNTS MY GHOSTY NIGHTMARES!
FRIENDS, WE WILL TAKE THIS MONSTER DOWN! I LEAVE THREE QUARTERS UP TO YOU, BUT THIS BEAST WILL HAVE NO QUARTER...
...FROM DIXIE!
ERRRGGHHHH!
NO QUARTER?
MORE LIKE A PENNY WASTED.
NOW, BOYZ--

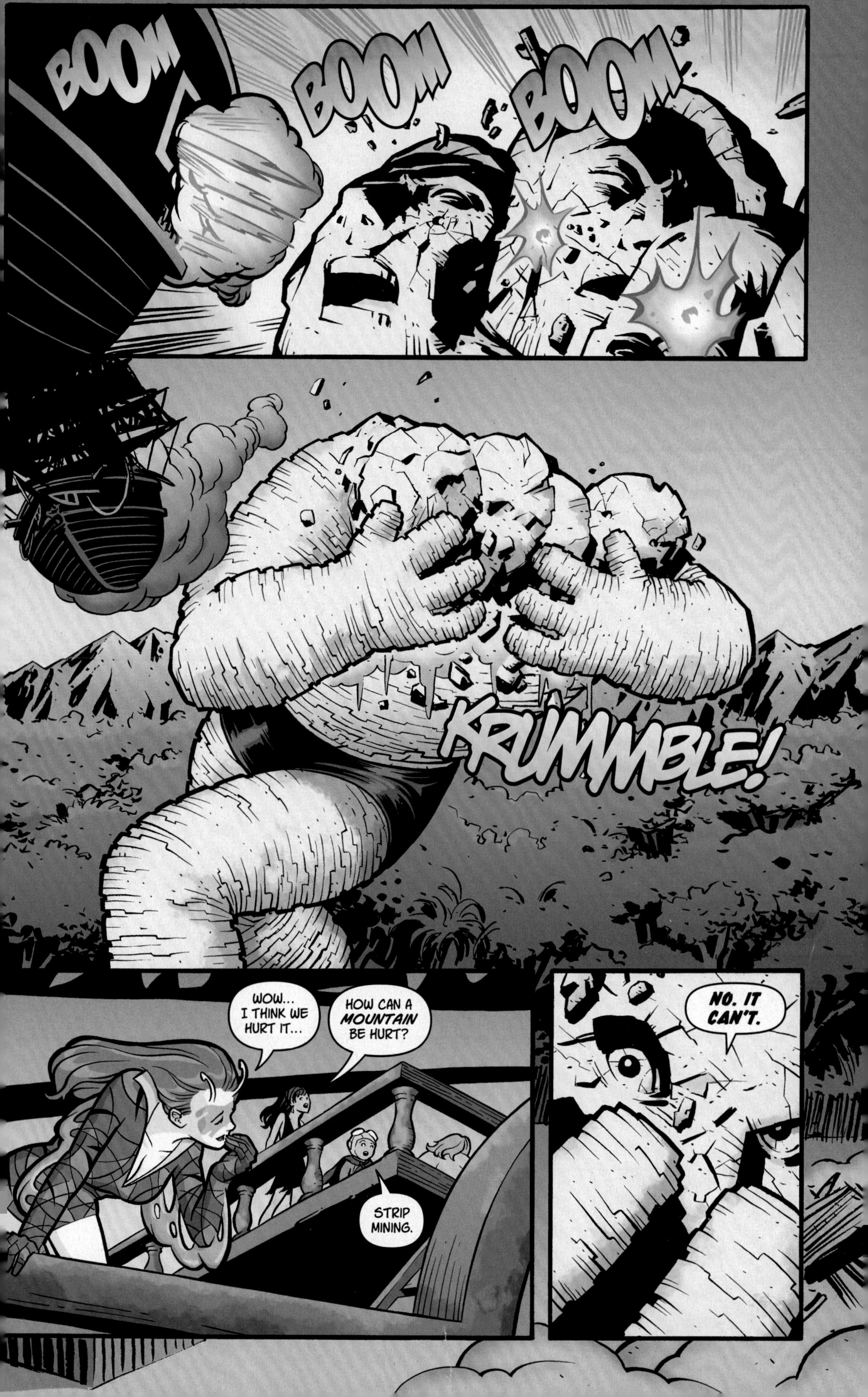
BOOM
BOOM
BOOM
KRUMMBLE!
WOW... I THINK WE HURT IT...
HOW CAN A *MOUNTAIN* BE HURT?
STRIP MINING.
NO. IT CAN'T.

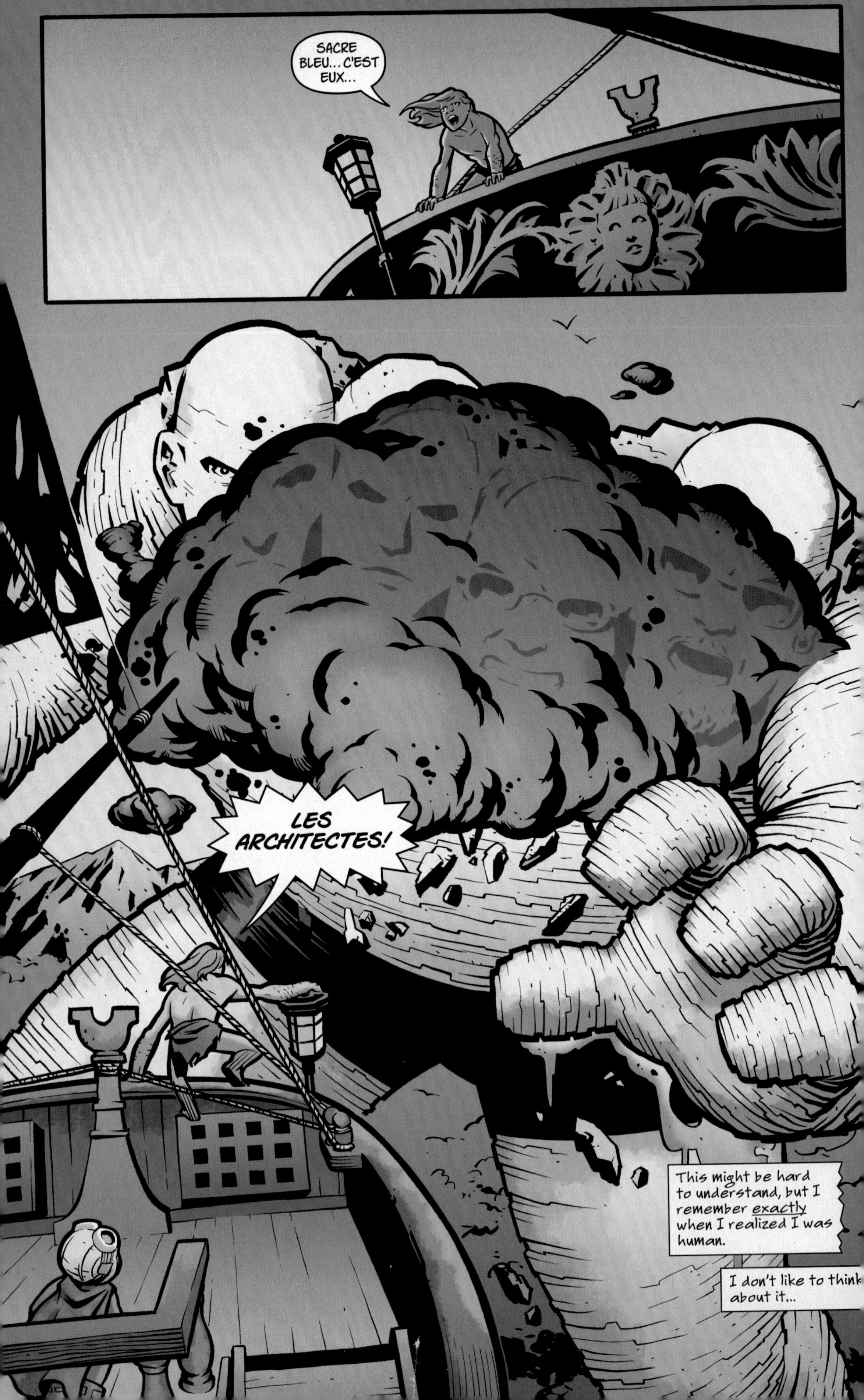
SACRE BLEU... C'EST EUX...
LES ARCHITECTES!
This might be hard to understand, but I remember exactly when I realized I was human.
I don't like to think about it...

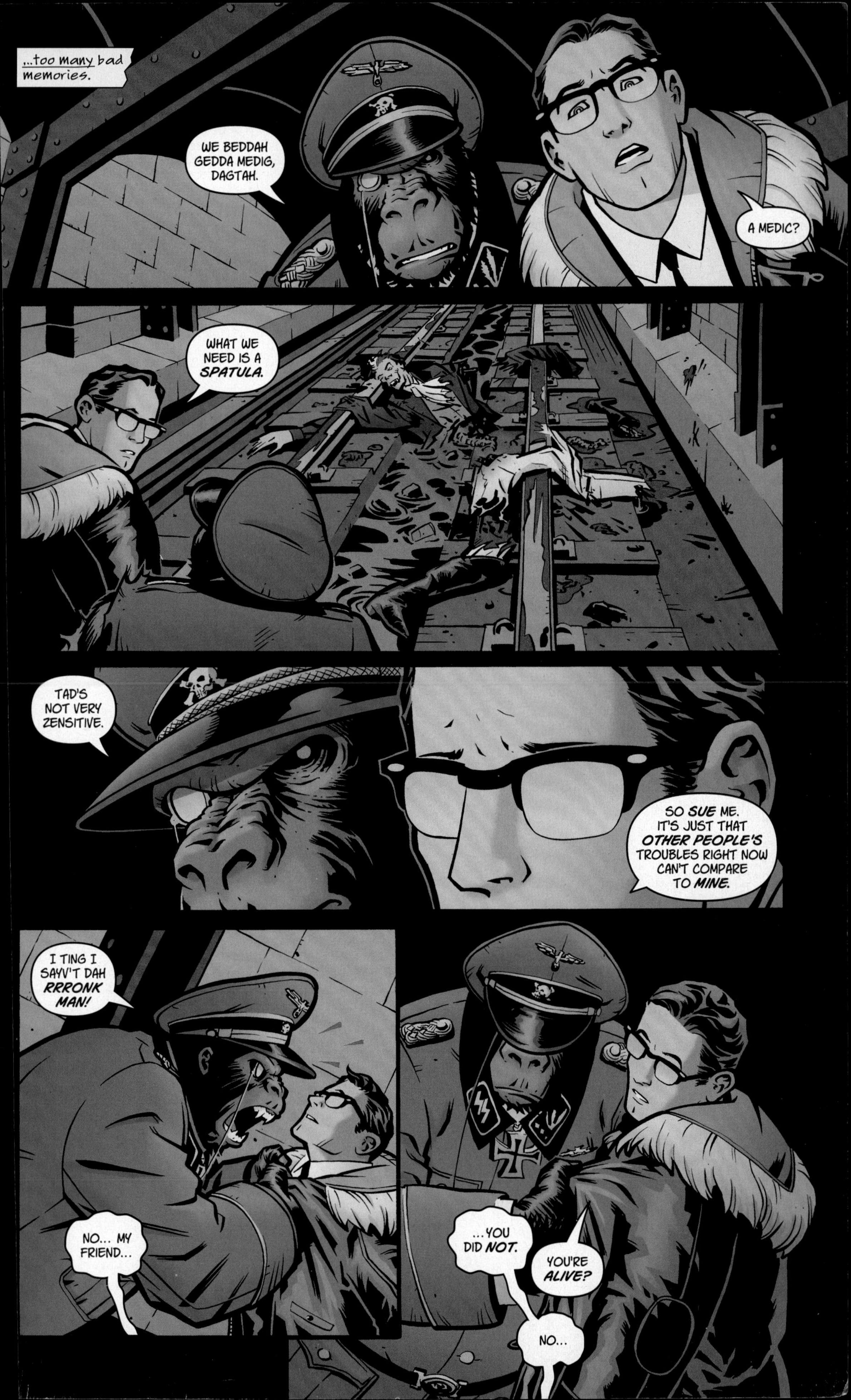
...too many bad memories.
WE BEDDAH GEDDA MEDIG, DAGTAH.
A MEDIC?
WHAT WE NEED IS A SPATULA.
TAD'S NOT VERY ZENSITIVE.
SO SUE ME. IT'S JUST THAT OTHER PEOPLE'S TROUBLES RIGHT NOW CAN'T COMPARE TO MINE.
I TING I SAYV'T DAH RRRONK MAN!
NO... MY FRIEND...
...YOU DID NOT.
YOU'RE ALIVE?
NO...

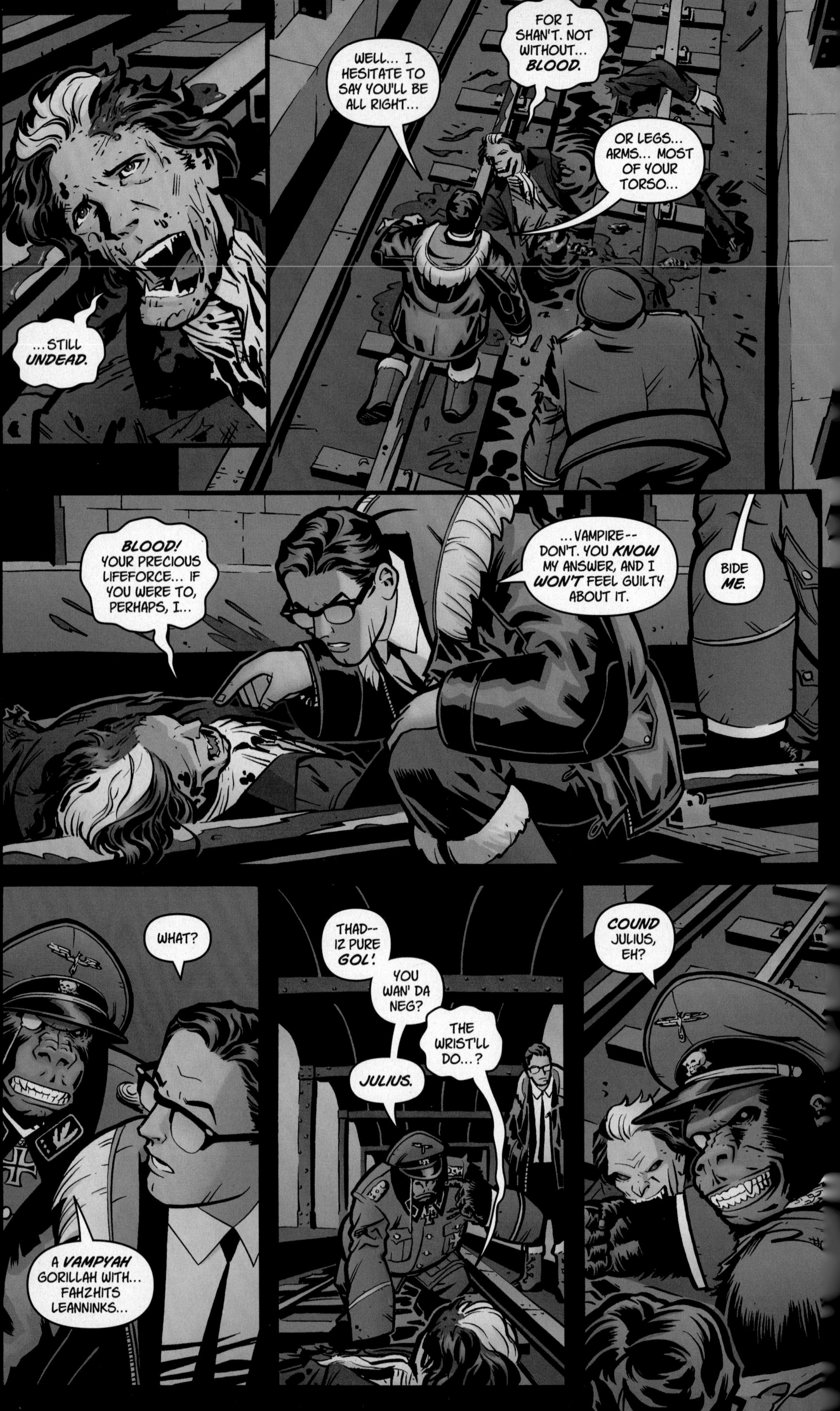

...STILL UNDEAD.
WELL... I HESITATE TO SAY YOU'LL BE ALL RIGHT...
FOR I SHAN'T. NOT WITHOUT... BLOOD.
OR LEGS... ARMS... MOST OF YOUR TORSO...
BLOOD! YOUR PRECIOUS LIFEFORCE... IF YOU WERE TO, PERHAPS, I...
...VAMPIRE-- DON'T. YOU KNOW MY ANSWER, AND I WON'T FEEL GUILTY ABOUT IT.
BIDE ME.
WHAT?
A VAMPYAH GORILLAH WITH... FAHZHITS LEANNINKS...
THAD-- IZ PURE GOL'.
YOU WAN' DA NEG?
JULIUS.
THE WRIST'LL DO...?
COUND JULIUS, EH?

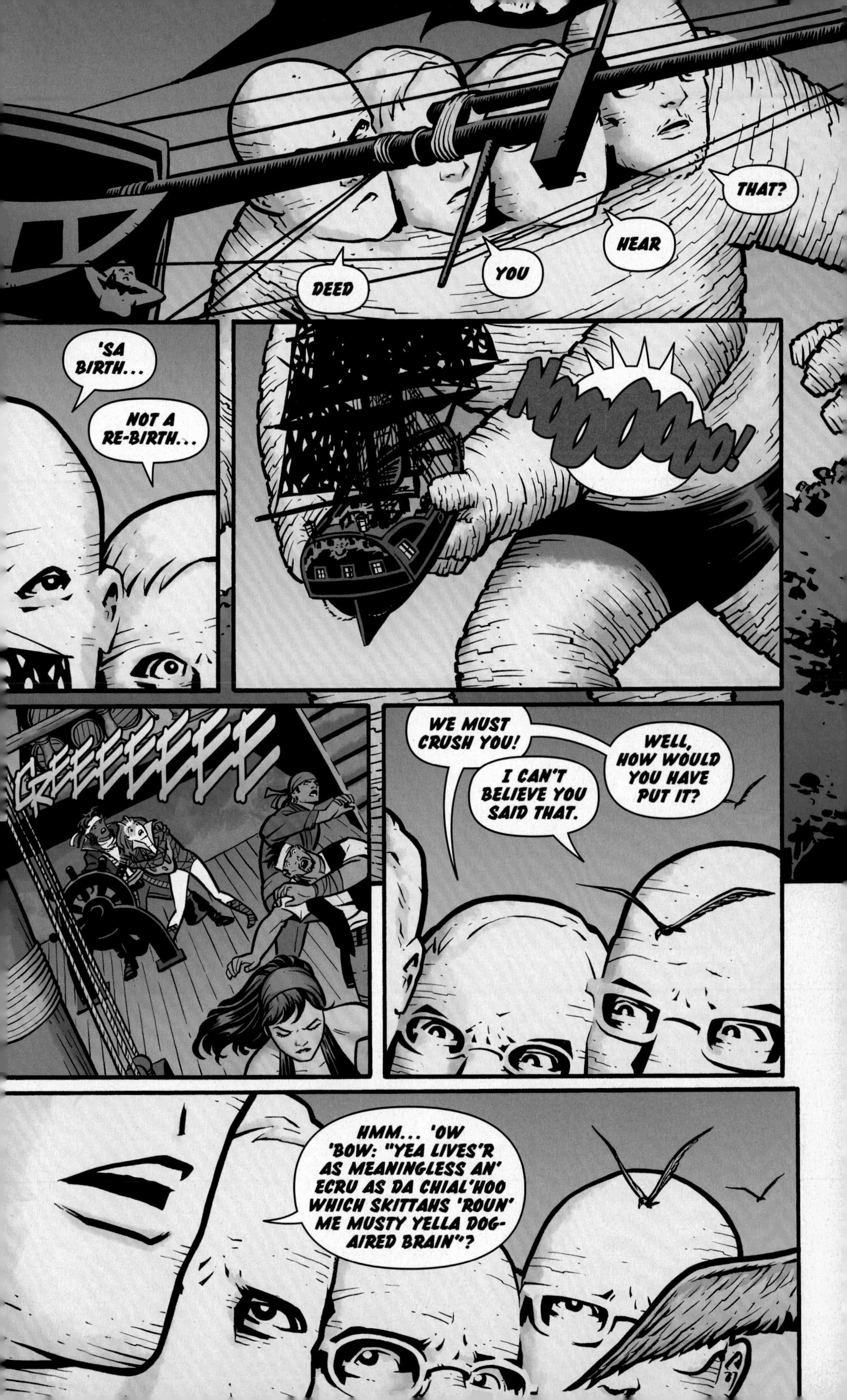
DEED
YOU
HEAR
THAT?
'SA BIRTH...
NOT A RE-BIRTH...
NOOOOOOO!
GREEEEEEEE
WE MUST CRUSH YOU!
I CAN'T BELIEVE YOU SAID THAT.
WELL, HOW WOULD YOU HAVE PUT IT?
HMM... 'OW 'BOW: "YEA LIVES'R AS MEANINGLESS AN' ECRU AS DA CHIAL'HOO WHICH SKITTAHS 'ROUN' ME MUSTY YELLA DOG-AIRED BRAIN"?

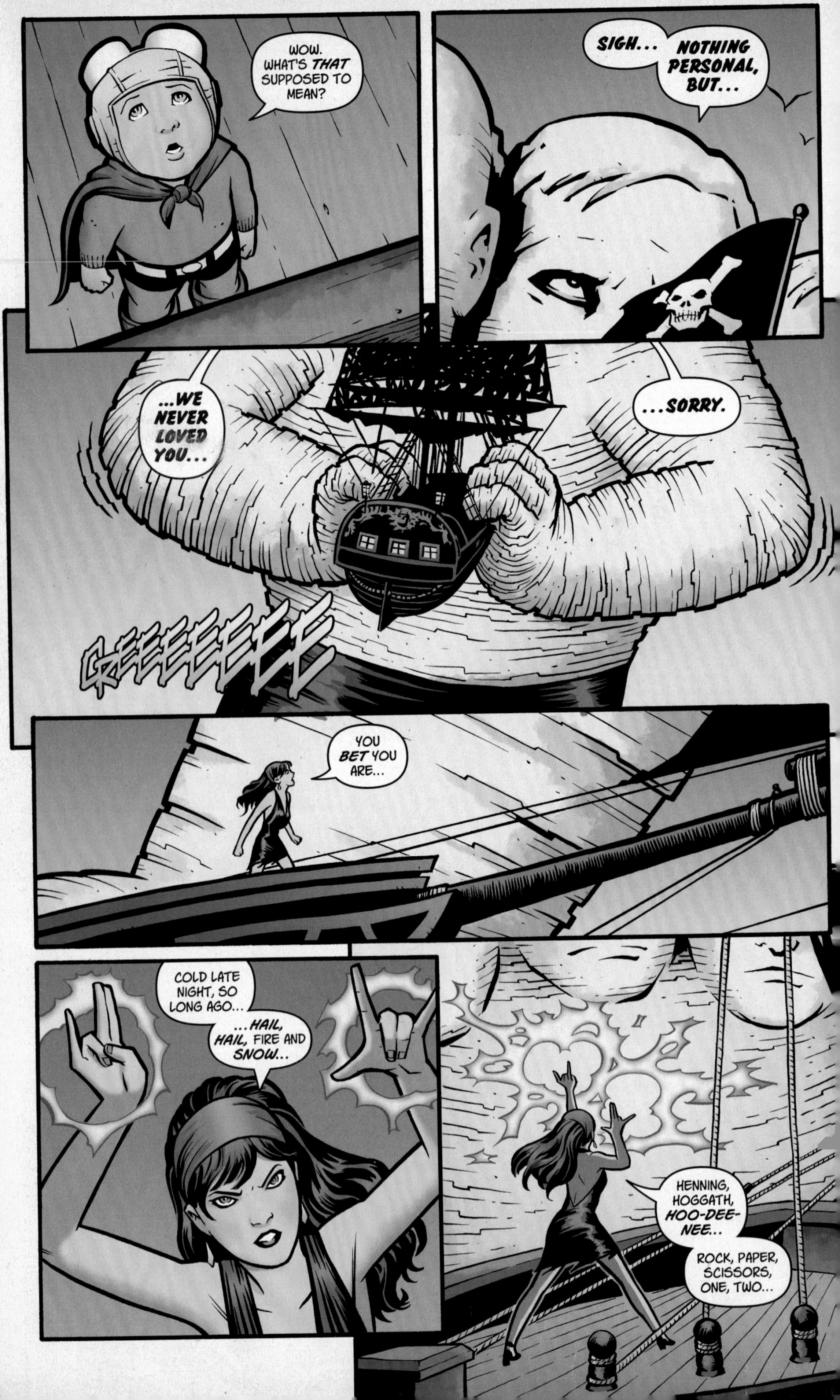
WOW. WHAT'S THAT SUPPOSED TO MEAN?
SIGH...
NOTHING PERSONAL, BUT...
...WE NEVER LOVED YOU...
...SORRY.
GREEEEEEE
YOU BET YOU ARE...
COLD LATE NIGHT, SO LONG AGO...
...HAIL, HAIL, FIRE AND SNOW...
HENNING, HOGGATH, HOO-DEE-NEE...
ROCK, PAPER, SCISSORS, ONE, TWO...

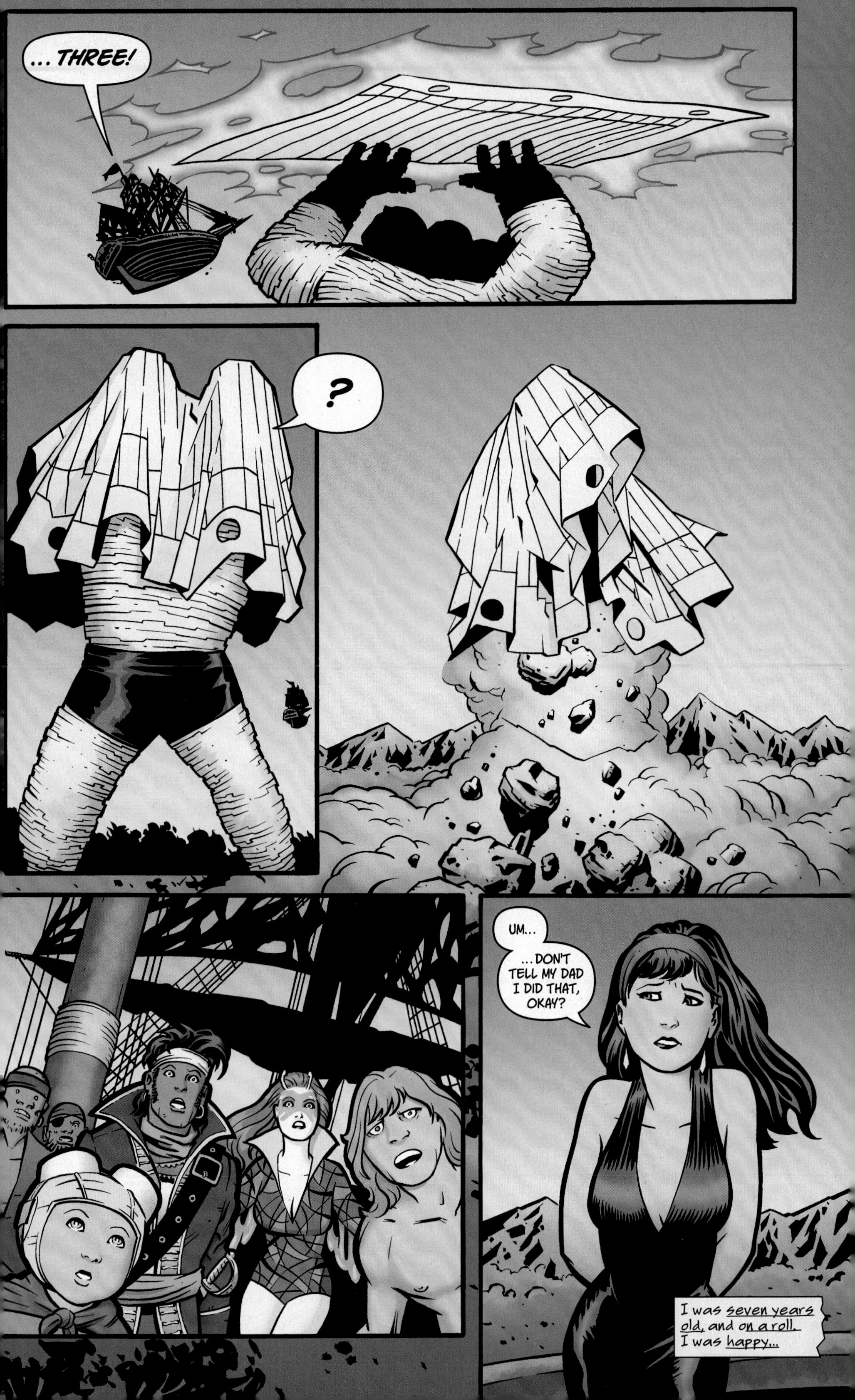
...THREE!
?
UM...
...DON'T TELL MY DAD I DID THAT, OKAY?
I was seven years old, and on a roll. I was happy...

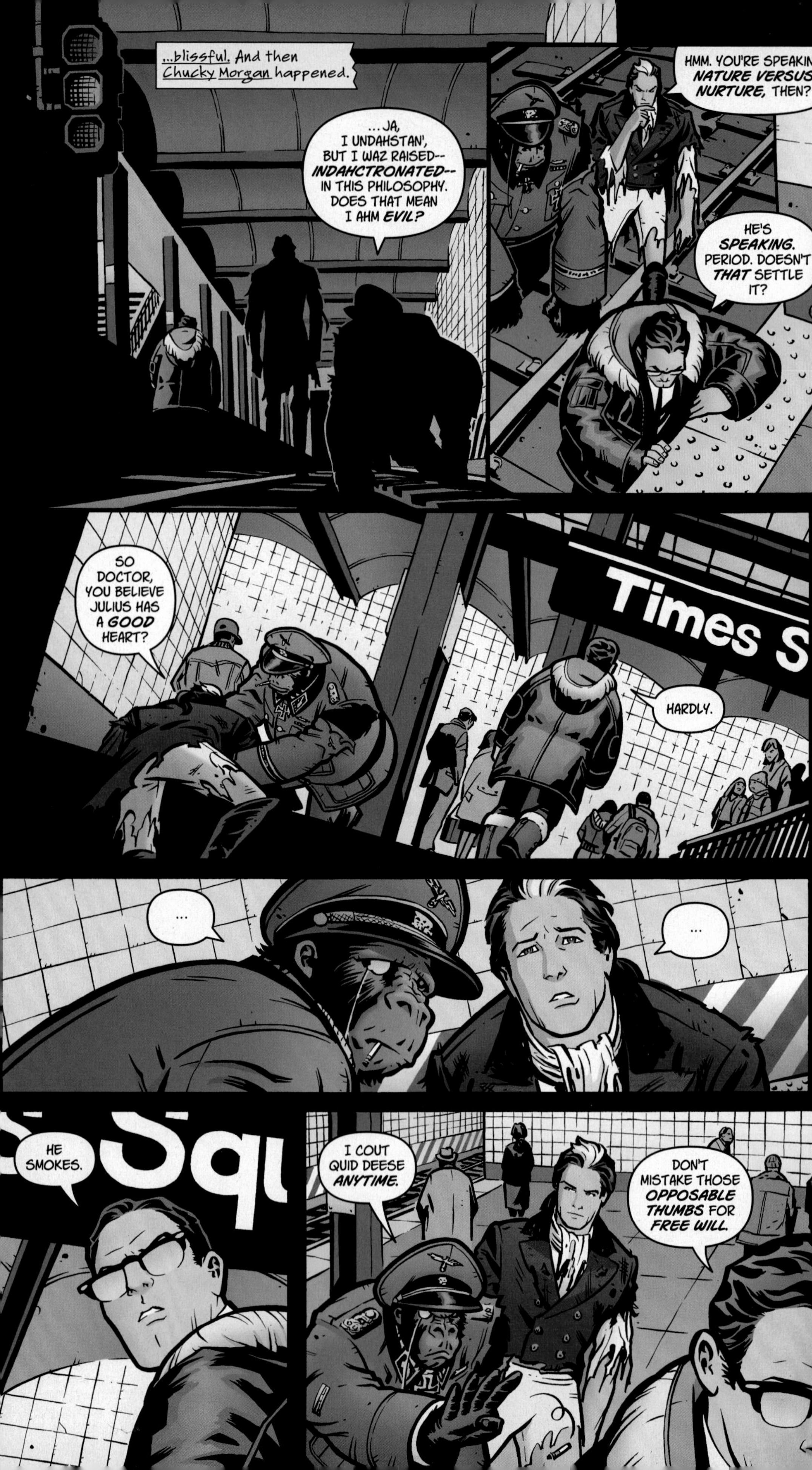
...blissful. And then Chucky Morgan happened.
...JA, I UNDAHSTAN', BUT I WAZ RAISED-- INDAHCTRONATED-- IN THIS PHILOSOPHY. DOES THAT MEAN I AHM EVIL?
HMM. YOU'RE SPEAKING NATURE VERSUS NURTURE, THEN?
HE'S SPEAKING. PERIOD. DOESN'T THAT SETTLE IT?
SO DOCTOR, YOU BELIEVE JULIUS HAS A GOOD HEART?
Times S
HARDLY.
...
...
Squ
HE SMOKES.
I COUT QUID DEESE ANYTIME.
DON'T MISTAKE THOSE OPPOSABLE THUMBS FOR FREE WILL.

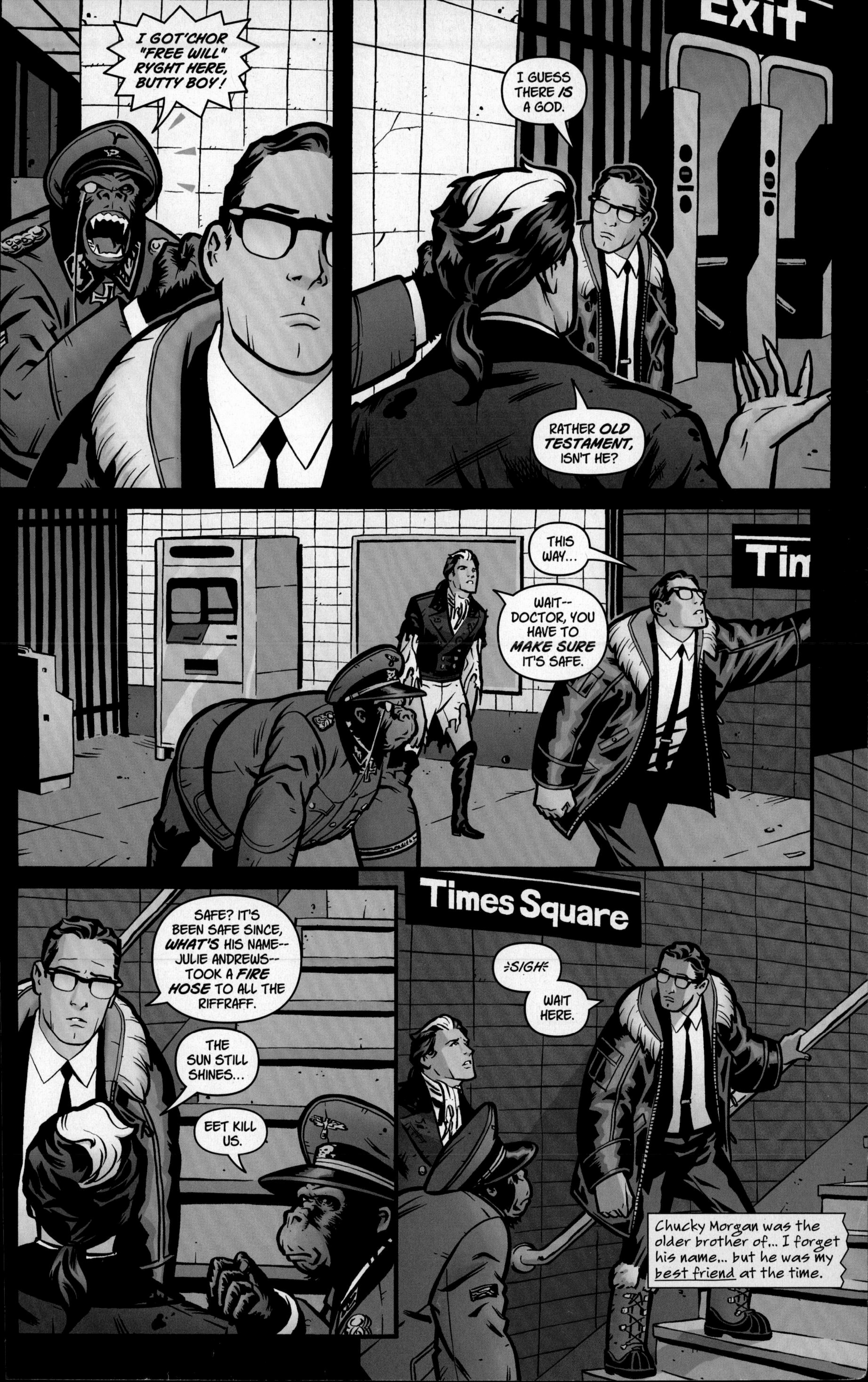
I GOT'CHOR "FREE WILL" RYGHT HERE, BUTTY BOY!
I GUESS THERE IS A GOD.
RATHER OLD TESTAMENT, ISN'T HE?
EXIT
THIS WAY...
WAIT-- DOCTOR, YOU HAVE TO MAKE SURE IT'S SAFE.
Tim
SAFE? IT'S BEEN SAFE SINCE, WHAT'S HIS NAME-- JULIE ANDREWS-- TOOK A FIRE HOSE TO ALL THE RIFFRAFF.
THE SUN STILL SHINES...
EET KILL US.
Times Square
SIGH
WAIT HERE.
Chucky Morgan was the older brother of... I forget his name... but he was my best friend at the time.

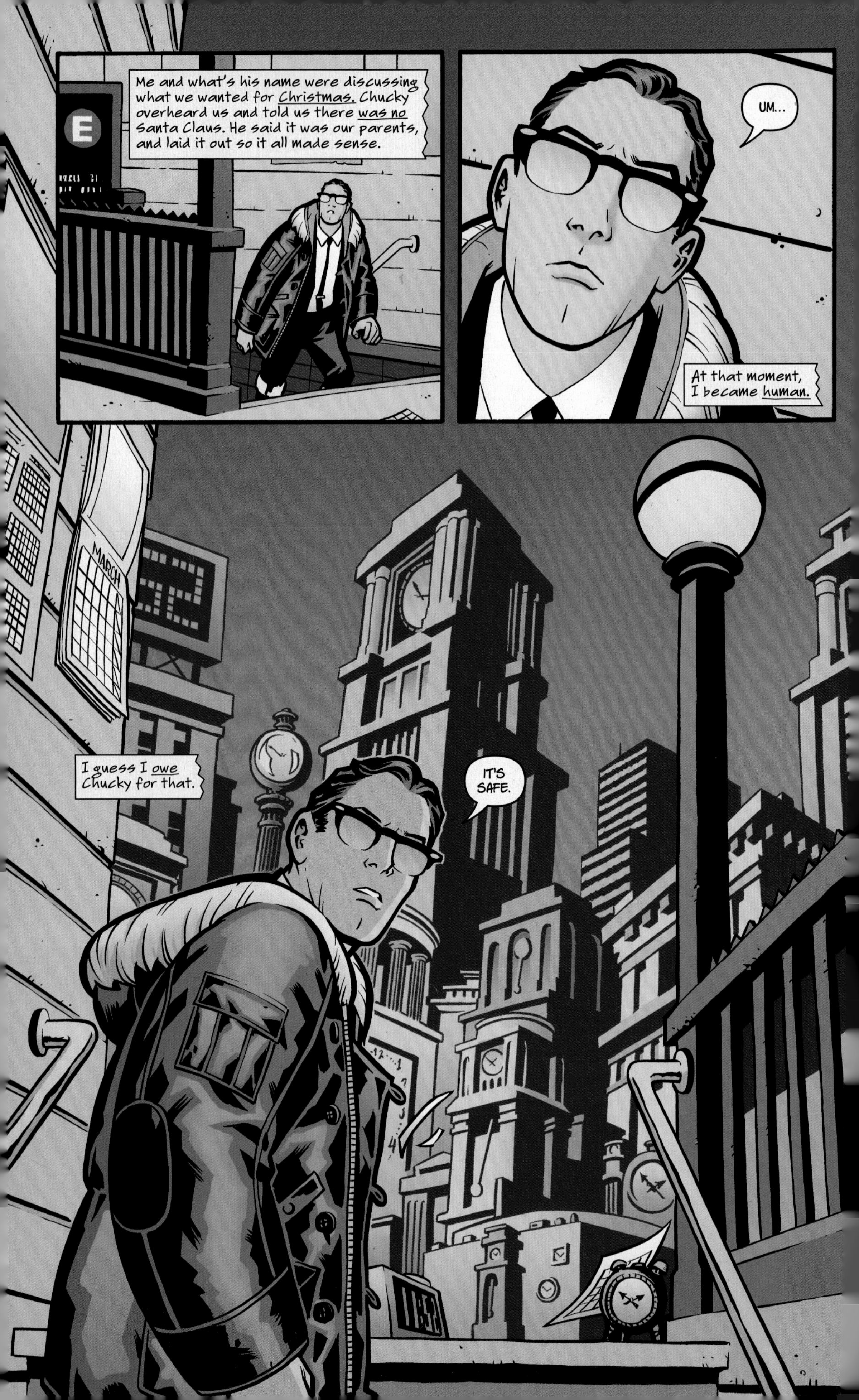
Me and what's his name were discussing what we wanted for Christmas. Chucky overheard us and told us there was no Santa Claus. He said it was our parents, and laid it out so it all made sense.
UM...
At that moment, I became human.
MARCH
I guess I owe Chucky for that.
IT'S SAFE.

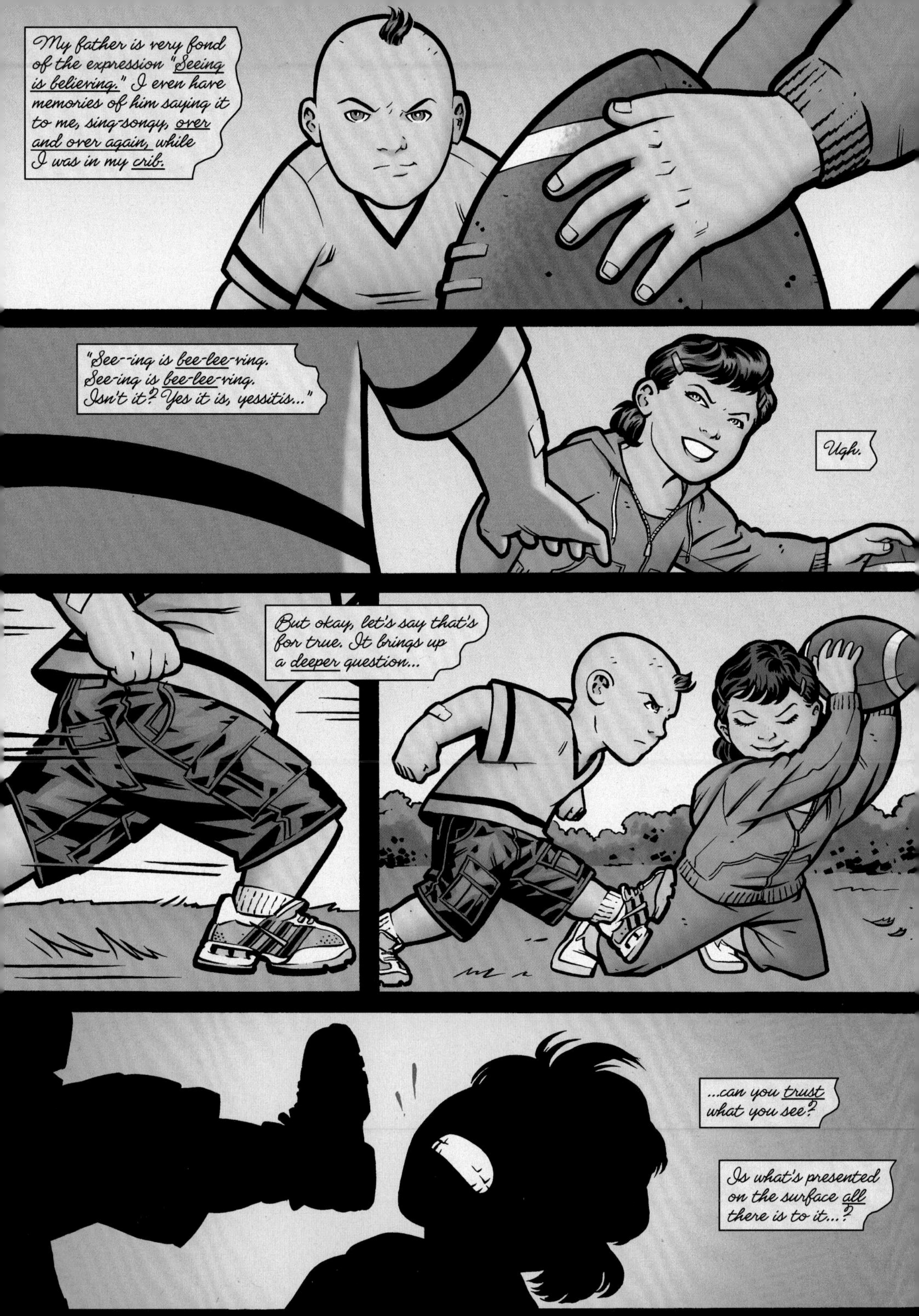
My father is very fond of the expression "Seeing is believing." I even have memories of him saying it to me, sing-songy, over and over again, while I was in my crib.
"See--ing is bee-lee-ving. See-ing is bee-lee-ving. Isn't it? Yes it is, yessitis..."
Ugh.
But okay, let's say that's for true. It brings up a deeper question...
...can you trust what you see?
Is what's presented on the surface all there is to it...?

CHAPTER 7

# MONKEY GROWN TO HEAVEN

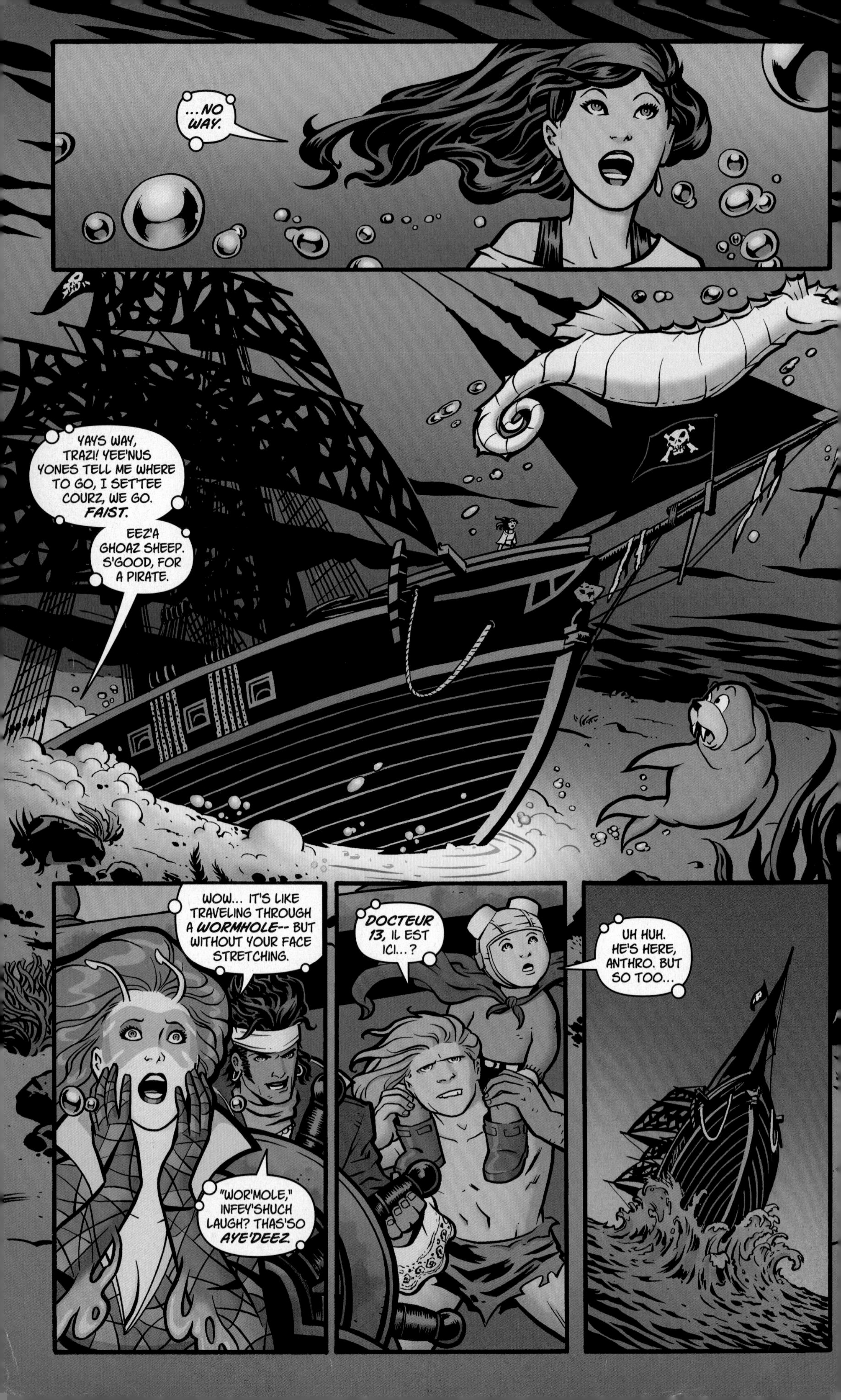
...NO WAY.
YAYS WAY, TRAZI! YEE'NUS YONES TELL ME WHERE TO GO, I SET'TEE COURZ, WE GO. FAIST.
EEZ'A GHOAZ SHEEP. S'GOOD, FOR A PIRATE.
WOW... IT'S LIKE TRAVELING THROUGH A WORMHOLE-- BUT WITHOUT YOUR FACE STRETCHING.
"WOR'MOLE," INFEY'SHUCH LAUGH? THAS'SO AYE'DEEZ.
DOCTEUR 13, IL EST ICI...?
UH HUH. HE'S HERE, ANTHRO. BUT SO TOO...

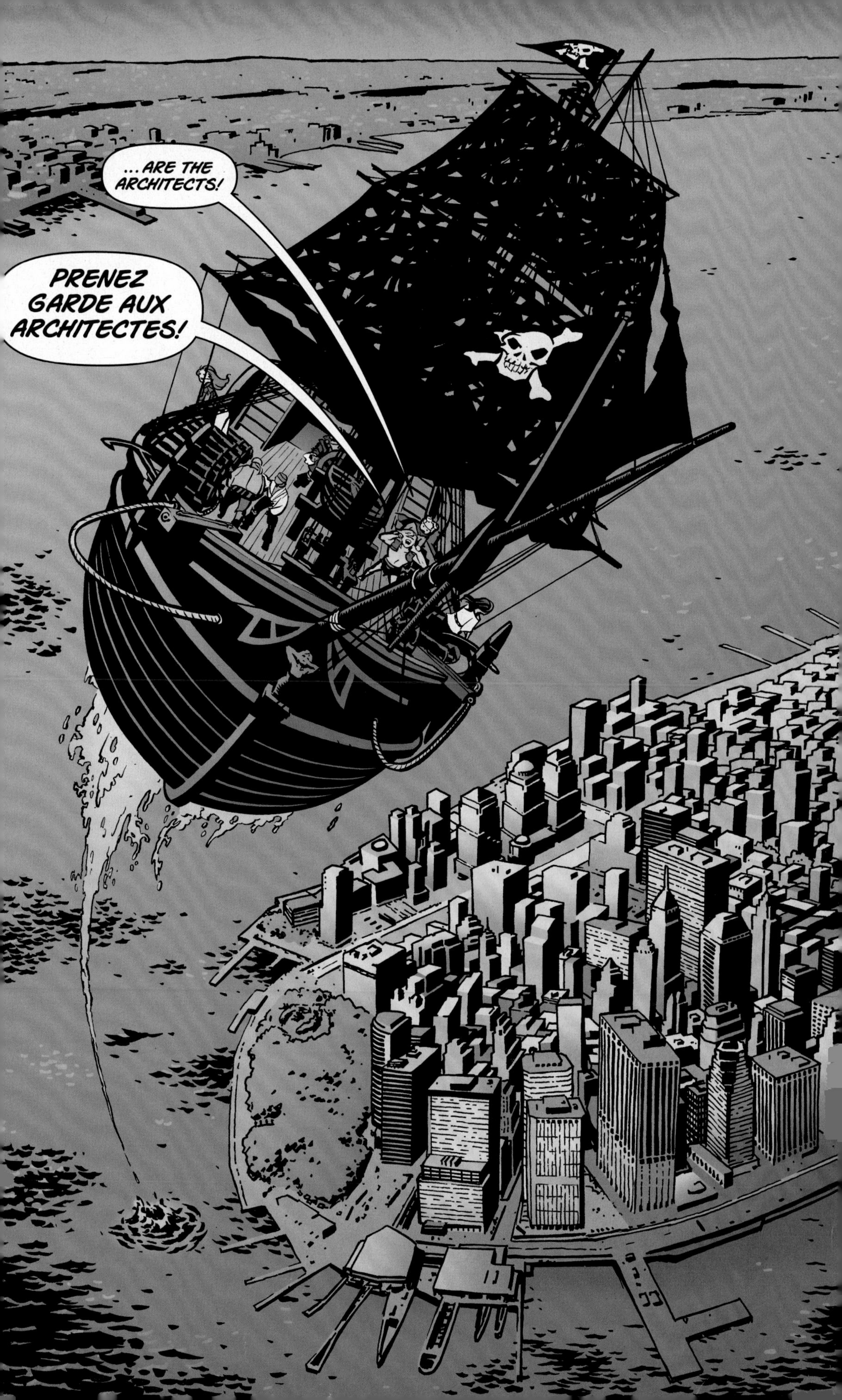
...ARE THE ARCHITECTS!
PRENEZ GARDE AUX ARCHITECTES!

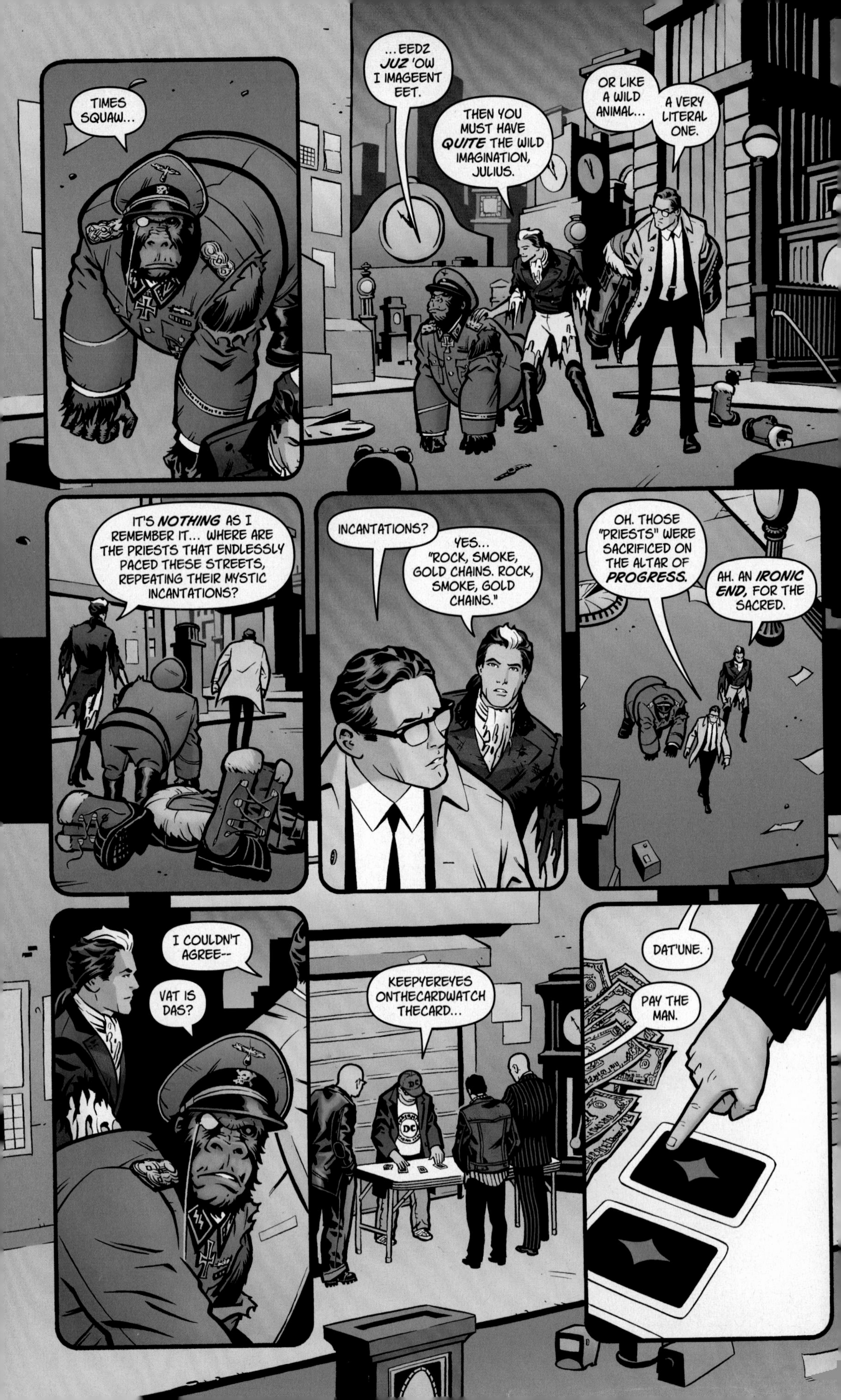

TIMES SQUAW...
...EEDZ JUZ 'OW I IMAGEENT EET.
THEN YOU MUST HAVE QUITE THE WILD IMAGINATION, JULIUS.
OR LIKE A WILD ANIMAL...
A VERY LITERAL ONE.
IT'S NOTHING AS I REMEMBER IT... WHERE ARE THE PRIESTS THAT ENDLESSLY PACED THESE STREETS, REPEATING THEIR MYSTIC INCANTATIONS?
INCANTATIONS?
YES... "ROCK, SMOKE, GOLD CHAINS. ROCK, SMOKE, GOLD CHAINS."
OH. THOSE "PRIESTS" WERE SACRIFICED ON THE ALTAR OF PROGRESS.
AH. AN IRONIC END, FOR THE SACRED.
I COULDN'T AGREE--
VAT IS DAS?
KEEPYEREYES ONTHECARDWATCH THECARD...
DAT'UNE.
PAY THE MAN.

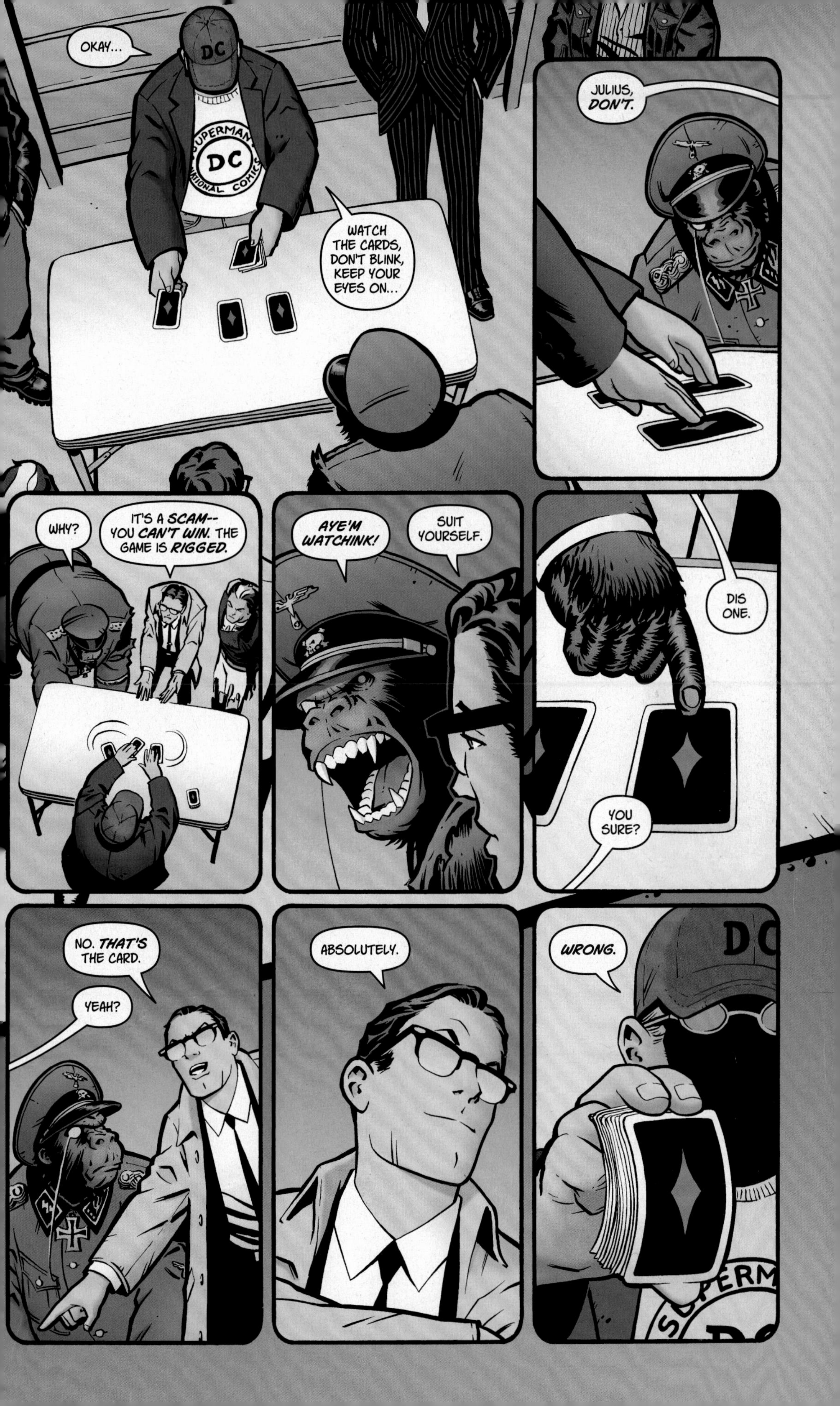
OKAY...
WATCH THE CARDS, DON'T BLINK, KEEP YOUR EYES ON...
JULIUS, DON'T.
WHY?
IT'S A SCAM-- YOU CAN'T WIN. THE GAME IS RIGGED.
AYE'M WATCHINK!
SUIT YOURSELF.
DIS ONE.
YOU SURE?
NO. THAT'S THE CARD.
YEAH?
ABSOLUTELY.
WRONG.

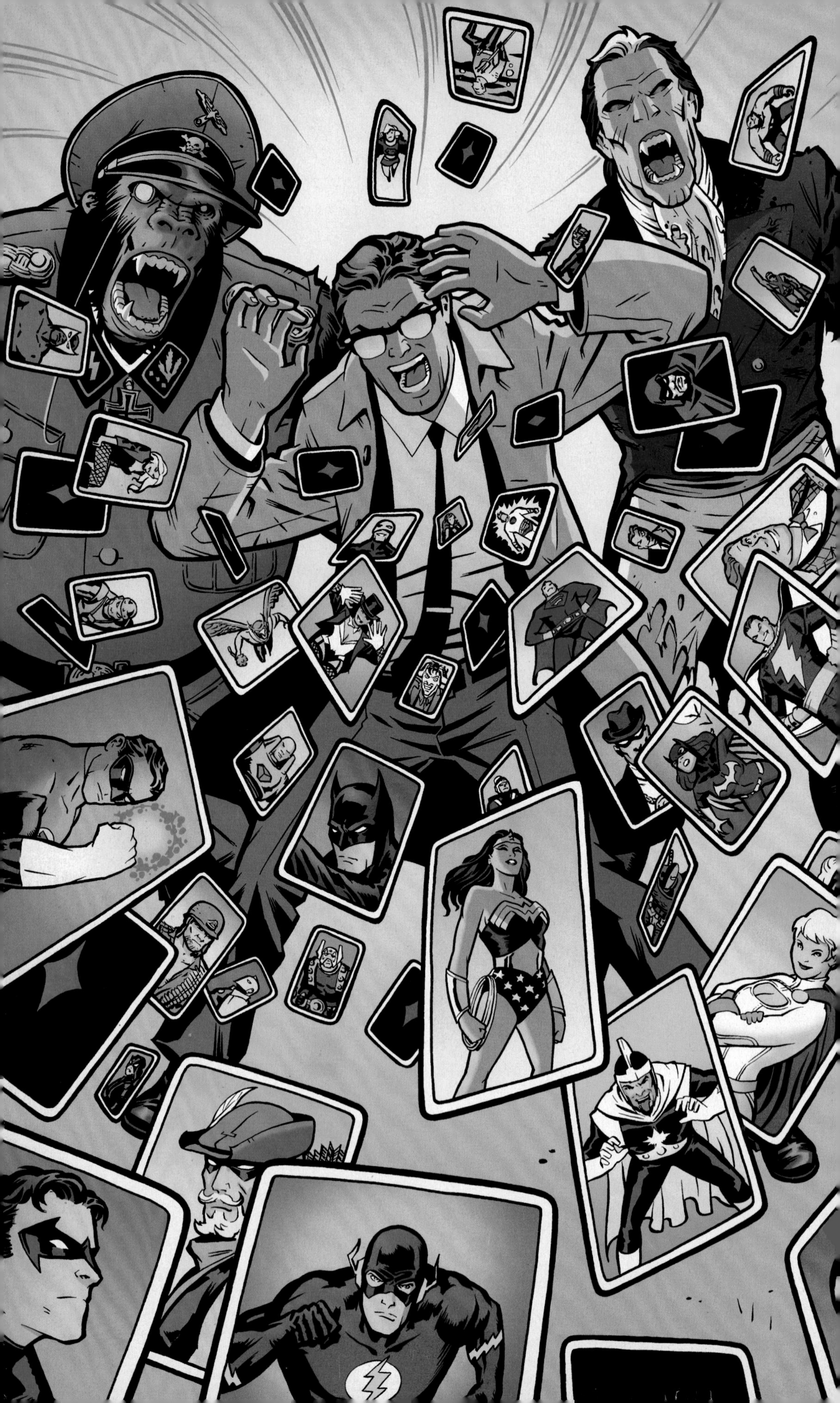

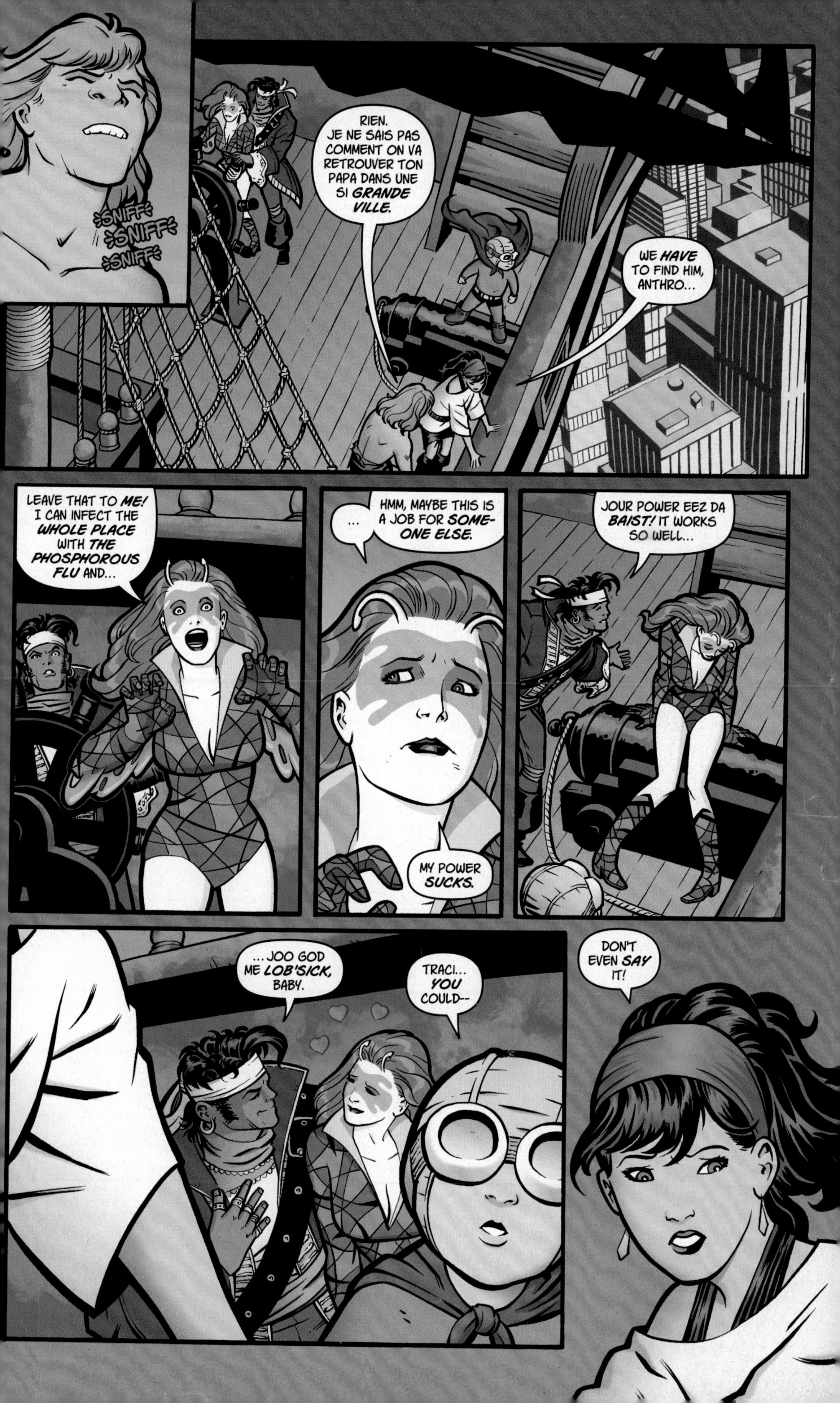
SNIFF SNIFF SNIFF
RIEN. JE NE SAIS PAS COMMENT ON VA RETROUVER TON PAPA DANS UNE SI GRANDE VILLE.
WE HAVE TO FIND HIM, ANTHRO...
LEAVE THAT TO ME! I CAN INFECT THE WHOLE PLACE WITH THE PHOSPHOROUS FLU AND...
...
HMM, MAYBE THIS IS A JOB FOR SOME-ONE ELSE.
MY POWER SUCKS.
JOUR POWER EEZ DA BAIST! IT WORKS SO WELL...
...JOO GOD ME LOB'SICK, BABY.
TRACI... YOU COULD--
DON'T EVEN SAY IT!

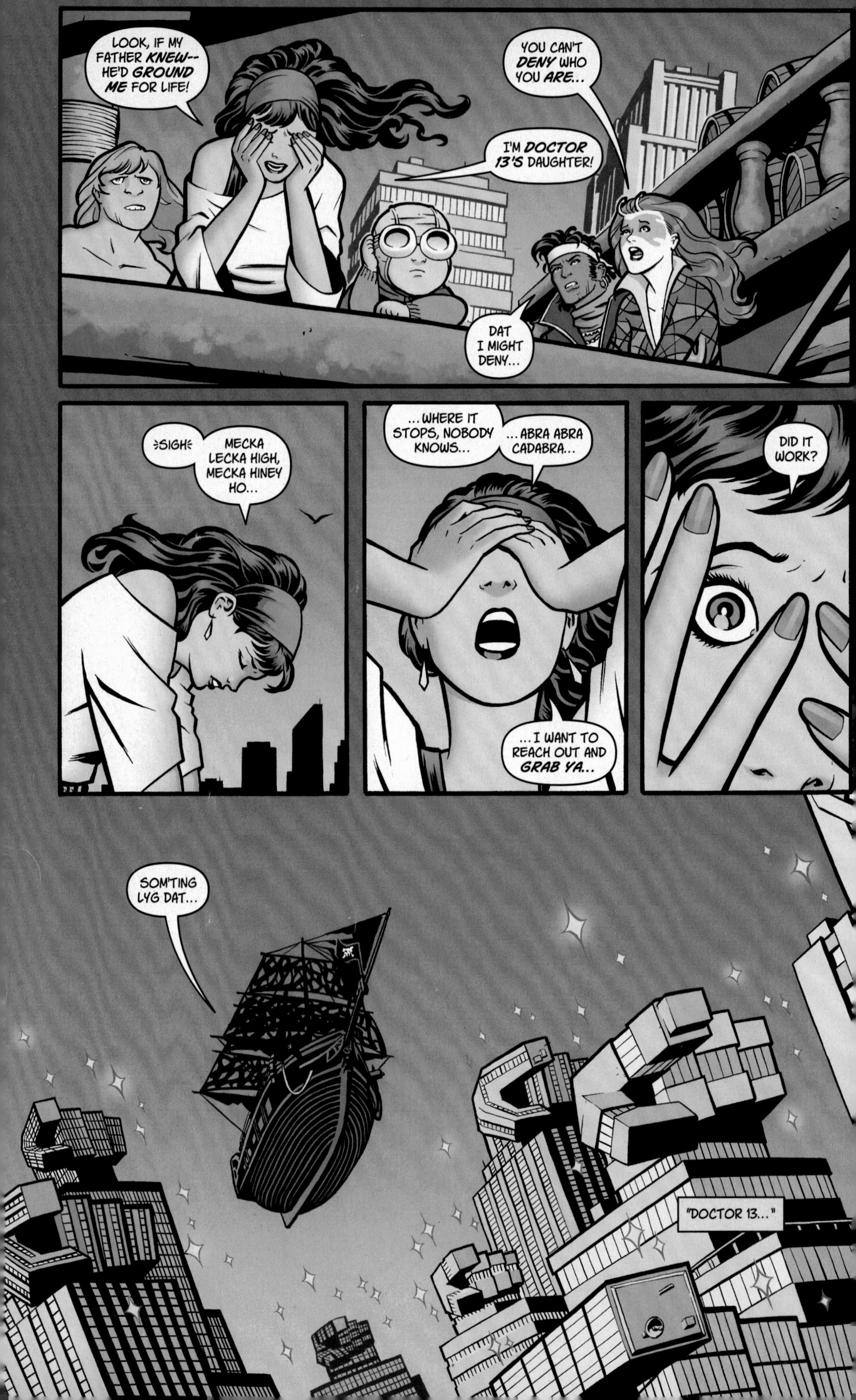
LOOK, IF MY FATHER KNEW-- HE'D GROUND ME FOR LIFE!
YOU CAN'T DENY WHO YOU ARE...
I'M DOCTOR 13'S DAUGHTER!
DAT I MIGHT DENY...
*SIGH*
MECKA LECKA HIGH, MECKA HINEY HO...
...WHERE IT STOPS, NOBODY KNOWS...
...ABRA ABRA CADABRA...
...I WANT TO REACH OUT AND GRAB YA...
DID IT WORK?
SOM'TING LYG DAT...
"DOCTOR 13..."

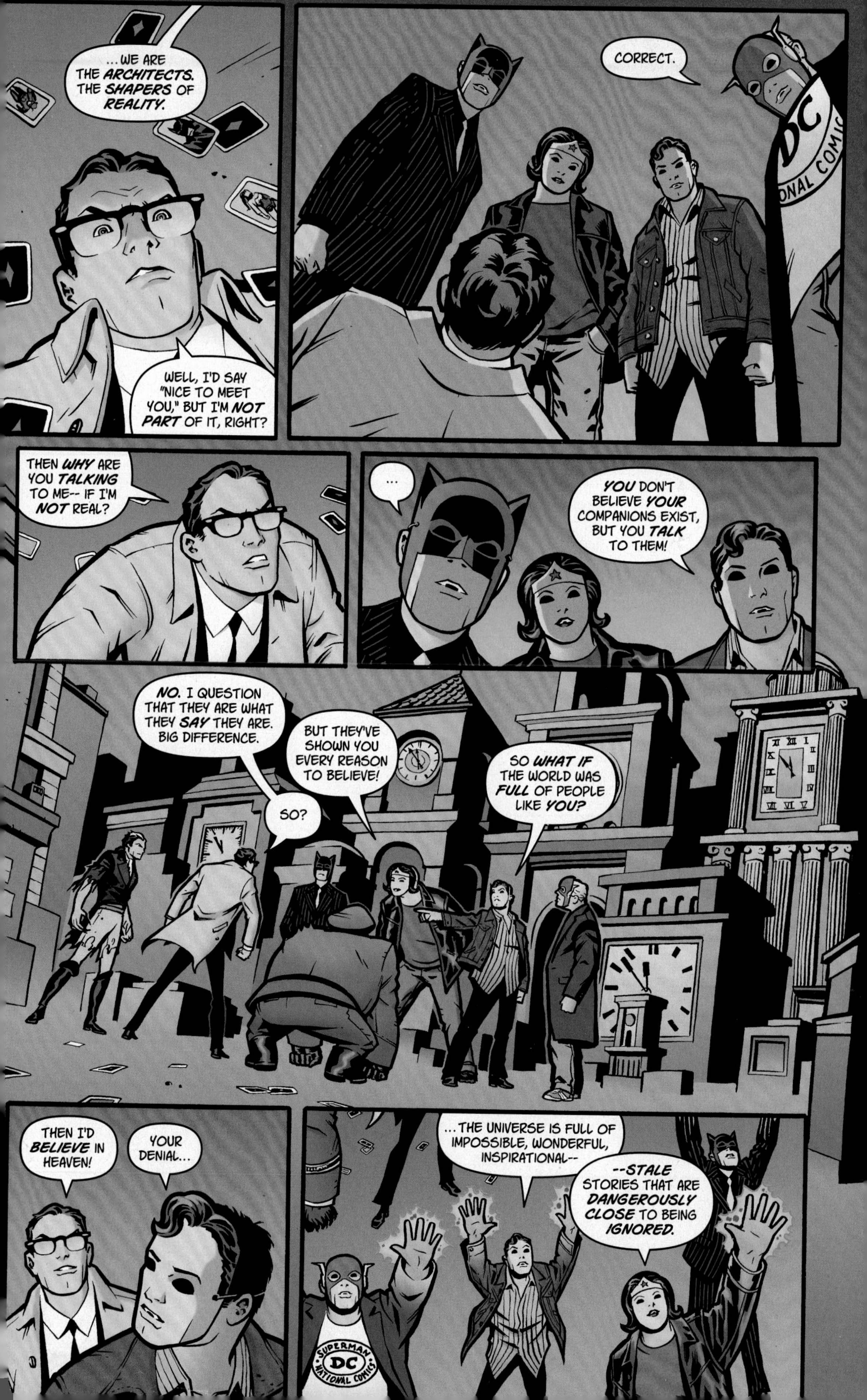

...WE ARE THE ARCHITECTS. THE SHAPERS OF REALITY.
WELL, I'D SAY "NICE TO MEET YOU," BUT I'M NOT PART OF IT, RIGHT?
CORRECT.
DC
NATIONAL COMIC
THEN WHY ARE YOU TALKING TO ME-- IF I'M NOT REAL?
...
YOU DON'T BELIEVE YOUR COMPANIONS EXIST, BUT YOU TALK TO THEM!
NO. I QUESTION THAT THEY ARE WHAT THEY SAY THEY ARE. BIG DIFFERENCE.
BUT THEY'VE SHOWN YOU EVERY REASON TO BELIEVE!
SO?
SO WHAT IF THE WORLD WAS FULL OF PEOPLE LIKE YOU?
THEN I'D BELIEVE IN HEAVEN!
YOUR DENIAL...
...THE UNIVERSE IS FULL OF IMPOSSIBLE, WONDERFUL, INSPIRATIONAL--
--STALE STORIES THAT ARE DANGEROUSLY CLOSE TO BEING IGNORED.
SUPERMAN DC NATIONAL COMICS

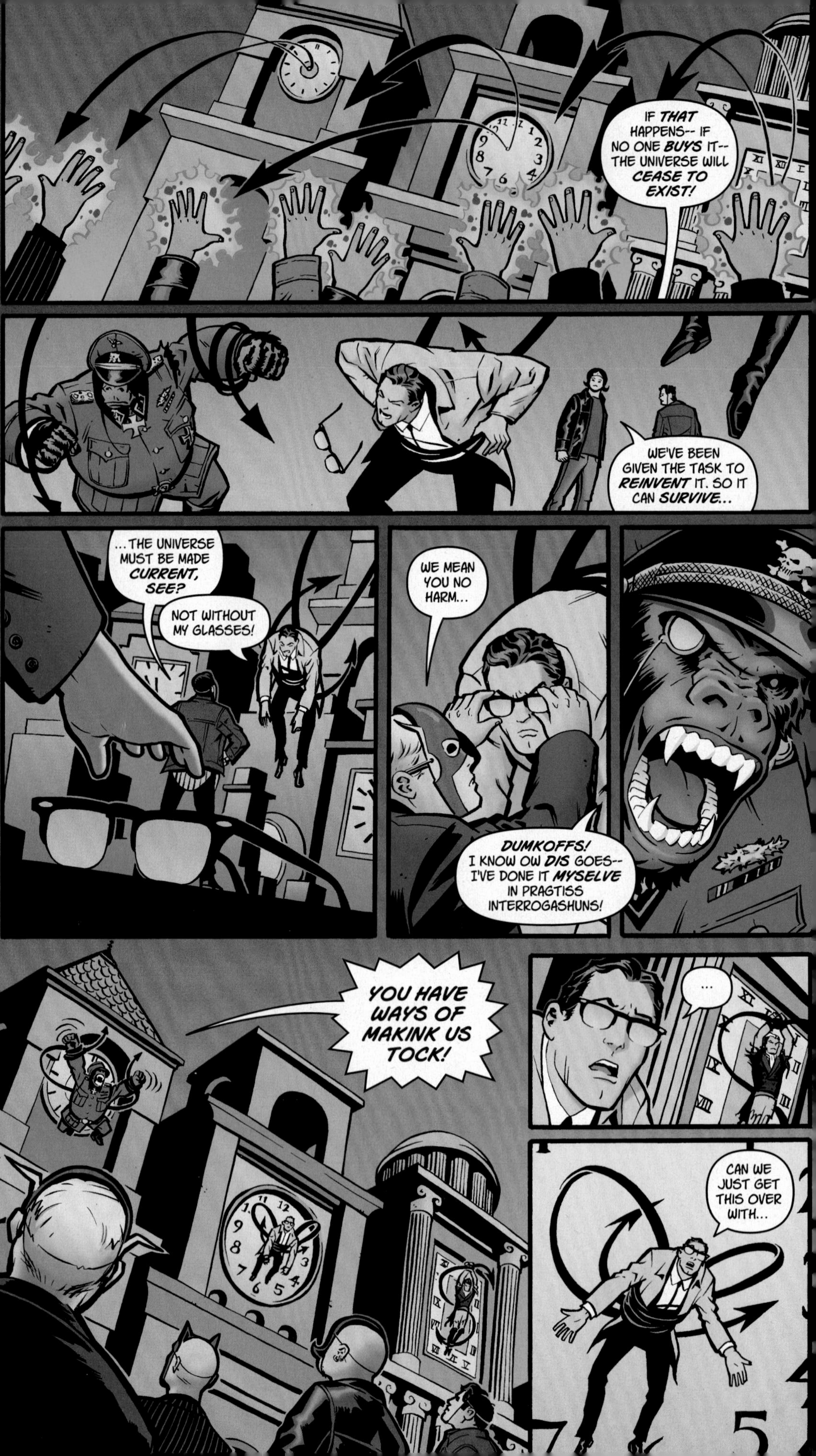
IF THAT HAPPENS-- IF NO ONE BUYS IT-- THE UNIVERSE WILL CEASE TO EXIST!
WE'VE BEEN GIVEN THE TASK TO REINVENT IT. SO IT CAN SURVIVE...
...THE UNIVERSE MUST BE MADE CURRENT, SEE?
NOT WITHOUT MY GLASSES!
WE MEAN YOU NO HARM...
DUMKOFFS! I KNOW OW DIS GOES-- I'VE DONE IT MYSELVE IN PRAGTISS INTERROGASHUNS!
YOU HAVE WAYS OF MAKINK US TOCK!
...
CAN WE JUST GET THIS OVER WITH...

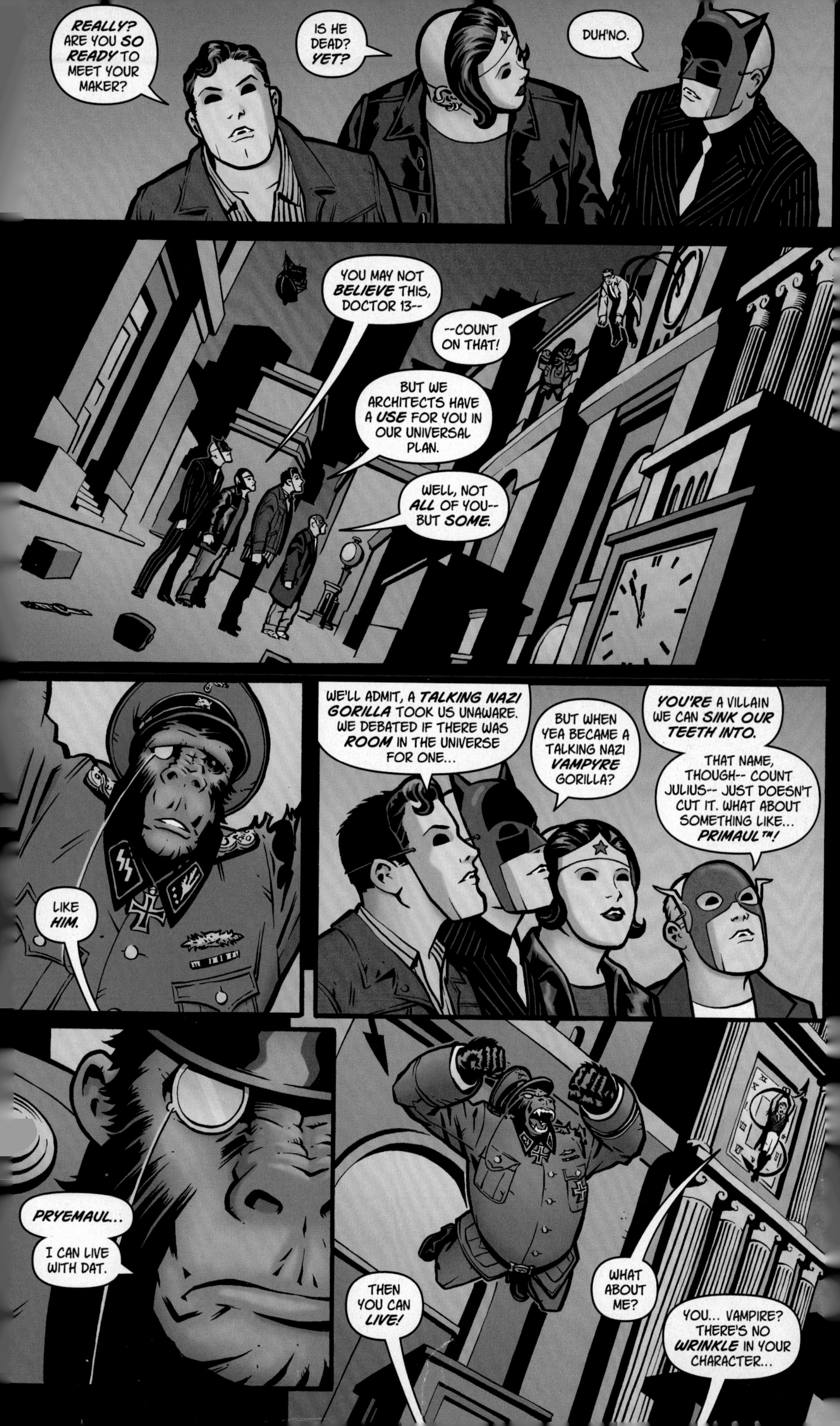
REALLY? ARE YOU SO READY TO MEET YOUR MAKER?
IS HE DEAD? YET?
DUH'NO.
YOU MAY NOT BELIEVE THIS, DOCTOR 13--
--COUNT ON THAT!
BUT WE ARCHITECTS HAVE A USE FOR YOU IN OUR UNIVERSAL PLAN.
WELL, NOT ALL OF YOU-- BUT SOME.
LIKE HIM.
WE'LL ADMIT, A TALKING NAZI GORILLA TOOK US UNAWARE. WE DEBATED IF THERE WAS ROOM IN THE UNIVERSE FOR ONE...
BUT WHEN YEA BECAME A TALKING NAZI VAMPYRE GORILLA?
YOU'RE A VILLAIN WE CAN SINK OUR TEETH INTO.
THAT NAME, THOUGH-- COUNT JULIUS-- JUST DOESN'T CUT IT. WHAT ABOUT SOMETHING LIKE... PRIMAUL™!
PRYEMAUL...
I CAN LIVE WITH DAT.
THEN YOU CAN LIVE!
WHAT ABOUT ME?
YOU... VAMPIRE? THERE'S NO WRINKLE IN YOUR CHARACTER...

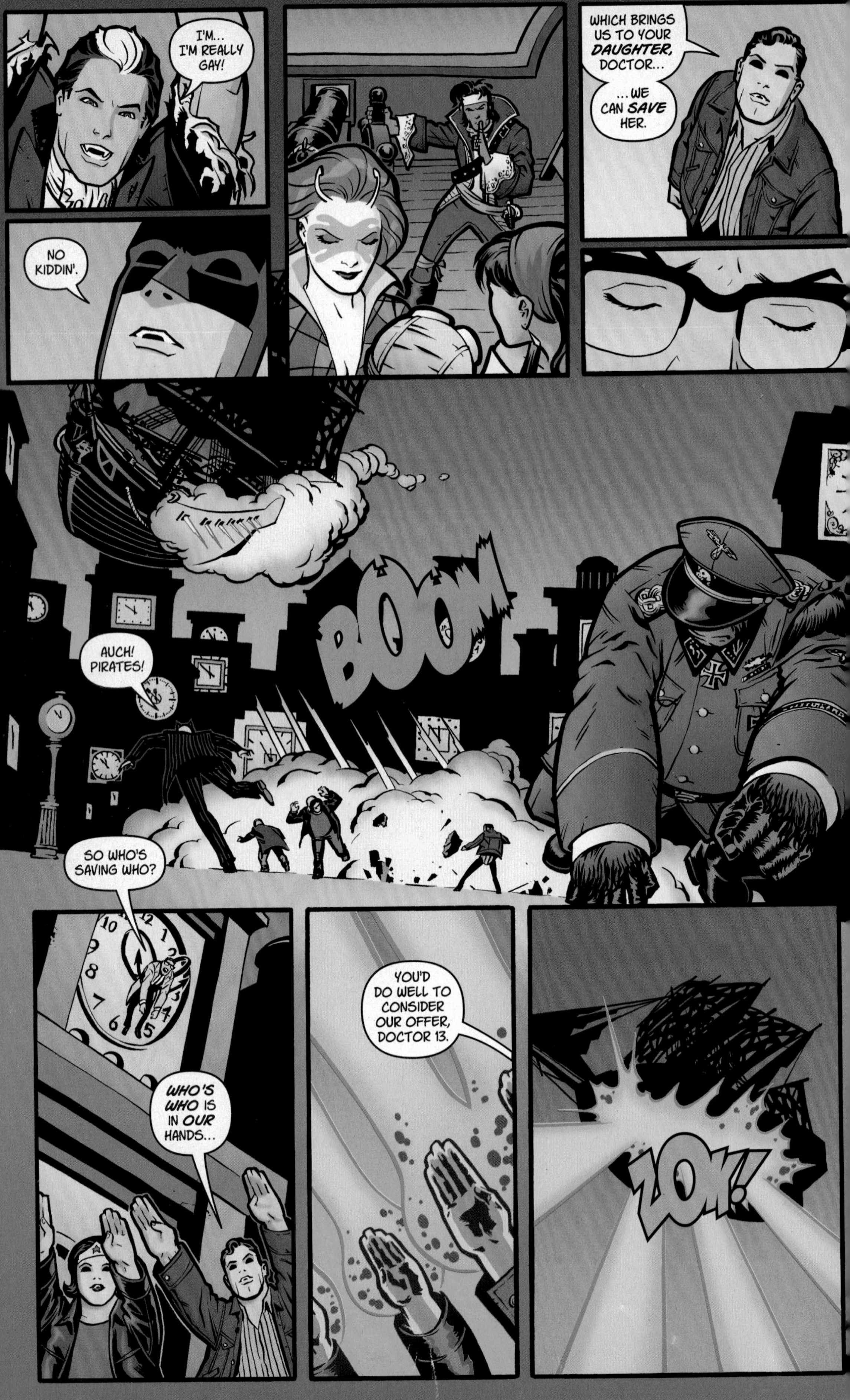
I'M... I'M REALLY GAY!
WHICH BRINGS US TO YOUR DAUGHTER, DOCTOR...
...WE CAN SAVE HER.
NO KIDDIN'.
BOOM
AUCH! PIRATES!
SO WHO'S SAVING WHO?
WHO'S WHO IS IN OUR HANDS...
YOU'D DO WELL TO CONSIDER OUR OFFER, DOCTOR 13.
ZOK!

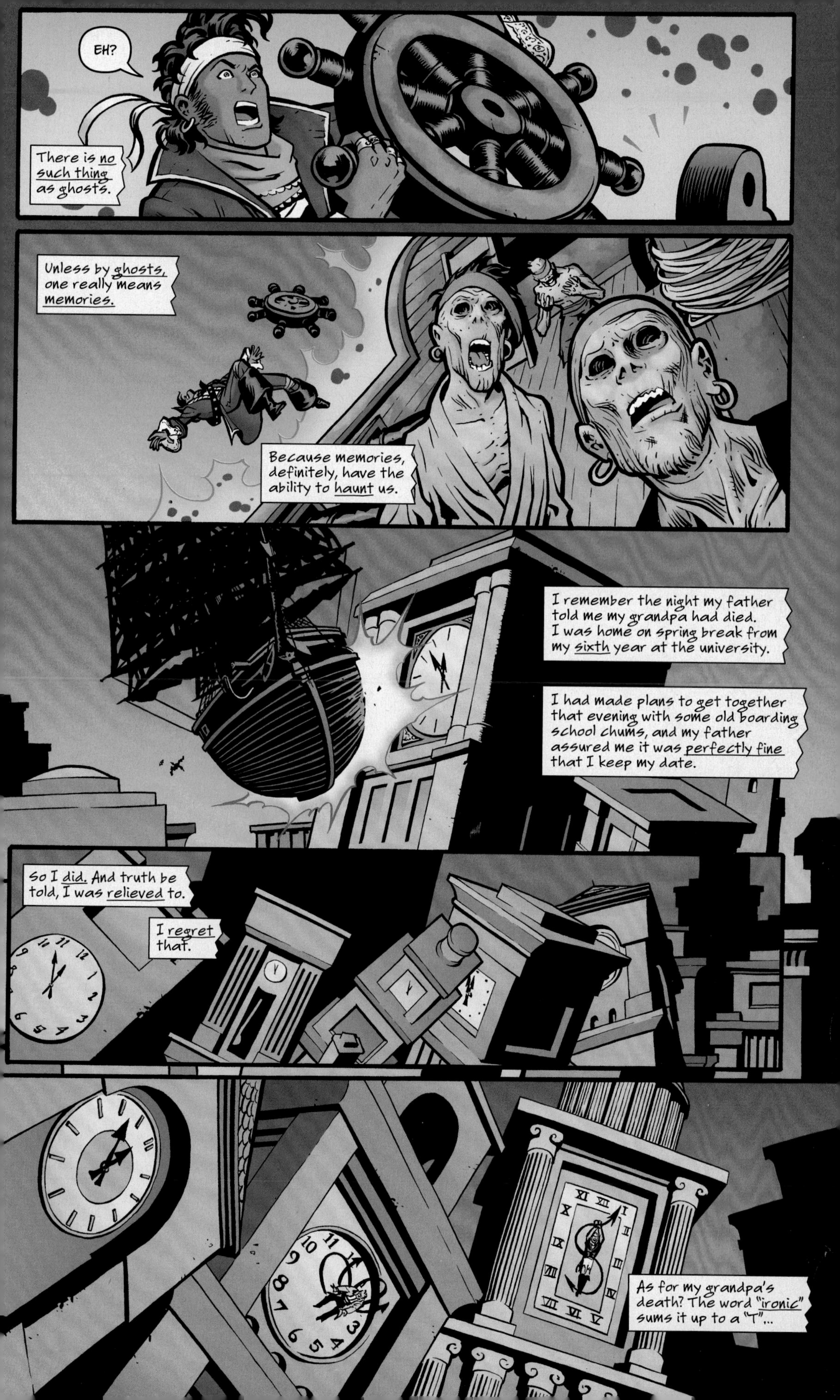
EH?
There is no such thing as ghosts.
Unless by ghosts, one really means memories.
Because memories, definitely, have the ability to haunt us.
I remember the night my father told me my grandpa had died. I was home on spring break from my sixth year at the university.
I had made plans to get together that evening with some old boarding school chums, and my father assured me it was perfectly fine that I keep my date.
So I did. And truth be told, I was relieved to.
I regret that.
As for my grandpa's death? The word "ironic" sums it up to a "T"...

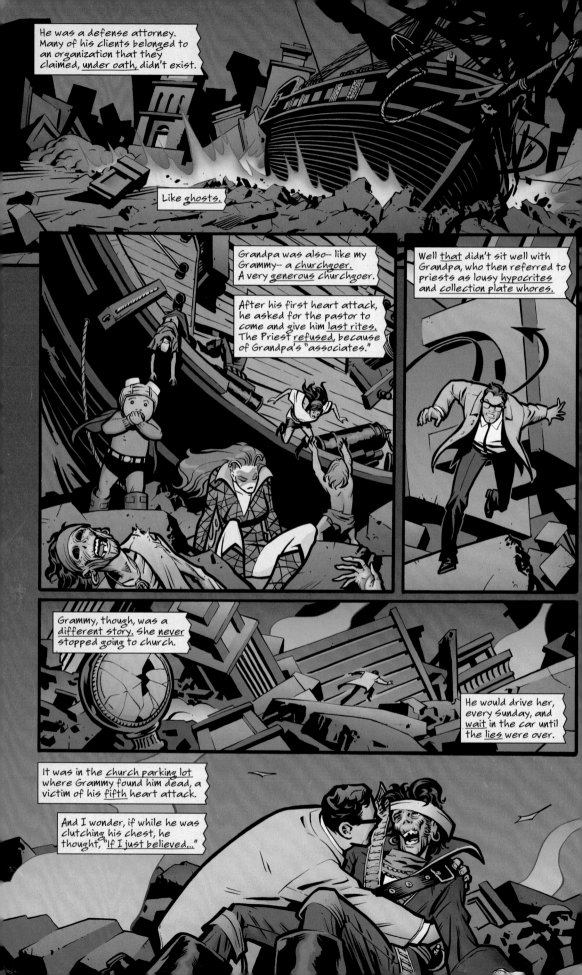

He was a defense attorney. Many of his clients belonged to an organization that they claimed, <u>under oath,</u> didn't exist.

Like <u>ghosts.</u>

Grandpa was also-- like my Grammy-- a <u>churchgoer.</u> A very <u>generous</u> churchgoer.

After his first heart attack, he asked for the pastor to come and give him <u>last rites.</u> The Priest <u>refused,</u> because of Grandpa's "associates."

Well <u>that</u> didn't sit well with Grandpa, who then referred to priests as lousy <u>hypocrites</u> and <u>collection plate whores.</u>

Grammy, though, was a <u>different story.</u> She <u>never</u> stopped going to church.

He would drive her, every Sunday, and <u>wait</u> in the car until the <u>lies</u> were over.

It was in the <u>church parking lot</u> where Grammy found him dead, a victim of his <u>fifth</u> heart attack.

And I wonder, if while he was clutching his chest, he thought, "<u>If I just believed...</u>"

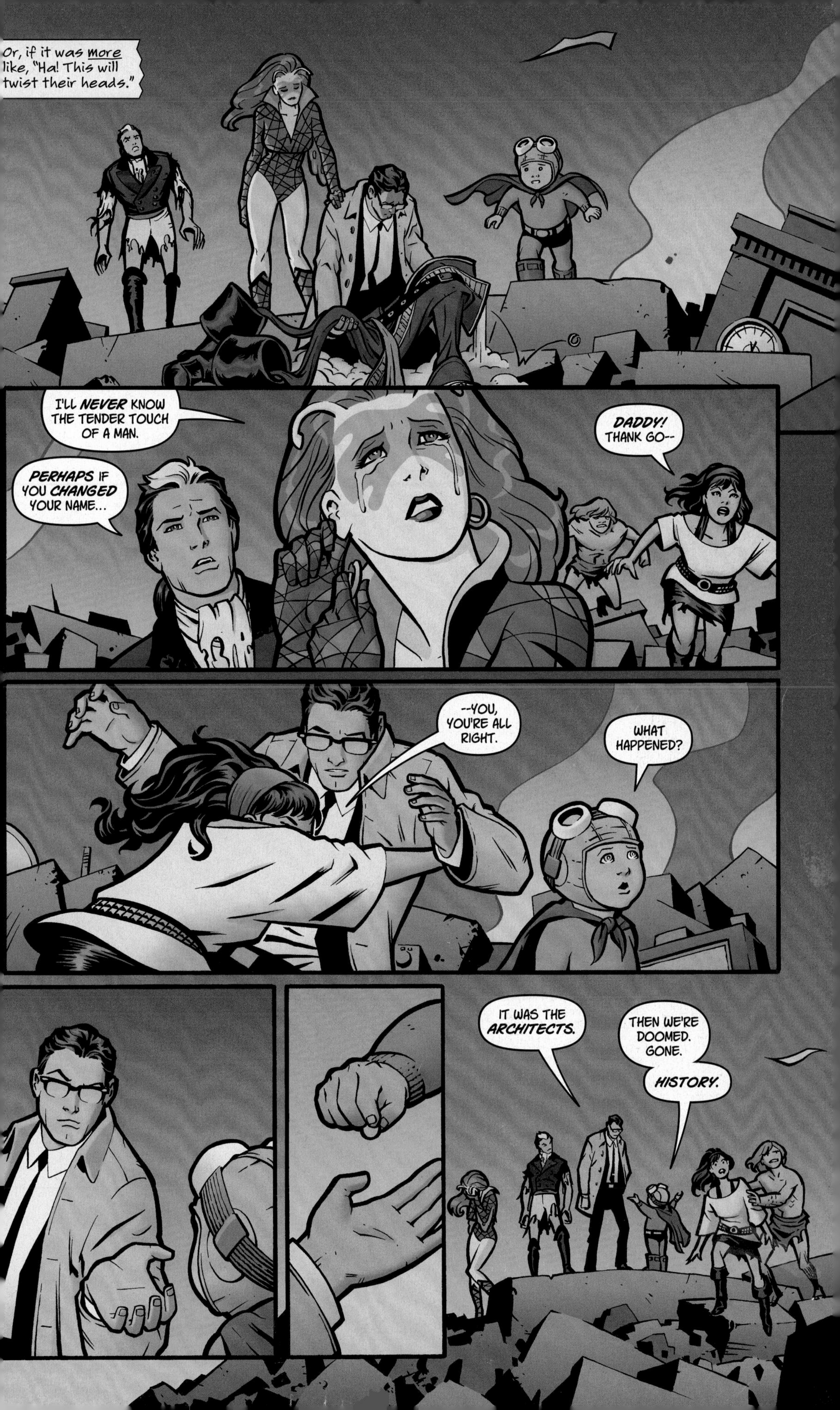
Or, if it was more like, "Ha! This will twist their heads."
I'LL NEVER KNOW THE TENDER TOUCH OF A MAN.
PERHAPS IF YOU CHANGED YOUR NAME...
DADDY! THANK GO--
--YOU, YOU'RE ALL RIGHT.
WHAT HAPPENED?
IT WAS THE ARCHITECTS.
THEN WE'RE DOOMED. GONE.
HISTORY.

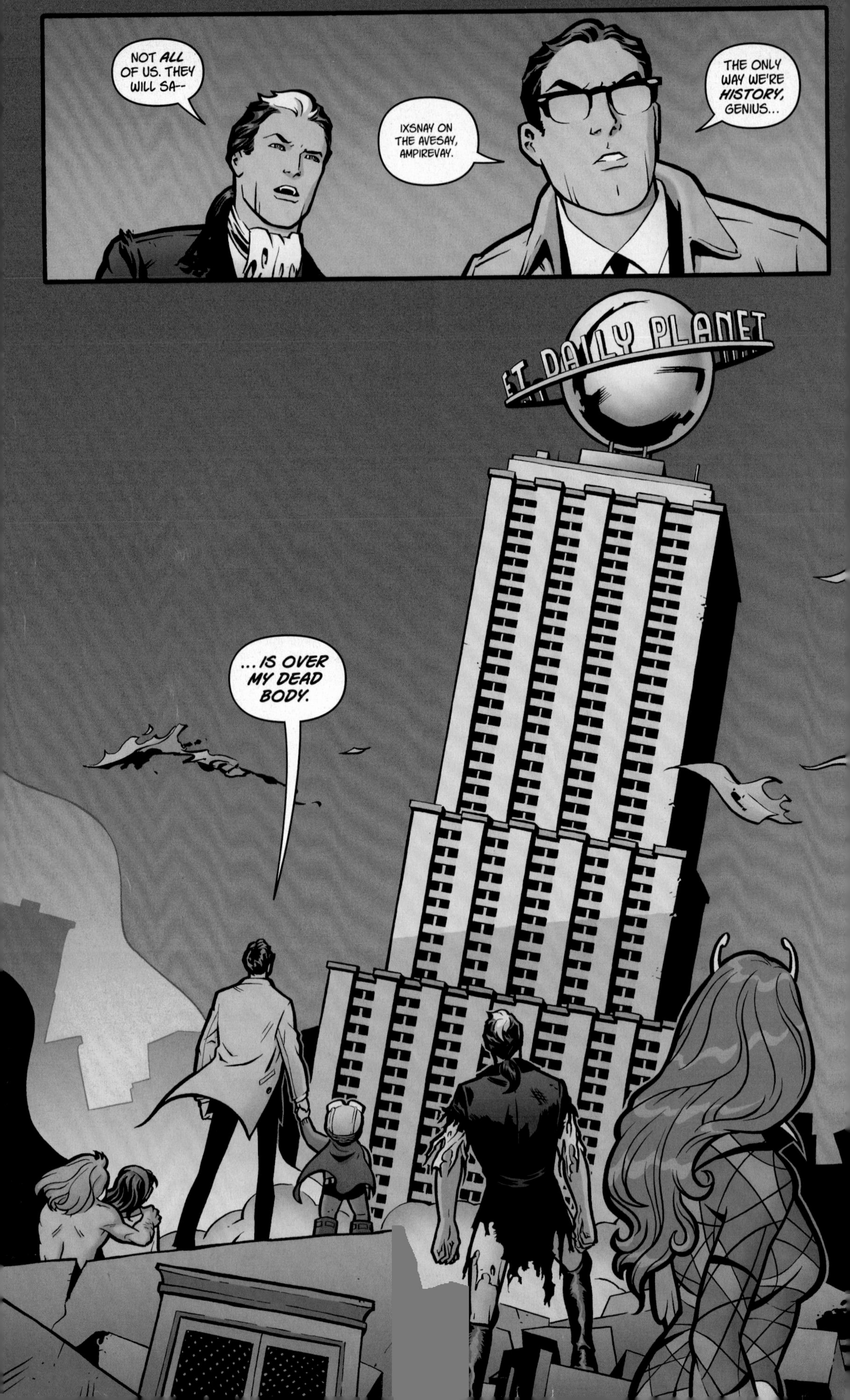
NOT ALL OF US. THEY WILL SA--
IXSNAY ON THE AVESAY, AMPIREVAY.
THE ONLY WAY WE'RE HISTORY, GENIUS...
DAILY PLANET
...IS OVER MY DEAD BODY.

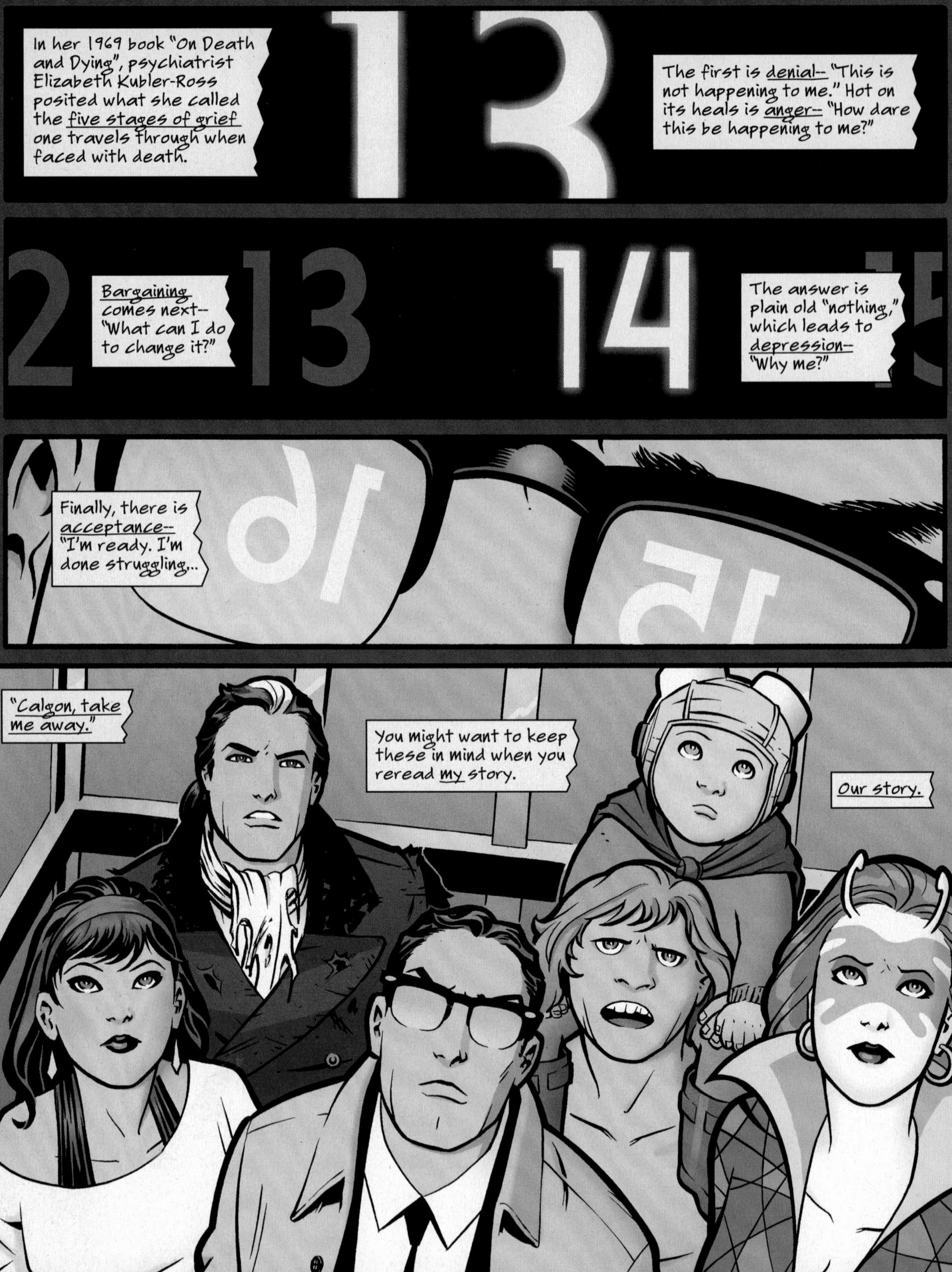
In her 1969 book "On Death and Dying", psychiatrist Elizabeth Kubler-Ross posited what she called the five stages of grief one travels through when faced with death.
The first is denial-- "This is not happening to me." Hot on its heals is anger-- "How dare this be happening to me?"
Bargaining comes next-- "What can I do to change it?"
The answer is plain old "nothing," which leads to depression-- "Why me?"
Finally, there is acceptance-- "I'm ready. I'm done struggling...
"Calgon, take me away."
You might want to keep these in mind when you reread my story.
Our story.

CHAPTER 8

# BEGGING THE BÉGUIN

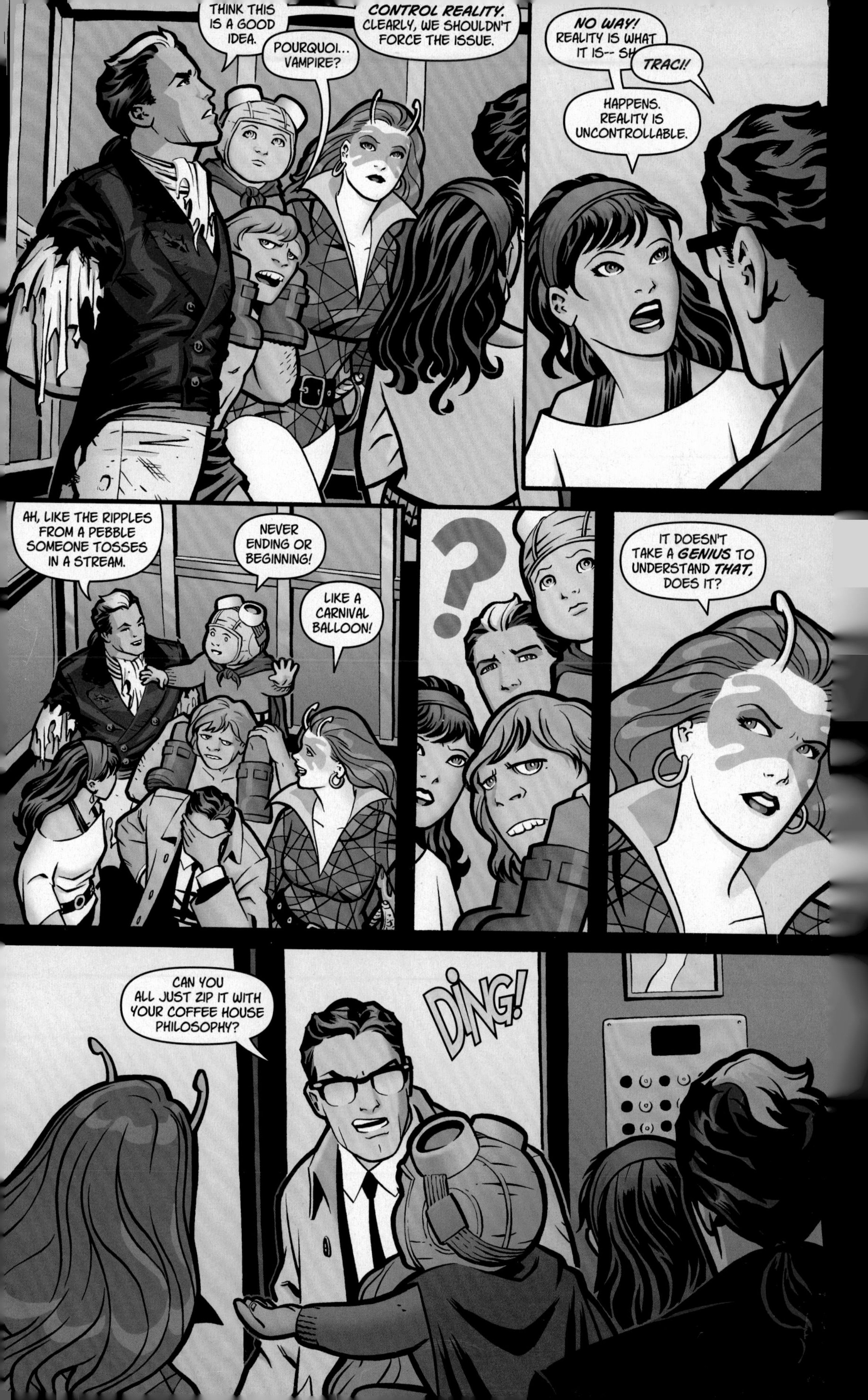
THINK THIS IS A GOOD IDEA.
POURQUOI... VAMPIRE?
CONTROL REALITY. CLEARLY, WE SHOULDN'T FORCE THE ISSUE.
NO WAY! REALITY IS WHAT IT IS-- SH
TRACI!
HAPPENS. REALITY IS UNCONTROLLABLE.
AH, LIKE THE RIPPLES FROM A PEBBLE SOMEONE TOSSES IN A STREAM.
NEVER ENDING OR BEGINNING!
LIKE A CARNIVAL BALLOON!
?
IT DOESN'T TAKE A GENIUS TO UNDERSTAND THAT, DOES IT?
CAN YOU ALL JUST ZIP IT WITH YOUR COFFEE HOUSE PHILOSOPHY?
DING!

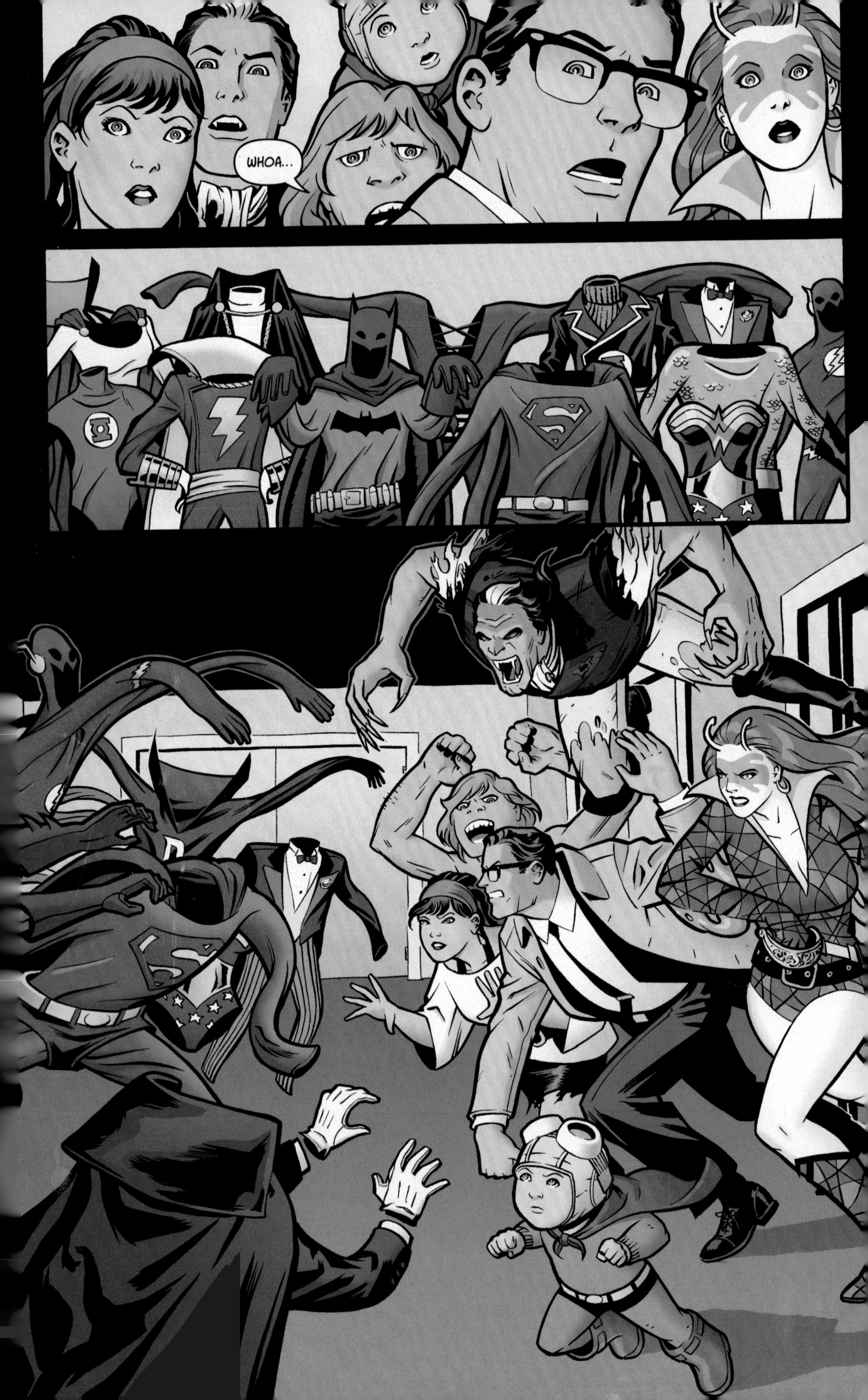
WHOA...

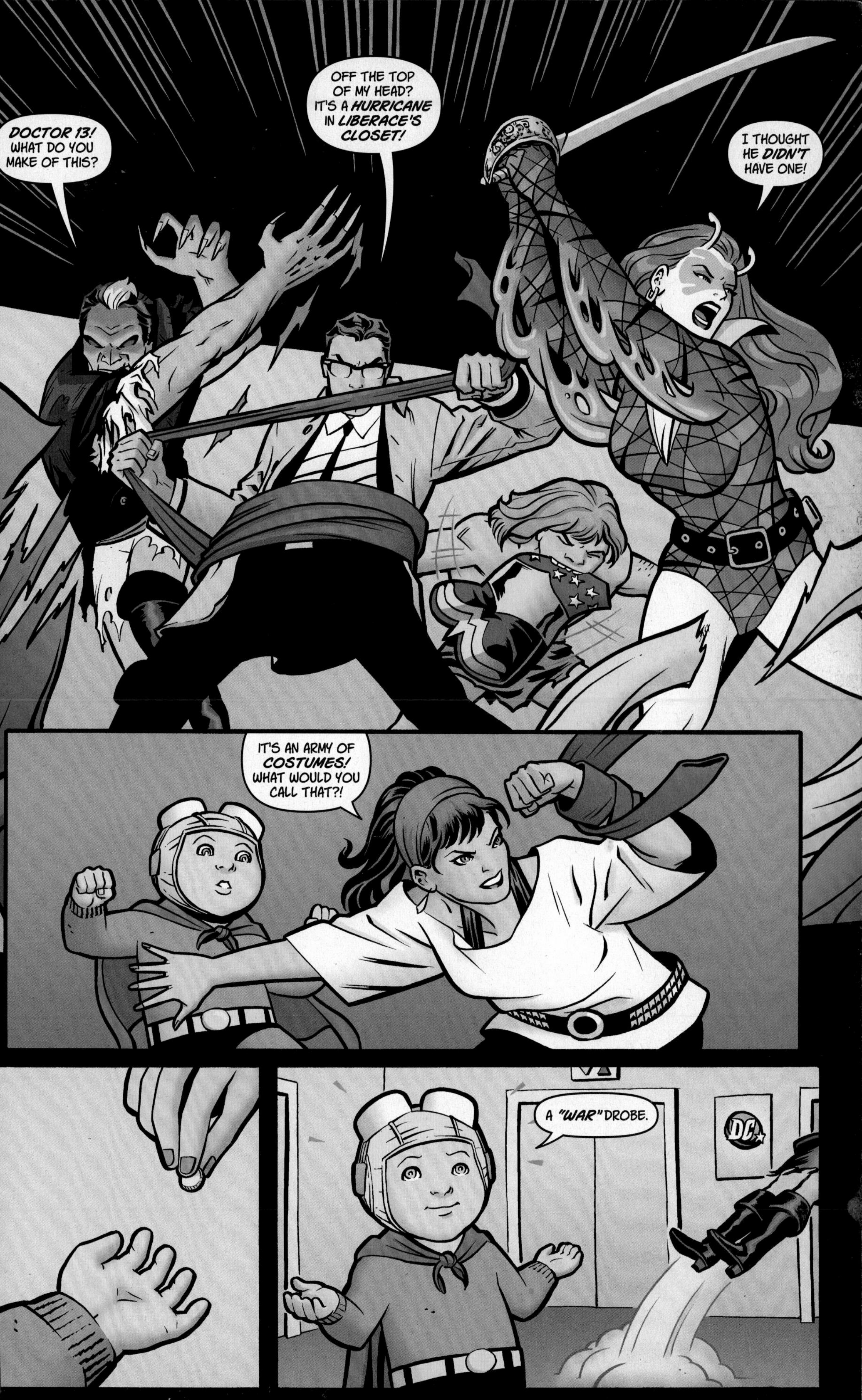
DOCTOR 13! WHAT DO YOU MAKE OF THIS?
OFF THE TOP OF MY HEAD? IT'S A HURRICANE IN LIBERACE'S CLOSET!
I THOUGHT HE DIDN'T HAVE ONE!
IT'S AN ARMY OF COSTUMES! WHAT WOULD YOU CALL THAT?!
A "WAR" DROBE.
DC

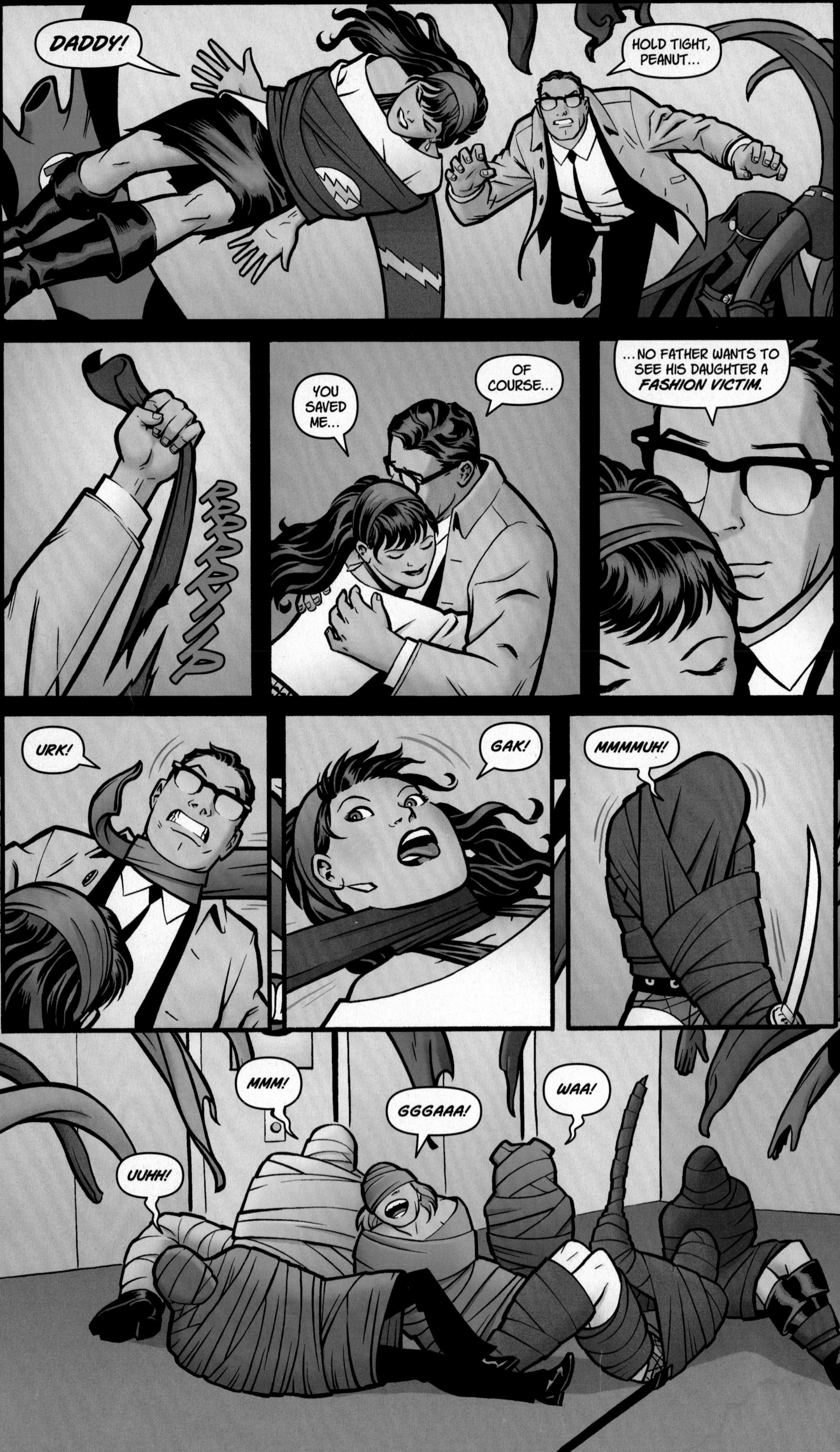
DADDY!
HOLD TIGHT, PEANUT...
RRRRIIIP
YOU SAVED ME...
OF COURSE...
...NO FATHER WANTS TO SEE HIS DAUGHTER A *FASHION VICTIM.*
URK!
GAK!
MMMMUH!
MMM!
GGGAAA!
WAA!
UUHH!

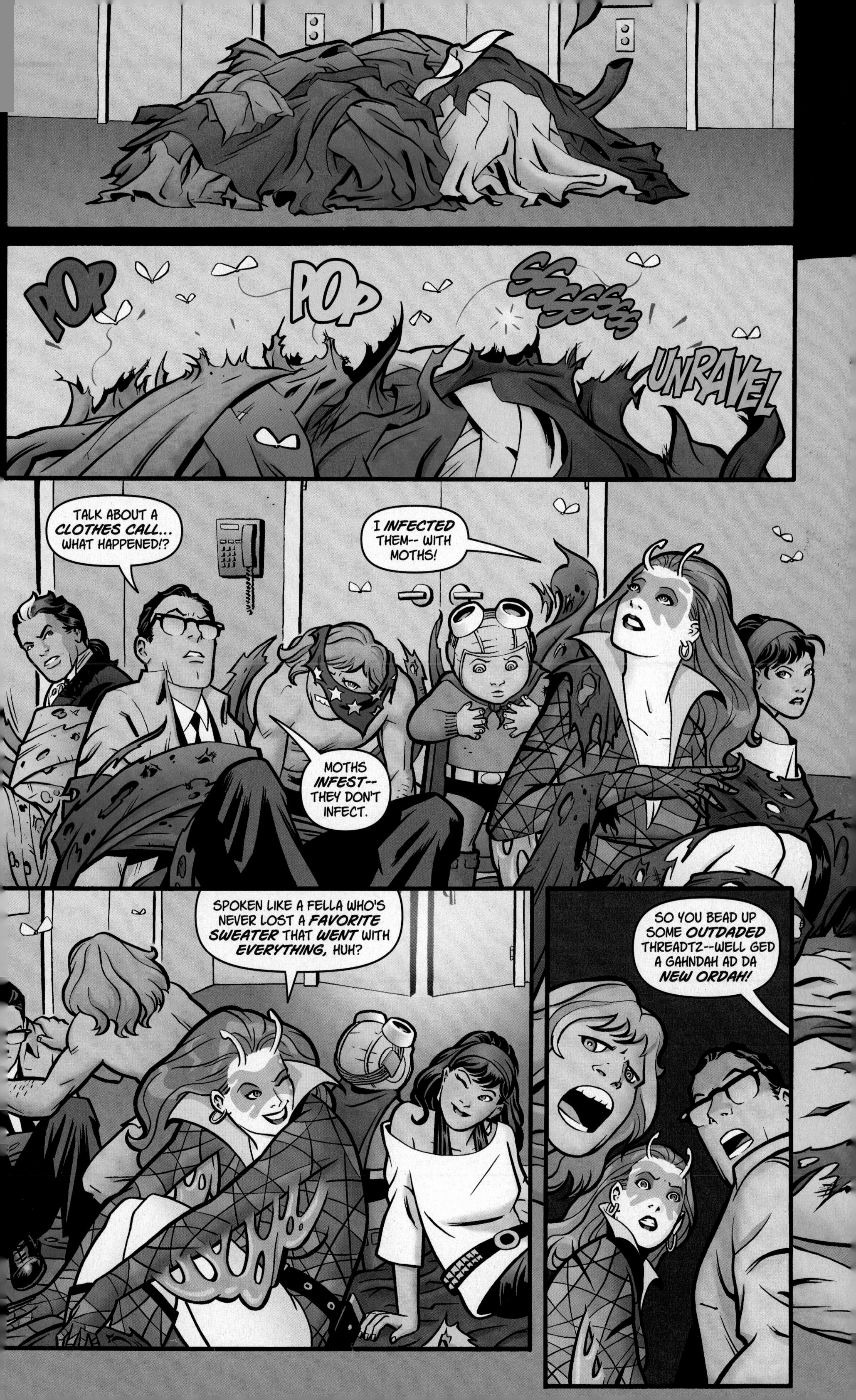

POP
POP
SSSSSSS
UNRAVEL
TALK ABOUT A CLOTHES CALL... WHAT HAPPENED!?
I INFECTED THEM-- WITH MOTHS!
MOTHS INFEST-- THEY DON'T INFECT.
SPOKEN LIKE A FELLA WHO'S NEVER LOST A FAVORITE SWEATER THAT WENT WITH EVERYTHING, HUH?
SO YOU BEAD UP SOME OUTDADED THREADTZ--WELL GED A GAHNDAH AD DA NEW ORDAH!

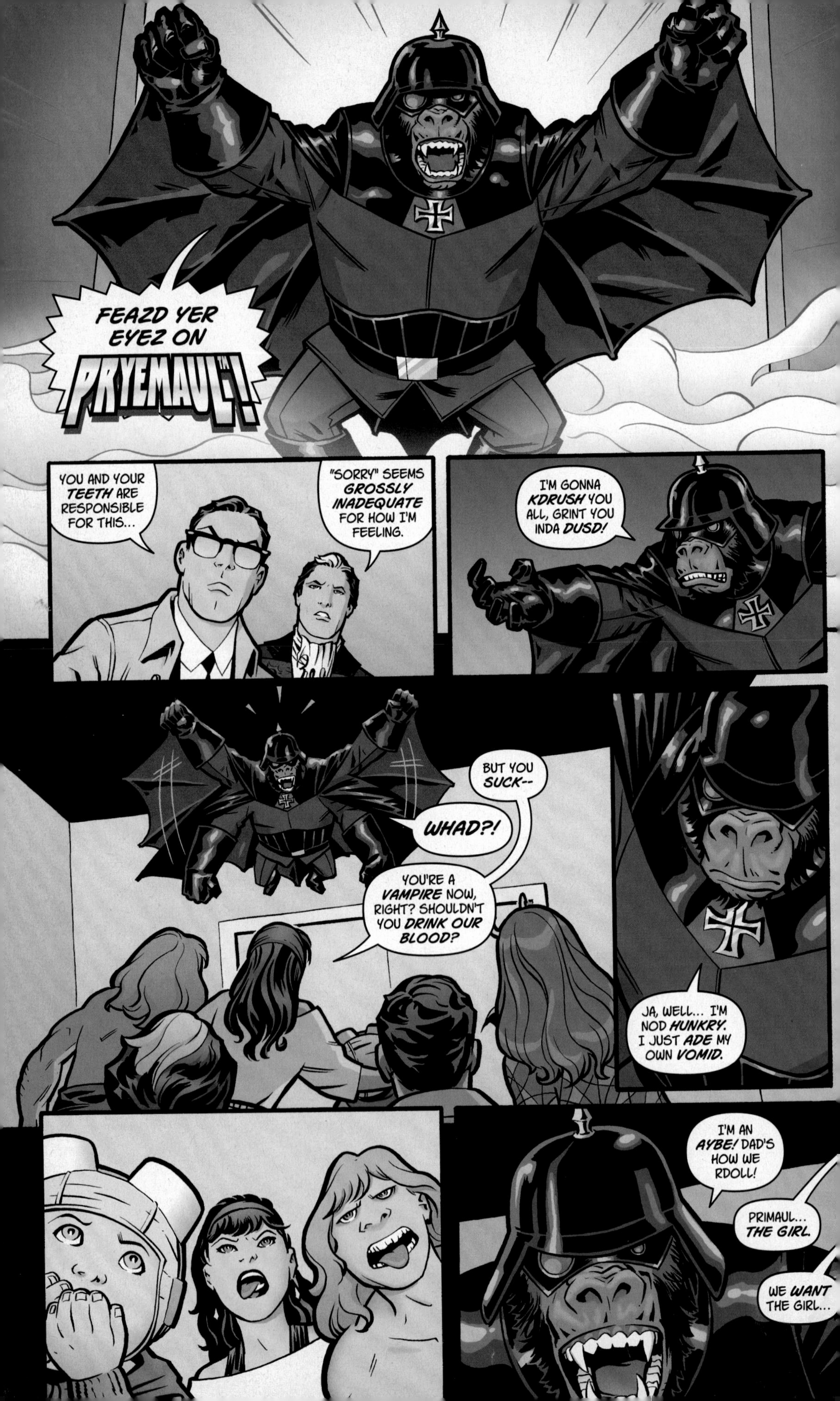

FEAZD YER EYEZ ON
PRYEMAUL™!
YOU AND YOUR TEETH ARE RESPONSIBLE FOR THIS...
"SORRY" SEEMS GROSSLY INADEQUATE FOR HOW I'M FEELING.
I'M GONNA KDRUSH YOU ALL, GRINT YOU INDA DUSD!
BUT YOU SUCK--
WHAD?!
YOU'RE A VAMPIRE NOW, RIGHT? SHOULDN'T YOU DRINK OUR BLOOD?
JA, WELL... I'M NOD HUNKRY. I JUST ADE MY OWN VOMID.
I'M AN AYBE! DAD'S HOW WE RDOLL!
PRIMAUL... THE GIRL.
WE WANT THE GIRL...

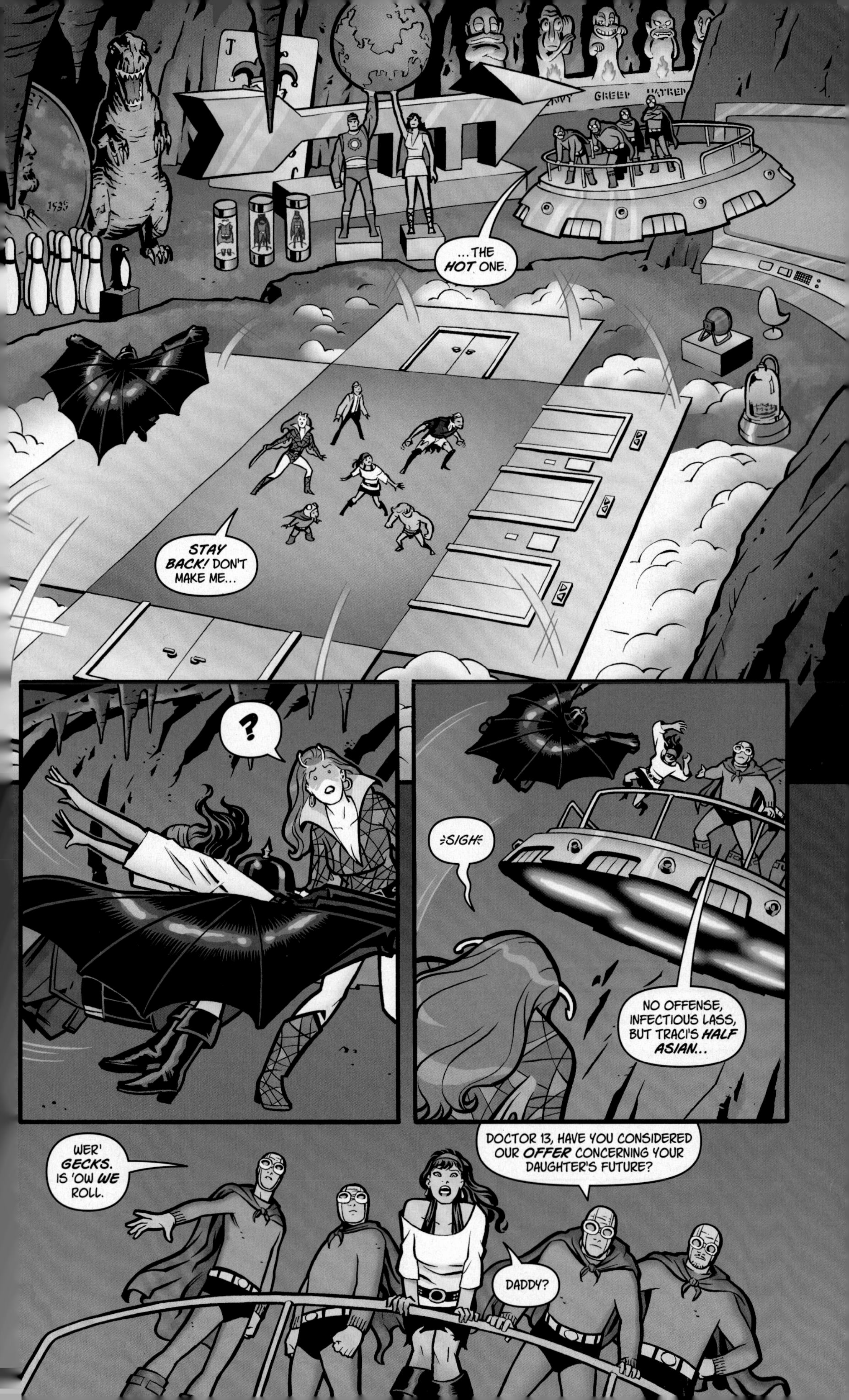
GREED
HATRED
...THE *HOT* ONE.
*STAY BACK!* DON'T MAKE ME...
?
SIGH
NO OFFENSE, INFECTIOUS LASS, BUT TRACI'S *HALF ASIAN...*
WER' *GECKS.* IS 'OW *WE* ROLL.
DOCTOR 13, HAVE YOU CONSIDERED OUR *OFFER* CONCERNING YOUR DAUGHTER'S FUTURE?
DADDY?

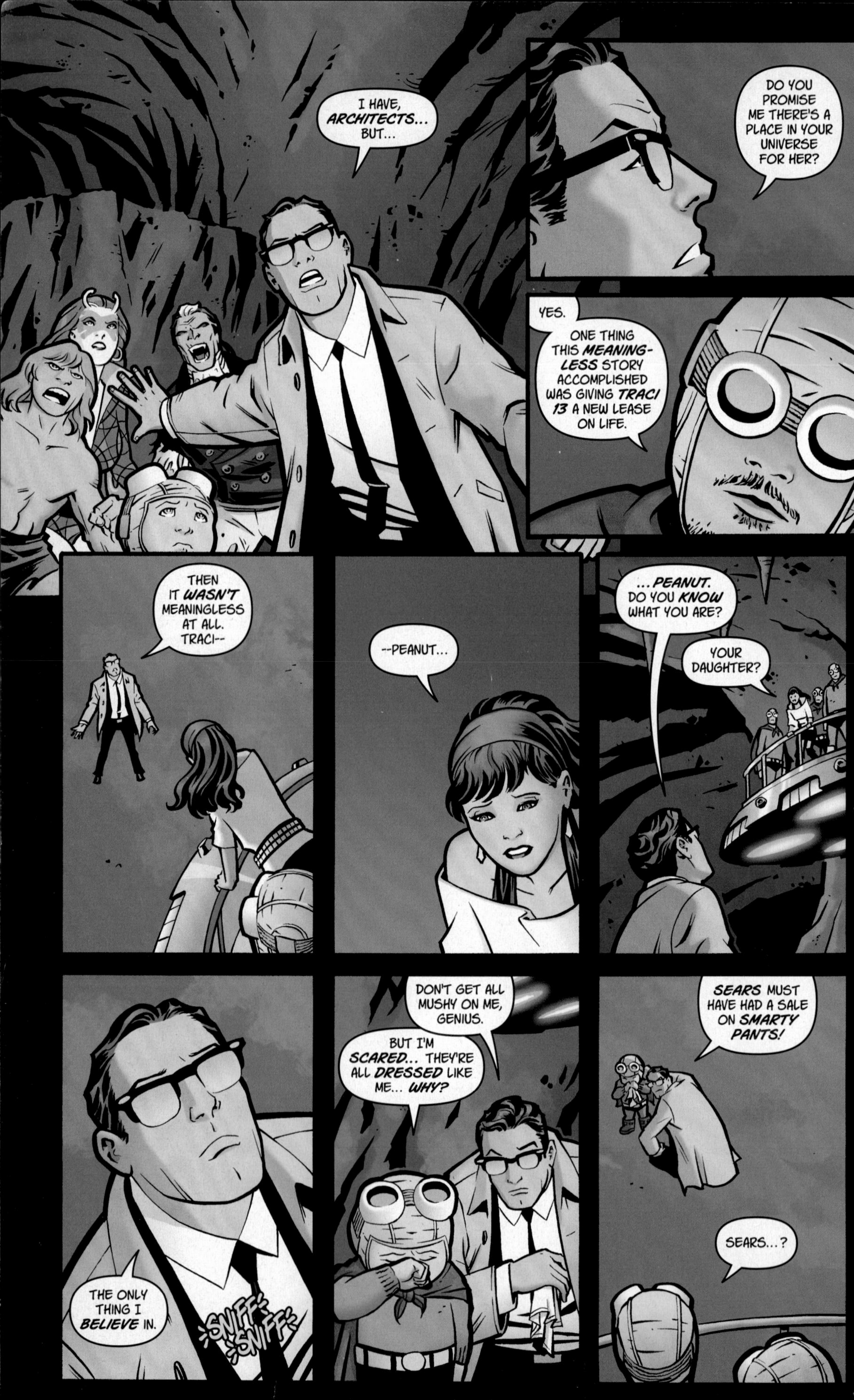
I HAVE, ARCHITECTS... BUT...
DO YOU PROMISE ME THERE'S A PLACE IN YOUR UNIVERSE FOR HER?
YES.
ONE THING THIS MEANINGLESS STORY ACCOMPLISHED WAS GIVING TRACI 13 A NEW LEASE ON LIFE.
THEN IT WASN'T MEANINGLESS AT ALL. TRACI--
--PEANUT...
...PEANUT. DO YOU KNOW WHAT YOU ARE?
YOUR DAUGHTER?
THE ONLY THING I BELIEVE IN.
SNIFF SNIFF
DON'T GET ALL MUSHY ON ME, GENIUS.
BUT I'M SCARED... THEY'RE ALL DRESSED LIKE ME... WHY?
SEARS MUST HAVE HAD A SALE ON SMARTY PANTS!
SEARS...?

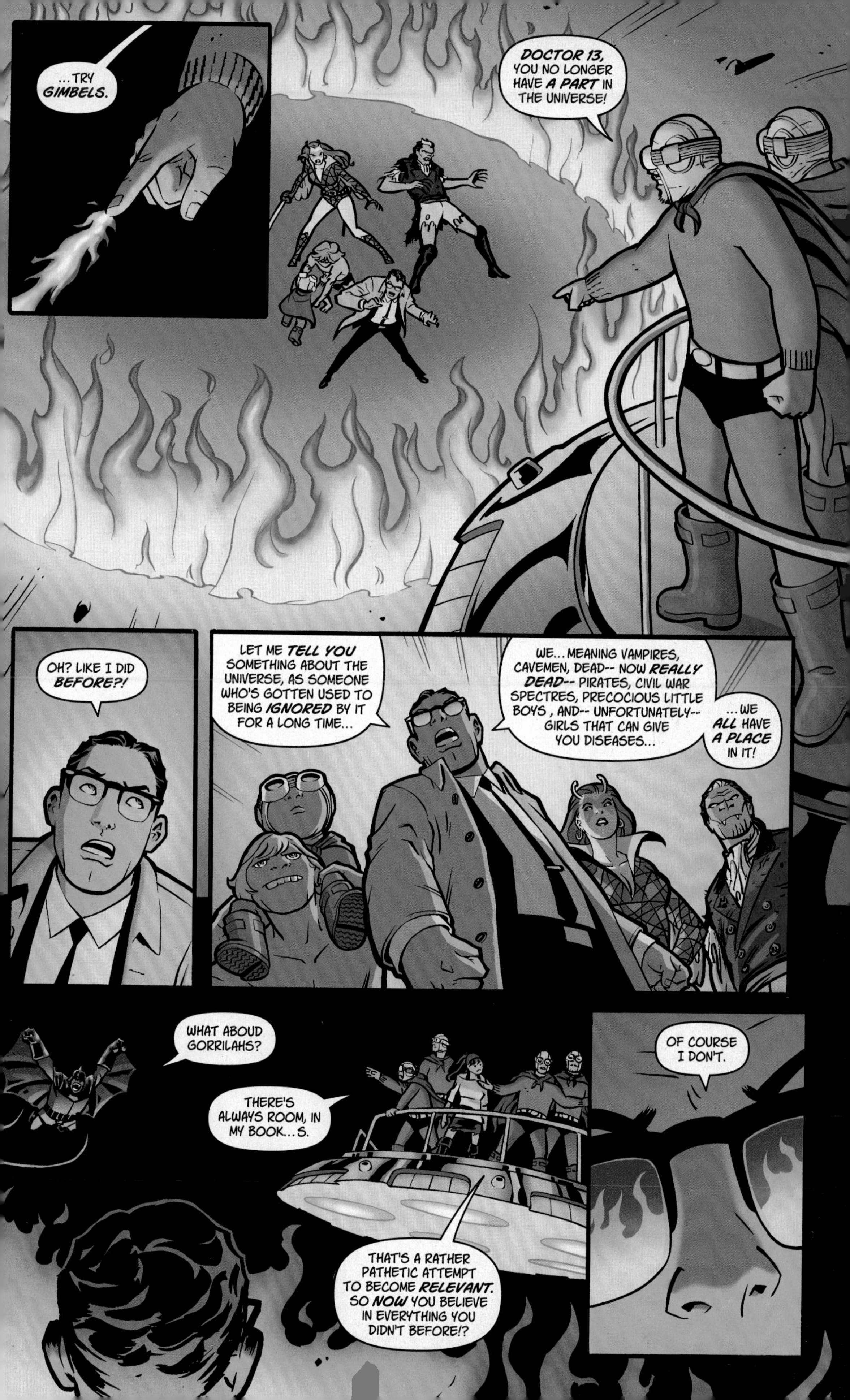
...TRY GIMBELS.
DOCTOR 13, YOU NO LONGER HAVE A PART IN THE UNIVERSE!
OH? LIKE I DID BEFORE?!
LET ME TELL YOU SOMETHING ABOUT THE UNIVERSE, AS SOMEONE WHO'S GOTTEN USED TO BEING IGNORED BY IT FOR A LONG TIME...
WE... MEANING VAMPIRES, CAVEMEN, DEAD-- NOW REALLY DEAD-- PIRATES, CIVIL WAR SPECTRES, PRECOCIOUS LITTLE BOYS , AND-- UNFORTUNATELY-- GIRLS THAT CAN GIVE YOU DISEASES...
...WE ALL HAVE A PLACE IN IT!
WHAT ABOUD GORRILAHS?
THERE'S ALWAYS ROOM, IN MY BOOK...S.
THAT'S A RATHER PATHETIC ATTEMPT TO BECOME RELEVANT. SO NOW YOU BELIEVE IN EVERYTHING YOU DIDN'T BEFORE!?
OF COURSE I DON'T.

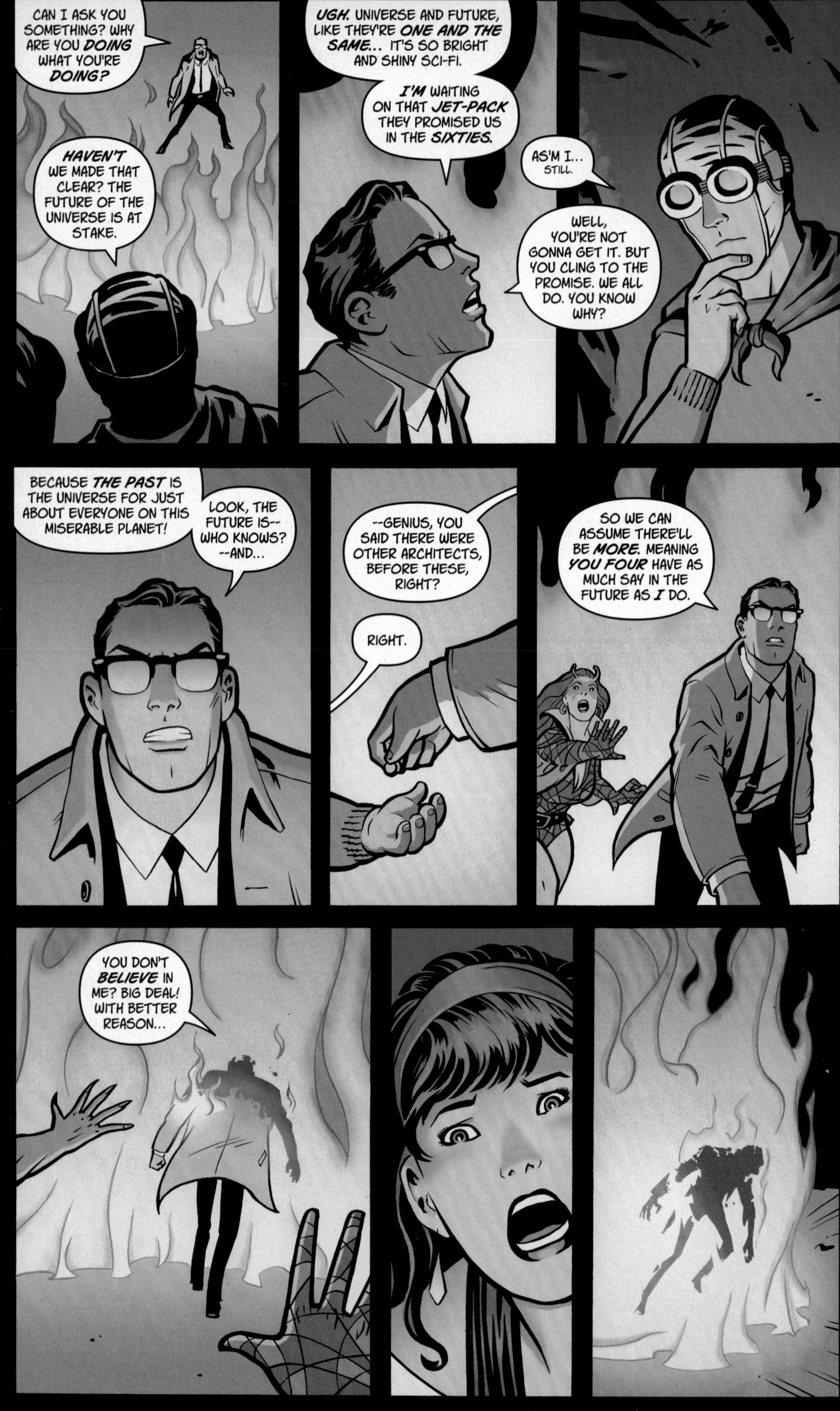

CAN I ASK YOU SOMETHING? WHY ARE YOU DOING WHAT YOU'RE DOING?
HAVEN'T WE MADE THAT CLEAR? THE FUTURE OF THE UNIVERSE IS AT STAKE.
UGH. UNIVERSE AND FUTURE, LIKE THEY'RE ONE AND THE SAME... IT'S SO BRIGHT AND SHINY SCI-FI.
I'M WAITING ON THAT JET-PACK THEY PROMISED US IN THE SIXTIES.
AS'M I... STILL.
WELL, YOU'RE NOT GONNA GET IT. BUT YOU CLING TO THE PROMISE. WE ALL DO. YOU KNOW WHY?
BECAUSE THE PAST IS THE UNIVERSE FOR JUST ABOUT EVERYONE ON THIS MISERABLE PLANET!
LOOK, THE FUTURE IS-- WHO KNOWS? --AND...
--GENIUS, YOU SAID THERE WERE OTHER ARCHITECTS, BEFORE THESE, RIGHT?
RIGHT.
SO WE CAN ASSUME THERE'LL BE MORE. MEANING YOU FOUR HAVE AS MUCH SAY IN THE FUTURE AS I DO.
YOU DON'T BELIEVE IN ME? BIG DEAL! WITH BETTER REASON...

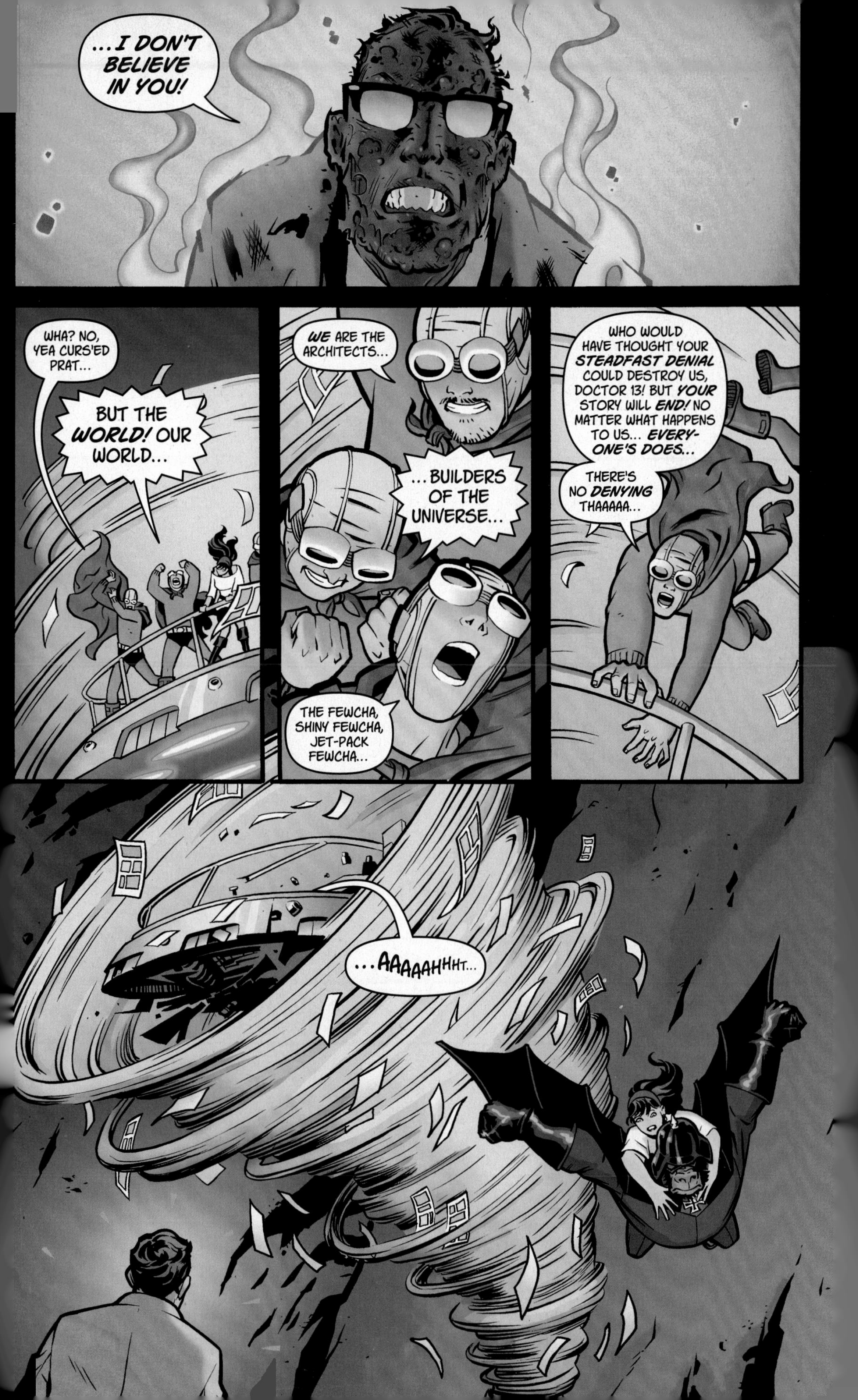
...I DON'T BELIEVE IN YOU!
WHA? NO, YEA CURS'ED PRAT...
BUT THE WORLD! OUR WORLD...
WE ARE THE ARCHITECTS...
...BUILDERS OF THE UNIVERSE...
THE FEWCHA, SHINY FEWCHA, JET-PACK FEWCHA...
WHO WOULD HAVE THOUGHT YOUR STEADFAST DENIAL COULD DESTROY US, DOCTOR 13! BUT YOUR STORY WILL END! NO MATTER WHAT HAPPENS TO US... EVERY-ONE'S DOES...
THERE'S NO DENYING THAAAAA...
...AAAAAHHHT...

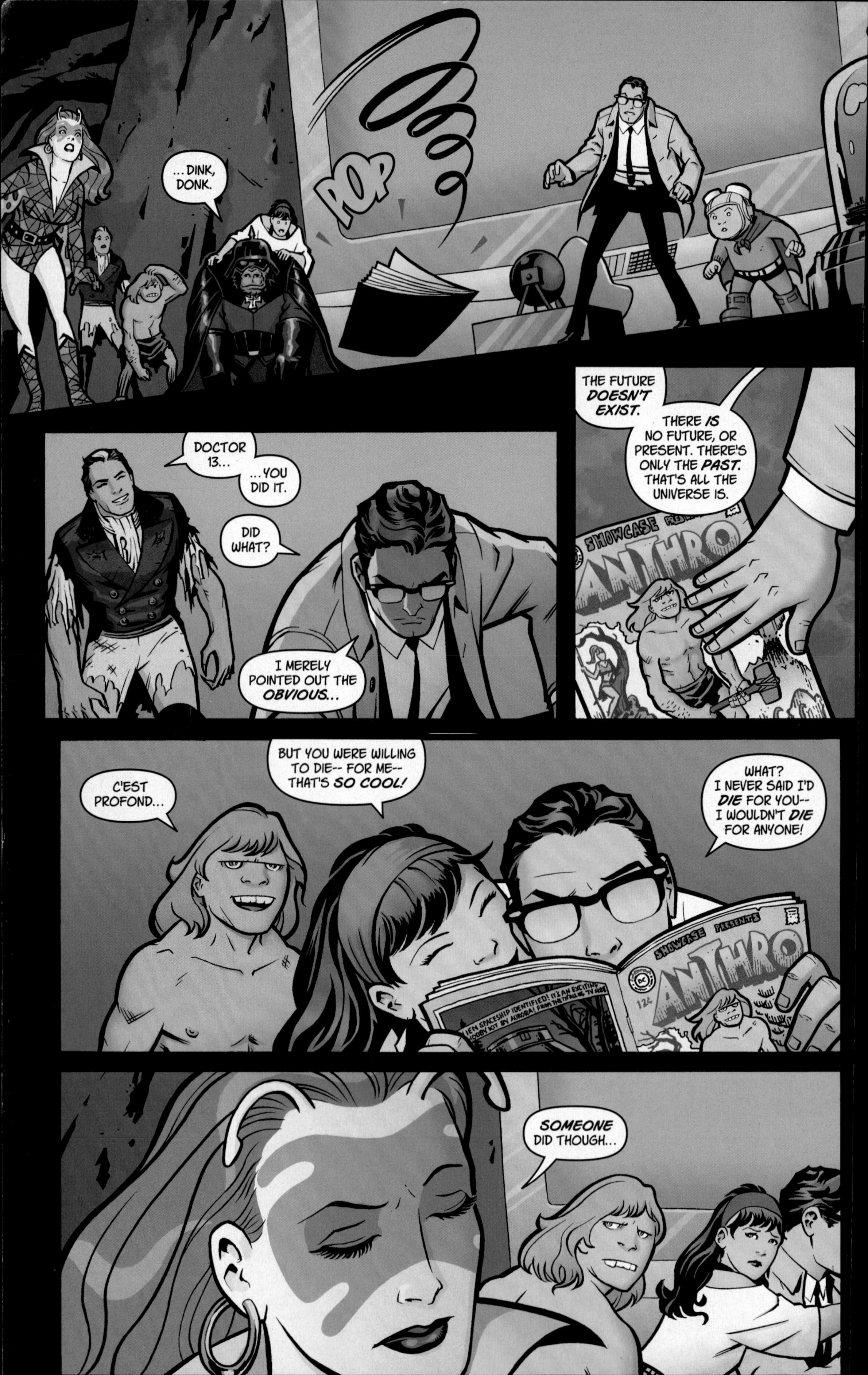

...DINK, DONK.
POP
DOCTOR 13...
...YOU DID IT.
DID WHAT?
I MERELY POINTED OUT THE OBVIOUS...
THE FUTURE DOESN'T EXIST.
THERE IS NO FUTURE, OR PRESENT. THERE'S ONLY THE PAST. THAT'S ALL THE UNIVERSE IS.
SHOWCASE
ANTHRO
C'EST PROFOND...
BUT YOU WERE WILLING TO DIE-- FOR ME-- THAT'S SO COOL!
WHAT? I NEVER SAID I'D DIE FOR YOU-- I WOULDN'T DIE FOR ANYONE!
SHOWCASE PRESENTS
ANTHRO
12¢
SOMEONE DID THOUGH...

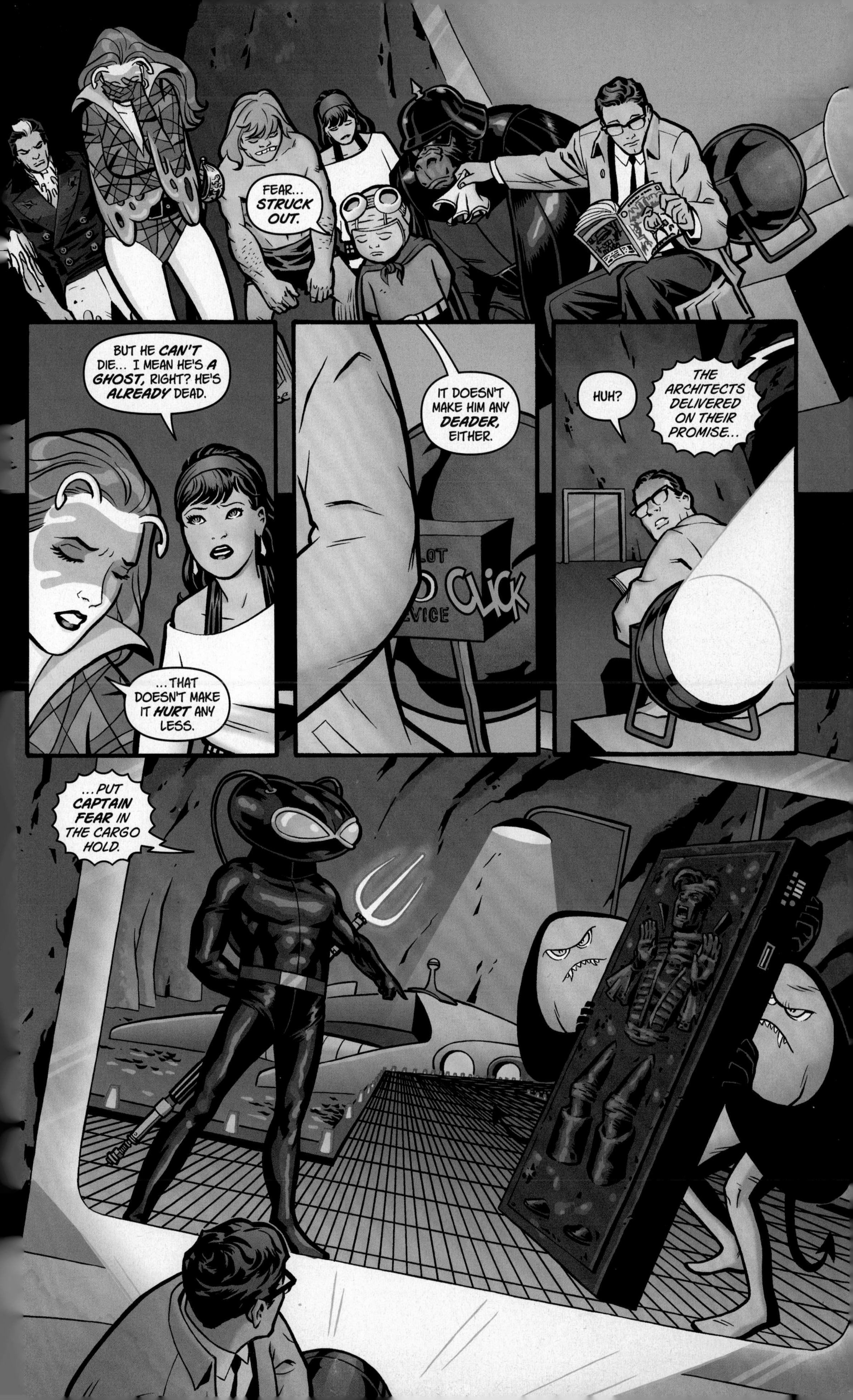
FEAR... STRUCK OUT.
BUT HE CAN'T DIE... I MEAN HE'S A GHOST, RIGHT? HE'S ALREADY DEAD.
...THAT DOESN'T MAKE IT HURT ANY LESS.
IT DOESN'T MAKE HIM ANY DEADER, EITHER.
CLICK
HUH?
THE ARCHITECTS DELIVERED ON THEIR PROMISE...
...PUT CAPTAIN FEAR IN THE CARGO HOLD.

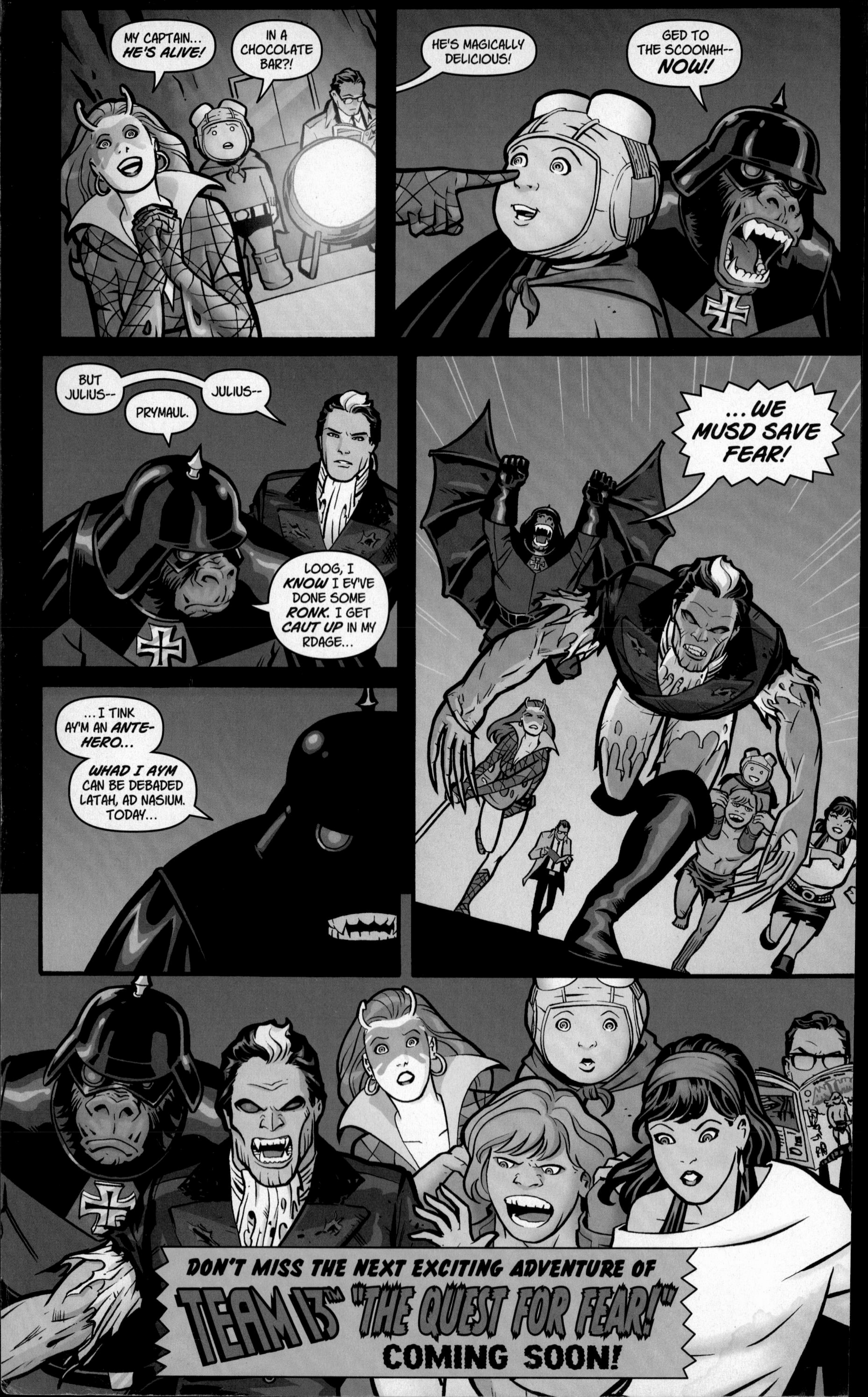
MY CAPTAIN... HE'S ALIVE!
IN A CHOCOLATE BAR?!
HE'S MAGICALLY DELICIOUS!
GED TO THE SCOONAH-- NOW!
BUT JULIUS--
PRYMAUL.
JULIUS--
LOOG, I KNOW I EY'VE DONE SOME RONK. I GET CAUT UP IN MY RDAGE...
...I TINK AY'M AN ANTE-HERO...
WHAD I AYM CAN BE DEBADED LATAH, AD NASIUM. TODAY...
...WE MUSD SAVE FEAR!
DON'T MISS THE NEXT EXCITING ADVENTURE OF
TEAM 13™ "THE QUEST FOR FEAR!"
COMING SOON!

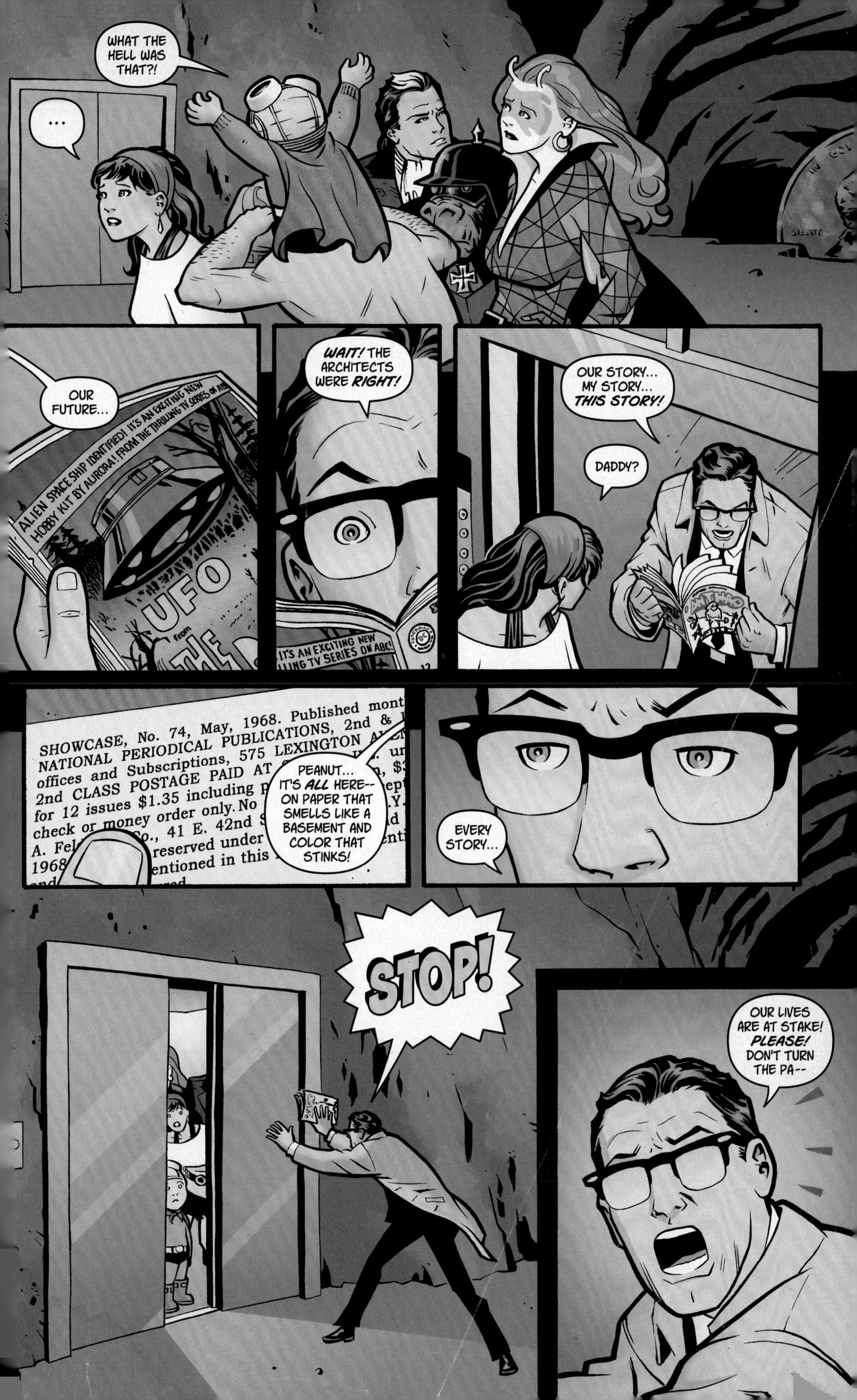
WHAT THE HELL WAS THAT?!
...
OUR FUTURE...
ALIEN SPACE SHIP IDENTIFIED! IT'S AN EXCITING NEW HOBBY KIT BY AURORA! FROM THE THRILLING TV SERIES ON
UFO
WAIT! THE ARCHITECTS WERE RIGHT!
IT'S AN EXCITING NEW
TV SERIES ON ABC!
OUR STORY... MY STORY... THIS STORY!
DADDY?
SHOWCASE, No. 74, May, 1968. Published mont
NATIONAL PERIODICAL PUBLICATIONS, 2nd &
offices and Subscriptions, 575 LEXINGTON
2nd CLASS POSTAGE PAID AT
for 12 issues $1.35 including
check or money order only. No
PEANUT... IT'S ALL HERE--ON PAPER THAT SMELLS LIKE A BASEMENT AND COLOR THAT STINKS!
EVERY STORY...
STOP!
OUR LIVES ARE AT STAKE! PLEASE! DON'T TURN THE PA--

# DOCTOR 13

## SKETCHES & DESIGNS

BY CLIFF CHIANG

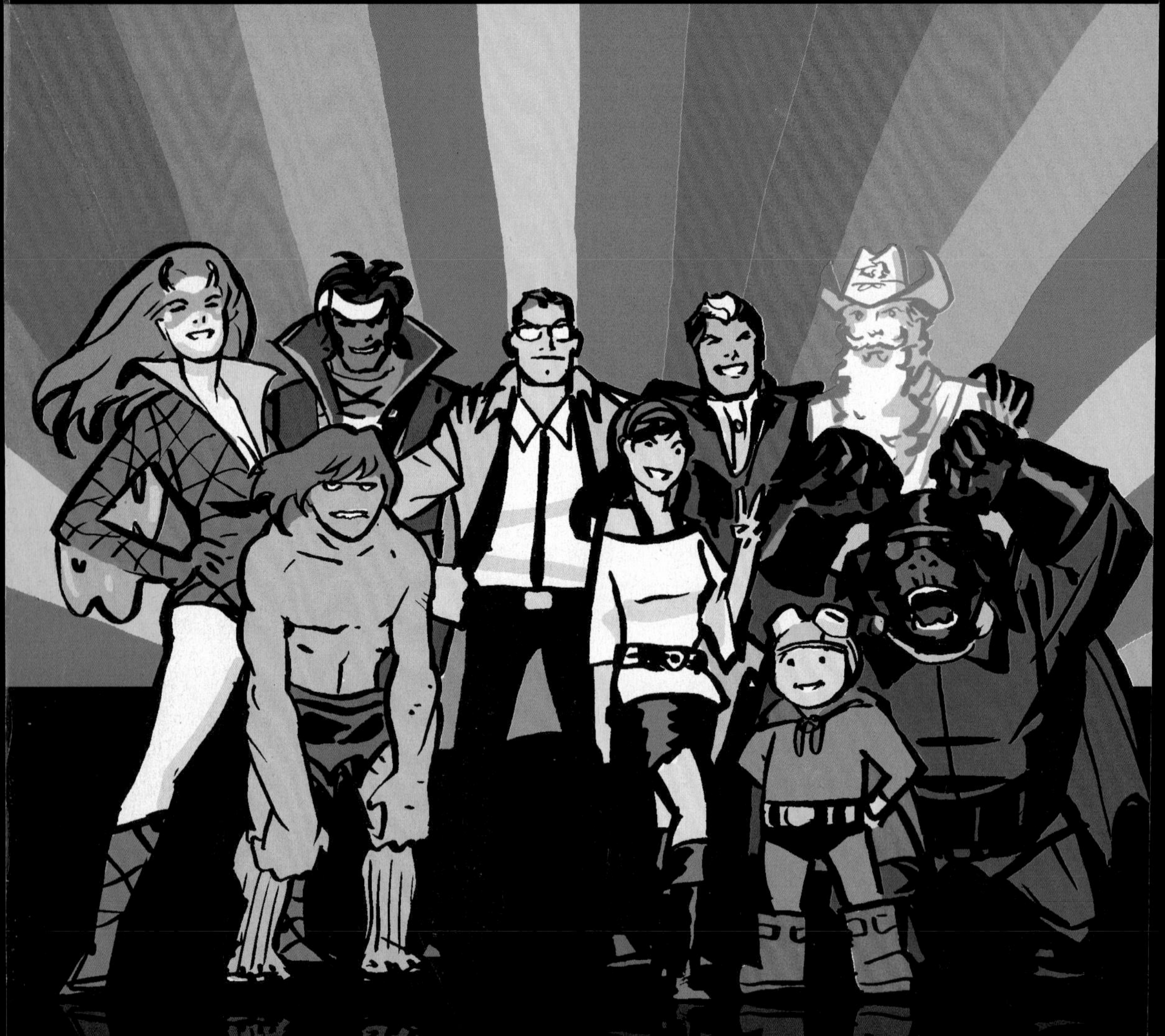

# DR. THIRTEEN

## ARCHITECTURE & MORTALITY

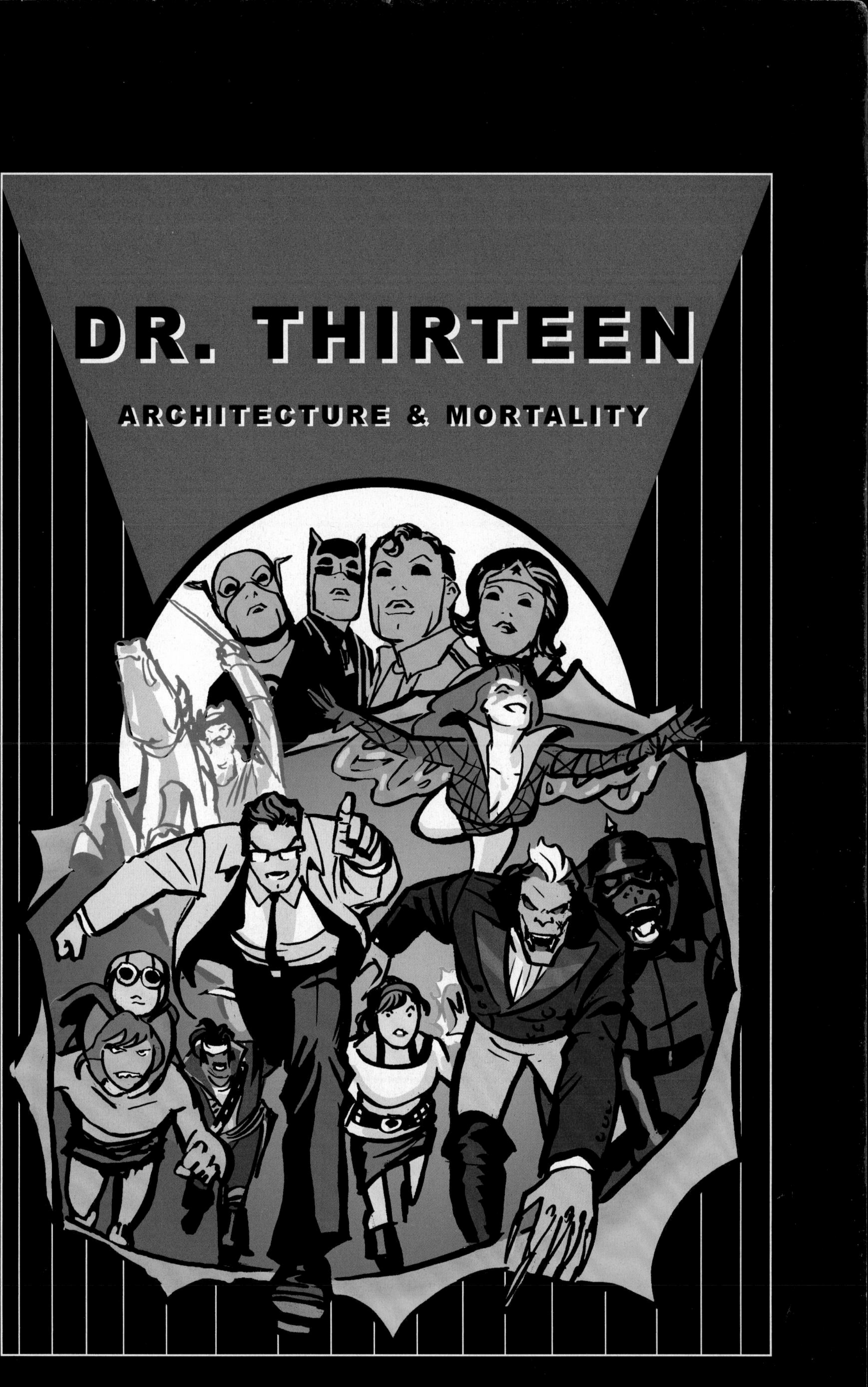

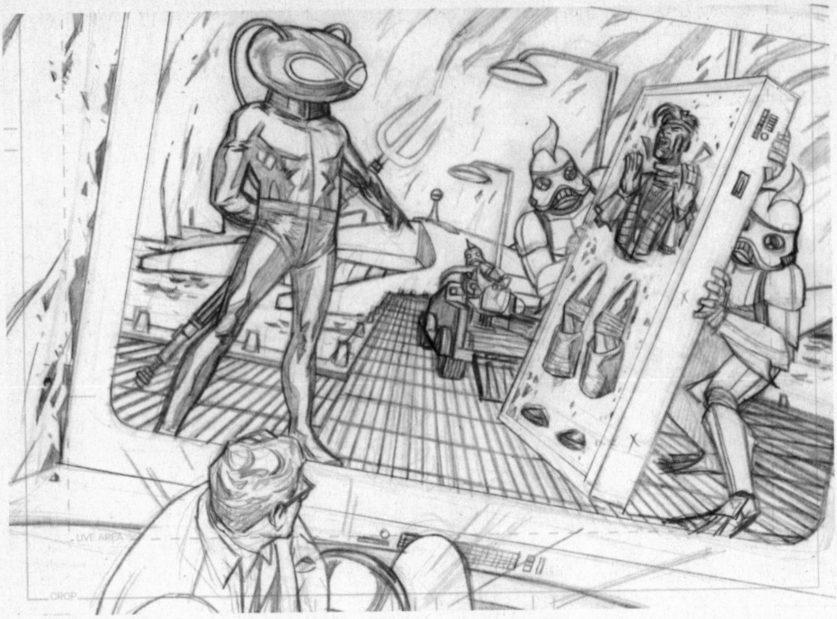
LIVE AREA
CROP

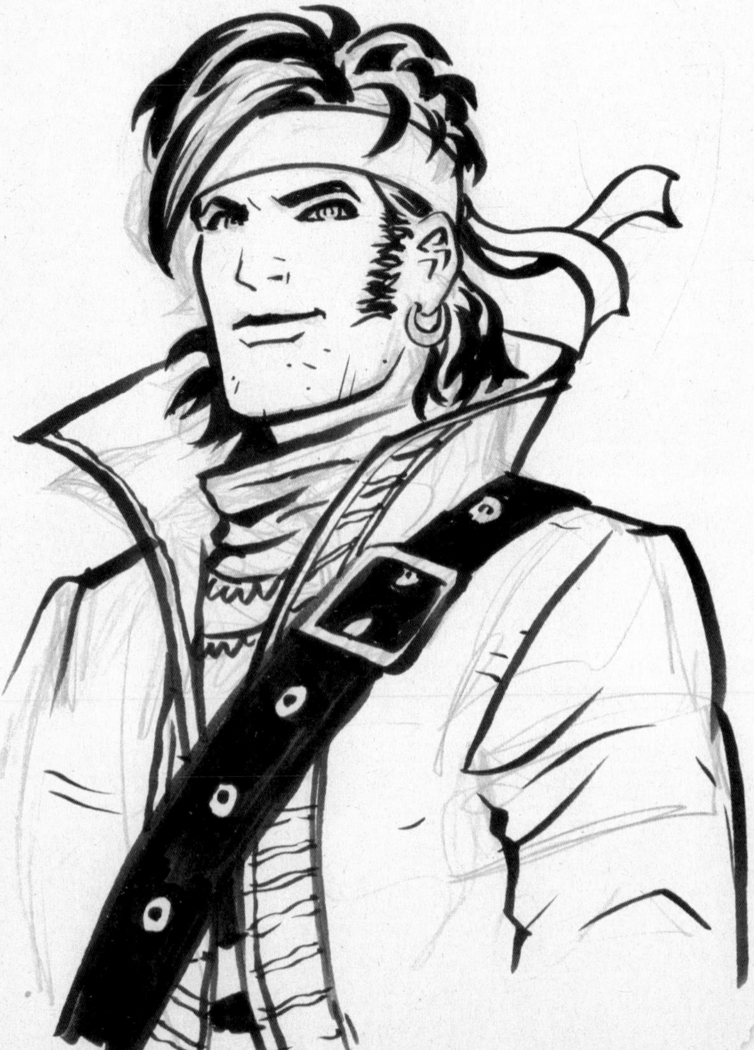

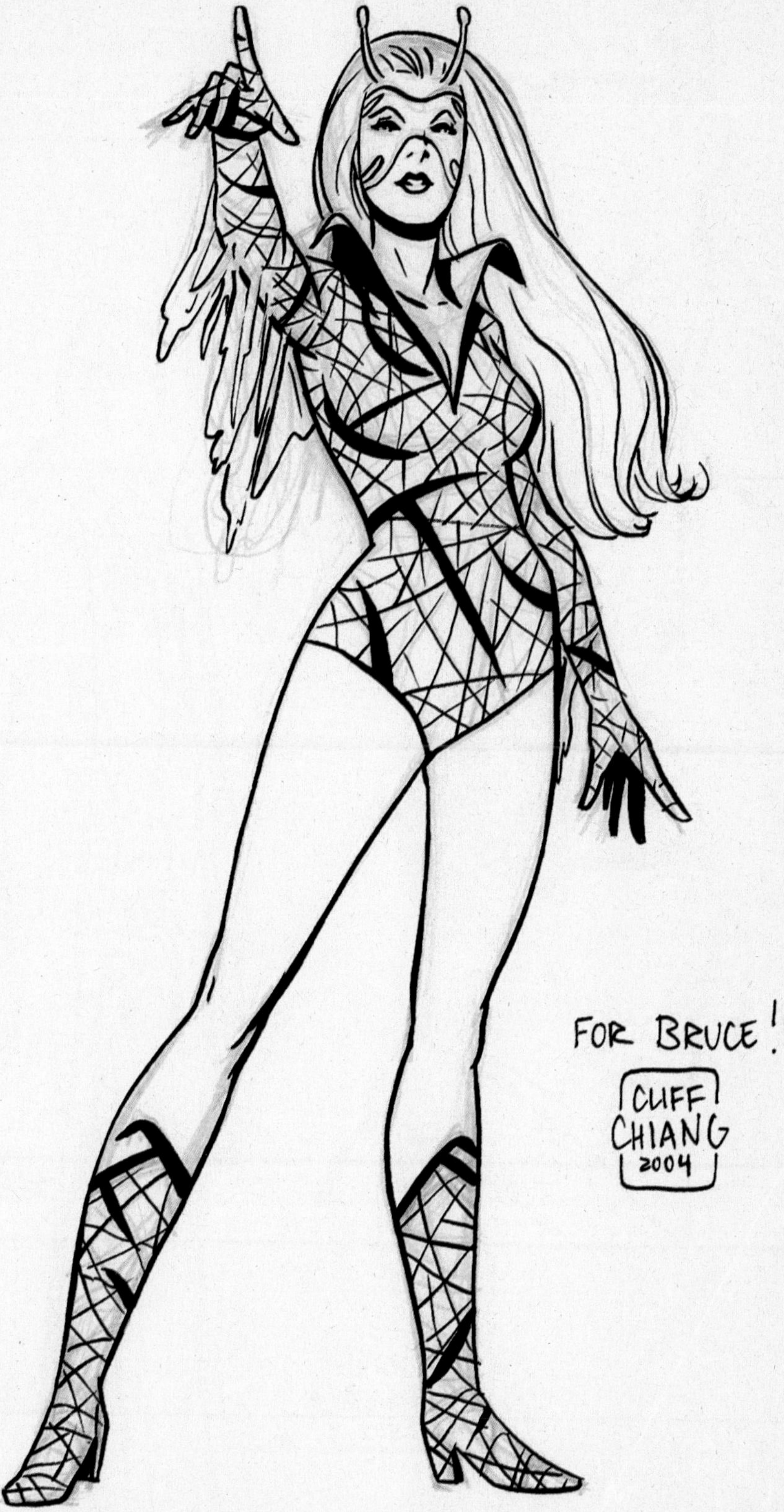
FOR BRUCE!
CLIFF CHIANG 2004

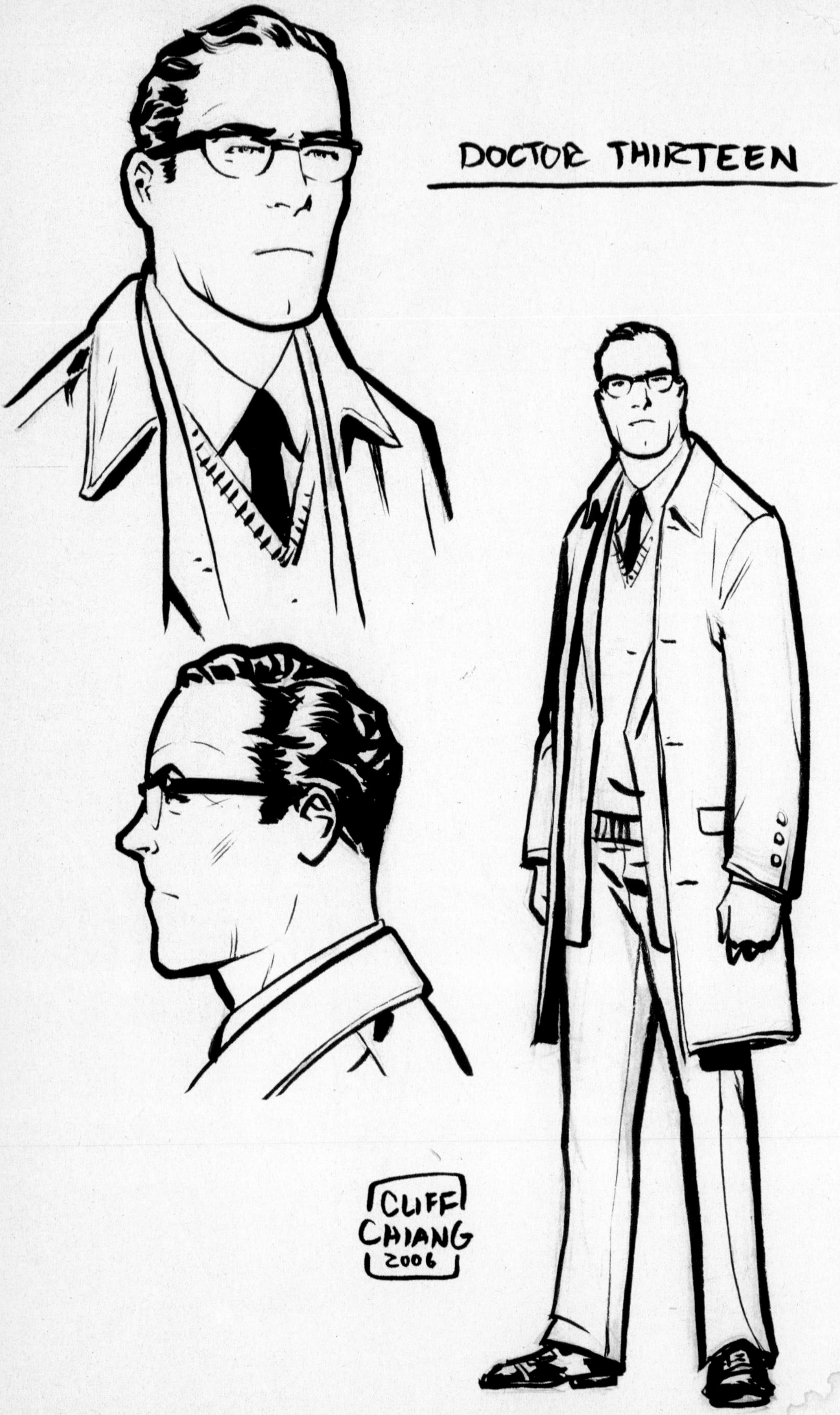
DOCTOR THIRTEEN
CLIFF
CHIANG
2006

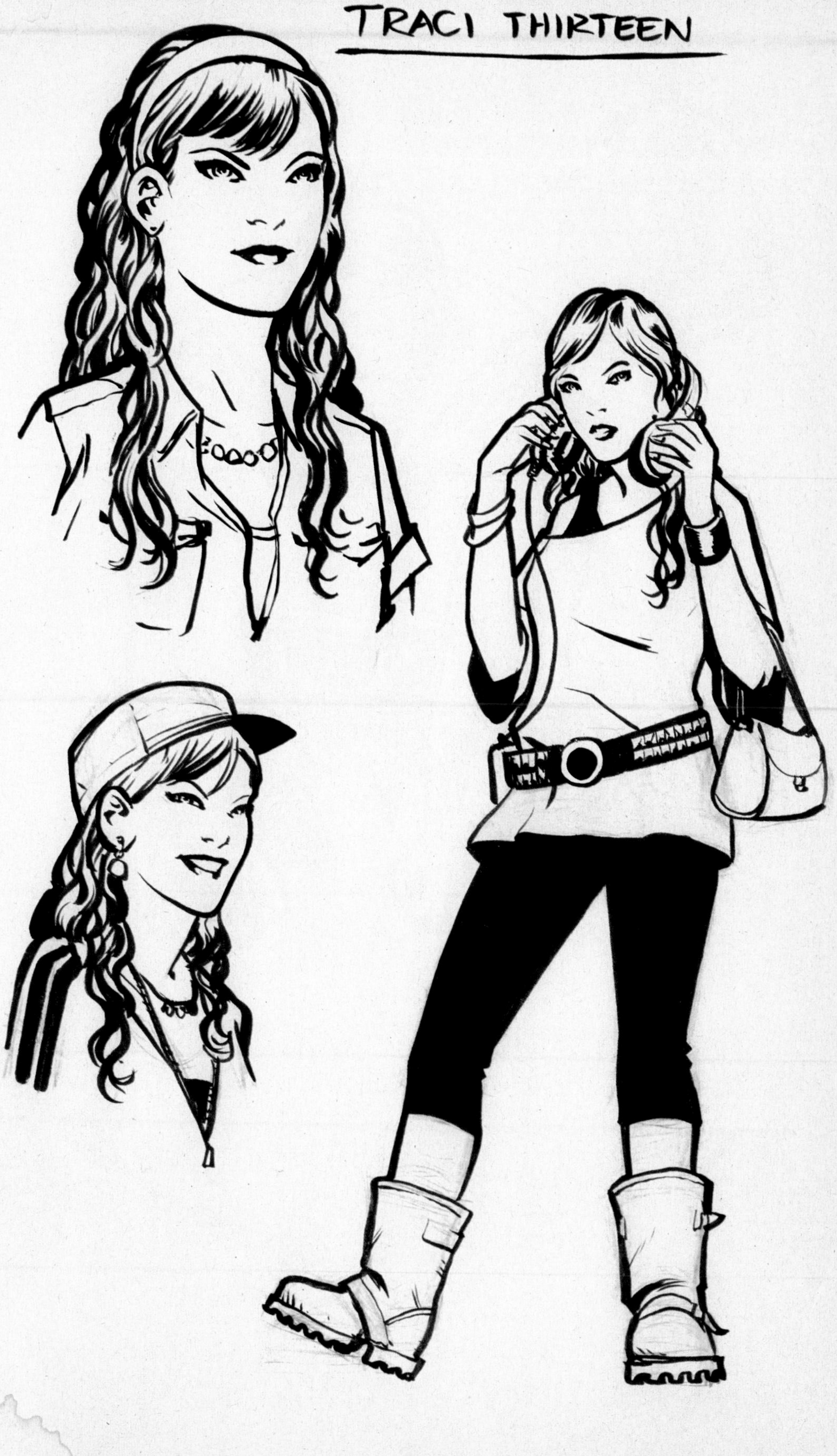
TRACI THIRTEEN

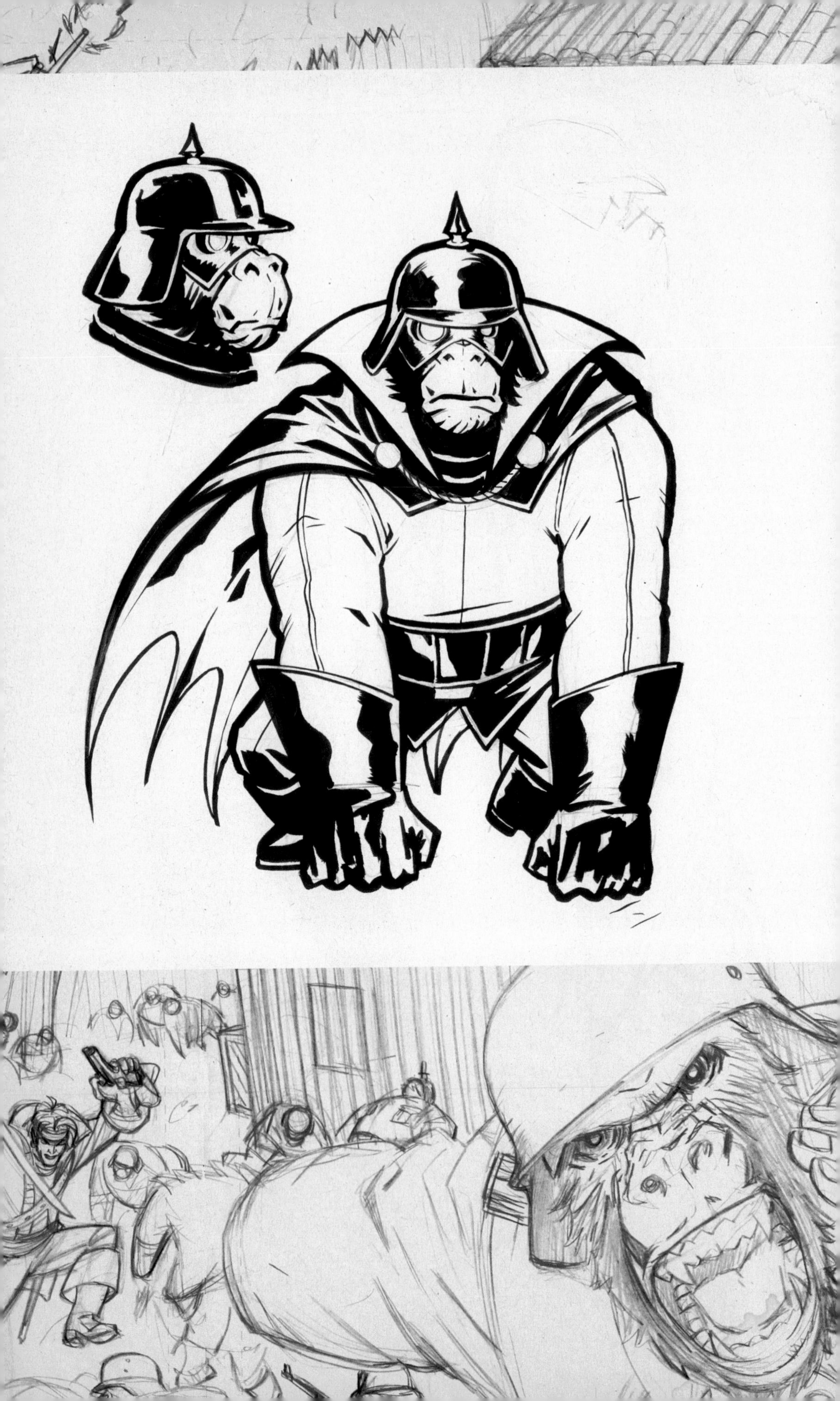

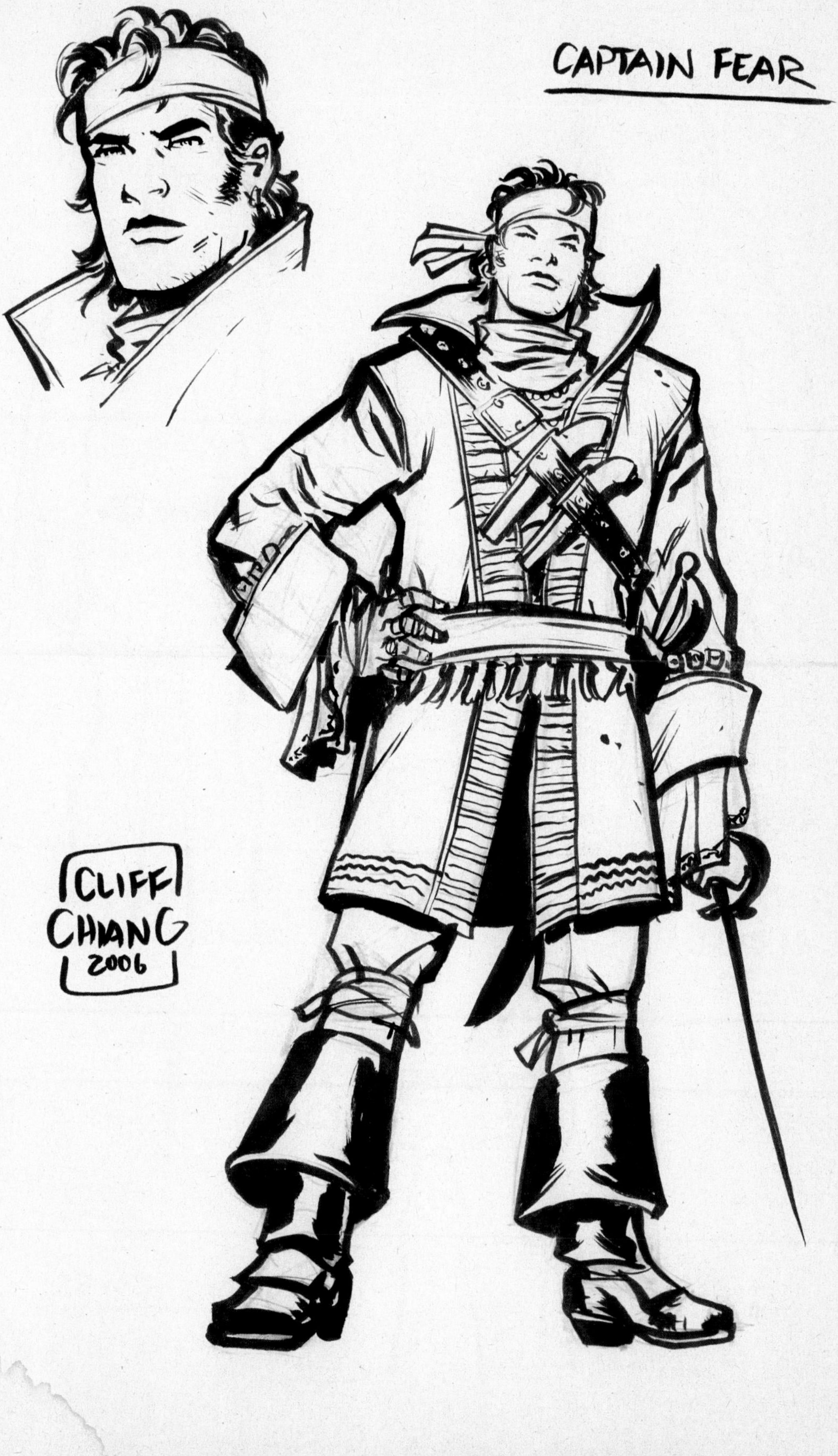
CAPTAIN FEAR
CLIFF
CHIANG
2006

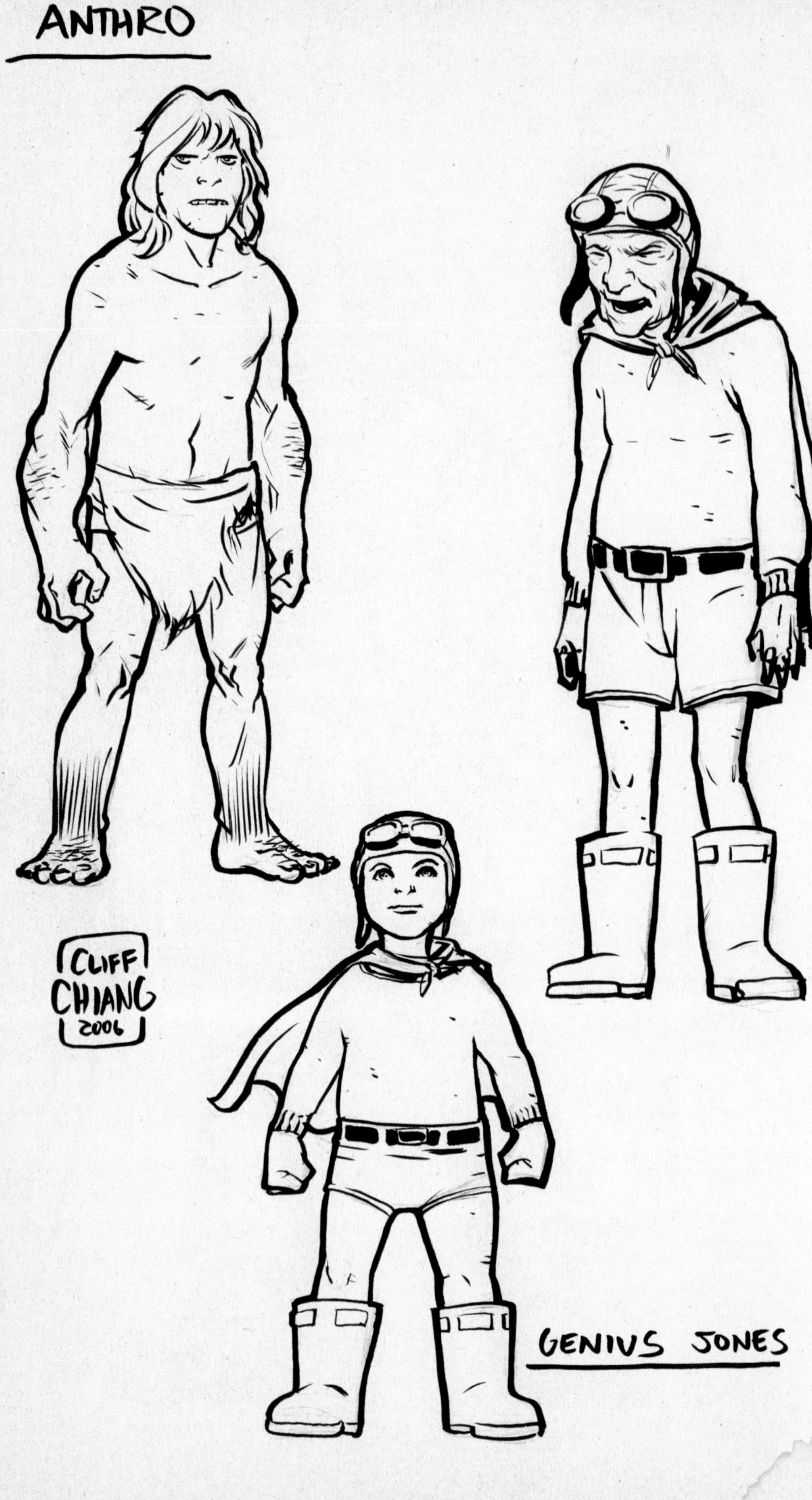
ANTHRO
CLIFF CHIANG 2006
GENIUS JONES

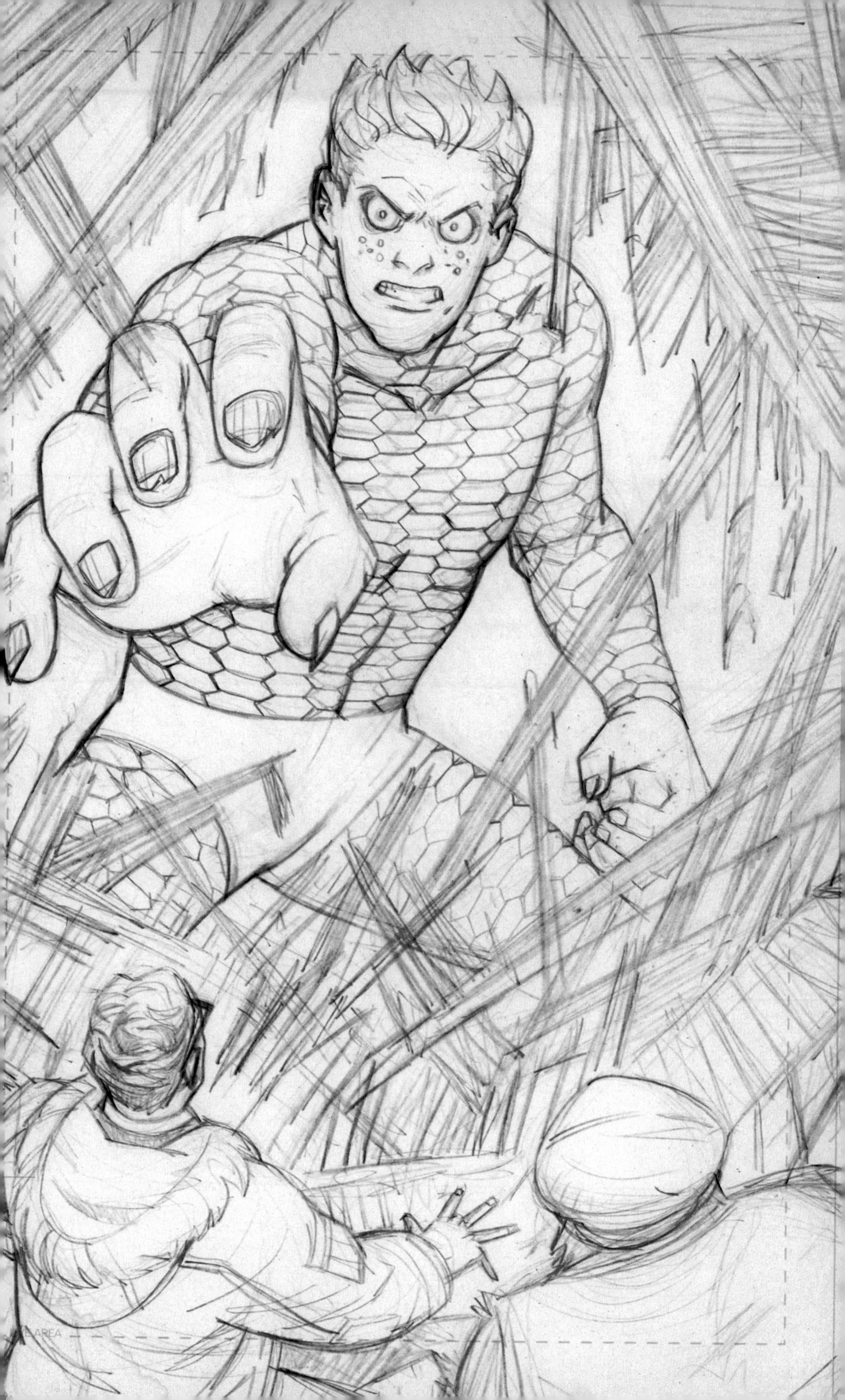

FAVORITE HEROES IN THESE COLLECTIONS FROM DC COMICS:

# KINGDOM COME

THE GREATEST SUPER-HERO EPIC OF TOMORROW!
KINGDOM COME
Mark WAID
Alex ROSS

**Mark Waid** and **Alex Ross** deliver a grim tale of youth versus experience, tradition versus change and what defines a hero. KINGDOM COME is a riveting story pitting the old guard — Superman, Batman, Wonder Woman and their peers — against a new uncompromising generation.

**WINNER OF FIVE EISNER AND HARVEY AWARDS, INCLUDING BEST LIMITED SERIES AND BEST ARTIST**

IDENTITY CRISIS

NEW YORK TIMES BEST-SELLING AUTHOR OF THE ZERO GAME
BRAD MELTZER
RAGS MORALES MICHAEL BAIR
IDENTITY CRISIS
Introduction by JOSS WHEDON, creator of BUFFY THE VAMPIRE SLAYER and FIREFLY

**BRAD MELTZER**
**RAGS MORALES**
**MICHAEL BAIR**

CRISIS ON INFINITE EARTHS

CRISIS
ON INFINITE EARTHS
MARV WOLFMAN
& GEORGE PÉREZ

**MARV WOLFMAN**
**GEORGE PÉREZ**

DC: THE NEW FRONTIER VOLUME 1

DC: The New Frontier
VOLUME ONE
BY DARWYN COOKE WITH DAVE STEWART

**DARWYN COOKE**
**DAVE STEWART**

SEARCH THE GRAPHIC NOVELS SECTION OF

**www.DCCOMICS.com**

FOR ART AND INFORMATION ON ALL OF OUR BOOKS

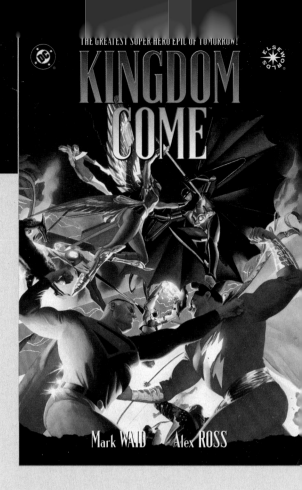

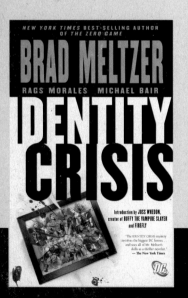

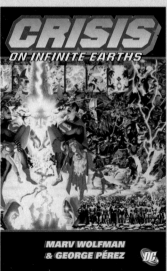

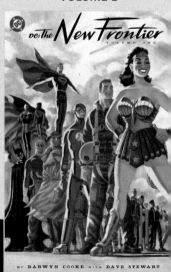